Calvin's Doctrine
of Biblical Authority

Calvin's Doctrine
of Biblical Authority

Abd-el-Masih Istafanous

WIPF & STOCK · Eugene, Oregon

CALVIN'S DOCTRINE OF BIBLICAL AUTHORITY

Copyright © 2010 Abd-el-Masih Istafanous. All rights reserved. Except for brief quotations in critical publications or reviews, no part of this book may be reproduced in any manner without prior written permission from the publisher. Write: Permissions, Wipf and Stock Publishers, 199 W. 8th Ave., Suite 3, Eugene, OR 97401.

Wipf & Stock
An Imprint of Wipf and Stock Publishers
199 W. 8th Ave., Suite 3
Eugene, OR 97401
www.wipfandstock.com

ISBN 13: 978-1-60899-644-5

Manufactured in the U.S.A.

All scripture quotations, unless otherwise indicated, are taken from the Holy Bible, New International Version®, NIV®. Copyright ©1973, 1978, 1984 by Biblica, Inc.™ Used by permission of Zondervan. All rights reserved worldwide.

To Isis

*My best friend, counselor, and dear wife
Who by the grace of God made this book possible . . .*

1 Cor 13:4–8a

Portrait of Calvin as he was preparing to go back to Geneva. It has the words: "I offer my troubled heart as a sacrifice to God." He wrote to Farel in Oct or Nov 1540 regarding going back to Geneva: "... I am not my own, I offer up my heart presented as a sacrifice to the Lord." [Calvin's Lat. Corresp. Opera, tom. ii. pp. 99, 100.]

Contents

Foreword by Thomas F. Torrance ix
Foreword by Professor Elsie A. McKee xi
Acknowledgments xiii
Note on Citations xv

Introduction xvii
  The Protestant Problem
    Twofold Knowledge of God and Twofold Knowledge
      of Ourselves
    Twofold Knowledge and Twofold Grace
  An Ecumenical Perspective
  Overview of the Book

Part One: Scripture and the Knowledge of God

1 Knowledge of God: The *Duplex Cognitio Domini* 3
    The Nature of the Twofold Knowledge
    Faith: The Basis of the Twofold Knowledge of God
    The Duplex *Cognitio Domini*
      The Correlative Character of Knowledge of God
      The Twofold Knowledge of God
        Knowledge of God the Creator
        Knowledge of God the Redeemer

2 Knowledge of God: The *Duplex Gratia Dei* 37
    Introductory Remarks on Faith
      Faith and Twofold Knowledge
      Faith as Knowledge
    Twofold Knowledge and Tension in the Life of Faith
      Knowledge of God the Creator
      Knowledge of God the Redeemer
      Note on Methodology

Toward a Definition of Faith
    First Definition of Faith
    Second Definition of Faith
The Duplex Cognitio Domini and the Duplex Gratia Dei
    The Duplex Gratia Dei
    The Grace of Sanctification and Knowledge of God the Creator
    The Grace of Justification and Knowledge of God the Redeemer
    Methodological Remarks
    Conclusion

PART TWO: WORD AND SPIRIT

3   Word and Spirit: Illumination of the Mind 93
    Faith and the Teaching Ministry of the Church
    Knowledge of God the Redeemer
    The Condemnatory Function of the Law
    Knowledge of God the Creator
    The Pedagogical Function of the Law
    The Twofold Knowledge

4   Word and Spirit: Sealing of the Heart 119
    Introductory Remarks
        The Roman Case against the Evangelicals
        Illumination and Sealing
        Sealing, Certainty, and Authority
    Biblical Authority and the Roman Church
    Biblical Authority and Humanism
    Biblical Authority and the Fanatics

5   Word and Spirit: A Corollary: The Doctrine of Inspiration 154
    The Case for Verbal Inerrancy
    The Case against Verbal Inerrancy
    Toward an Answer

    Concluding Summary 173
    Appendix: Calvin and Calvinism 181
    Bibliography 189
    Subject/Name Index 195

Foreword

Thomas F. Torrance

This is a very fine work which I have long felt should be made widely available in published form, for it takes us right back to the teaching of John Calvin himself, and sets it free from the framework of Protestant Scholasticism within which Calvin's own thought has so often been trapped and twisted. To me this book has several great merits. It is written by one who himself is a very able clear-headed scholar and who while familiar with relevant European and American literature, works with a refreshing independence of mind, and a freedom of interpretation in spite of the pressures of divergent interpretations and controversies in Calvin studies. Moreover, Dr. Istafanous has a distinctive sympathy and appreciation for the biblical and evangelical fidelity of John Calvin in his struggles to clarify and uphold the great truths of the Gospel in the face of distortion by humanists, Romanists, and fanatics. What strikes me most as a theologian about this work that in it Dr. Istafanous has set out the doctrine of biblical authority in such a way as to show how the word of God mediated to us through the Holy Scriptures is to be heard and received apart from any specific theory of inspiration. This is a book not only for scholars and theologians, however, but for all preachers and teachers of the Gospel who have missionary and pastoral tasks to fulfill. I believe it will have a particularly valuable contribution to make to the church today in the West as well as in the East, for it directs us straight back to the authority of the word of God himself as it sounds to us through the Bible.

Thomas F. Torrance

Foreword

Professor Elsie A. McKee

John Calvin's five-hundredth birthday is a very appropriate occasion to refresh and extend acquaintance with the life and teaching of this remarkable Biblical scholar and church leader. It is also a fitting time to revisit issues which have been a source of debate or even controversy, particularly when those topics are as central to Christian teaching as the understanding of scripture and faith.

It is thus a special pleasure to see that Professor Istafanous has brought forward his carefully developed and very helpful investigation of Calvin's teaching on the relationship of faith to the authority of scripture, to make this work available now in print. The author engages with the secondary literature to set out the debate about how scripture is authoritative for Calvin, and then delineates through his research a new perspective on resolving the conflict over interpretations. While attending to later use of Calvin, Dr. Istafanous works successfully to set Calvin in his own historical context; for example, pointing out that the issue of inspiration is essentially a modern problem. Particularly interesting is the way that this book brings together Calvin's views of the twofold knowledge of God and the twofold knowledge of ourselves, to propose a different and intriguing way to see the context for understanding the structure of the 1559 *Institutes of the Christian Religion.*

Although the original research for this book was undertaken many years ago, the insights which Dr. Istafanous presents have not been found in other works and thus the publication of this work today can provide access to that thoughtful investigation for today's students of Calvin. Also, the author has brought his thesis into conversation with more recent literature, demonstrating the continuing worth of his study. The appearance of this book about such an important subject is a welcome addition to the reformer's birthday celebration.

Speaking as one who followed Professor Istafanous as a student of John Calvin at Princeton Seminary and who, baptized and reared in the Church of Christ in Congo, holds very dear the work of the church in Africa to which Dr. Istafanous has so greatly contributed for many years, it is a privilege to share in welcoming this book as it appears on the public stage.

Elsie McKee,
Tshimunyi wa Ngulumingi
Princeton, December 1, 2009

Acknowledgments

I WISH TO EXPRESS my deep appreciation to many friends and colleagues at the Evangelical Theological Seminary in Cairo, Egypt, for their encouragement and continued assistance. I would especially like to thank the Rev. Dr. Atef M. Gendi, President, and the Rev. Dr. Darren Kennedy, Chair of the Theology Department, for their continued support. I am also grateful to Miss Elaine Pequegnat for her meticulous editing of most of the work.

I would like to express my deep thanks and appreciation to Professor Elsie Anne McKee of Princeton Theological Seminary for her continued advice, great encouragement, and foreword introducing this book.

Finally, I would like to acknowledge the friendship, support and encouragement of the late Professor T. F. Torrance of Edinburgh. He continued to inspire me to press on to complete the work and have it ready for publication.

Abd-el-Masih Istafanous

Note on Citations

References to the primary sources consist of two sets of symbols. The first set applies to any edition or translation while the second refers to the source in the original language. Citations from the *Institutes* are referred to by book, chapter, and section; e.g., *Inst.*, I, i, 1. These are followed by references in parentheses to the location in the *Calvini opera selecta*: the volume, page, and lines respectively as follows (O. S. III, 31, 6–10). References to passages from the *Commentaries* indicate the text where the passage can be found in any edition or translation; e.g., Com. Ezek 20:44. I have used modern translations as much as possible. These references are followed by citations in parentheses of the location of the passage in the *Calvini opera quae supersunt omnia* in the corresponding volume and column as follows (C. O. XL, 514). Citations from the treatises, catechisms, confessions, or other writings are referred to by page in the particular English translation whenever available. I have added in parentheses the corresponding reference from the O. S. or the C. O.

Introduction

The subject matter of this book presented itself while I was studying the authority of Scripture within the Westminster Standards. I was surprised by the depth of the insights to be learned from Calvin. It seems that his knowledge of Scripture and dedication to the word have ensured the relevancy of his theological system even in the twenty-first century. Furthermore, his doctrine of biblical authority has raised numerous questions among interpreters, a fact that necessitates careful renewed study.[1]

It is clear that we shall have to deal with the *Institutio Christianae religionis*[2] more frequently than any other of Calvin's writings, because as he himself clearly states,[3] it provides us with the most systematic presentation of his theology. In our study, however, we shall also make extensive use of Calvin's commentaries, treatises, and other writings.

To understand the *Institutes* in particular, we should keep in mind the purpose or purposes that Calvin had before him at the time of writing. In his *Prefatory Address to King Francis I of France*, he explains:

> My purpose was solely to transmit certain rudiments by which those who are touched with any zeal for religion might be shaped to true godliness. And I undertook this labor especially for our French countrymen, very many of whom I knew to be hungering and thirsting for Christ; but I saw very few who had been duly imbued with even a slight knowledge of Him. The book itself wit-

---

1. Dowey, *Knowledge of God in Calvin's Theology* (1952), 87–89; same page numbers are in the 1994 edition; Gerrish, "Biblical Authority," 353–54; Johnson, *Authority in Protestant Theology*, 43–45; Warfield, *Calvin and Calvinism*, 71–73.

2. The English translation of the *Institutes* used in this book is that of Ford L. Battles, Library of Christian Classics, vols. 20 and 21. This translation often inserts scriptural references not found in the original; these are quoted in the present work. Other translations will be used as needed.

3. Ibid., 4–5.

nesses that this was my intention, adapted as it is to a simple and, you may say, elementary form of teaching.⁴

To this initial purpose, Calvin added an apologetic one. The occasion for this apology was the persecution of the so-called Evangelicals, whereupon Calvin said to King Francis I, "From this [the *Institutes*] you may learn the nature of the doctrine against which those madmen burn with rage who today disturb your realm with fire and sword."⁵

Thus in the first edition of the *Institutes* (1536), we find two purposes going hand in hand in the same work. Calvin explains his dual purpose in the following manner, "It seemed to me that I should be doing something worthwhile if I both *gave instruction* to them [the abovementioned French countrymen] and *made confession* before you [King Francis I] with the same work."⁶ While expounding his beliefs before the King would necessarily emphasize an apologetic approach, instructing his French countrymen would definitely lead Calvin to stress the way of salvation. As Calvin himself thought, however, these two purposes are reconcilable and could be achieved through the same work.

From the edition of 1539 on through the later editions, the element of instruction receives more emphasis and the purpose of the work changes slightly. Addressing the reader, Calvin says:

> It has been my purpose in this labor to prepare and instruct candidates in sacred theology for the reading of the divine Word, in order that they may be able both to have easy access to it and to advance in it without stumbling. For I believe I have so embraced the sum of religion in all its parts, I have arranged it in such an order, that if anyone rightly grasps it, it will not be difficult for him to determine what he ought especially to seek in Scripture, and to what end he ought to relate its contents.⁷

This passage should not be understood to mean that Calvin's audience had become limited to the narrow circle of candidates in sacred theology. He constantly had in mind a more inclusive audience.⁸ After 1539 he himself translated every edition of the *Institutes* into the French

---

4. *Inst.* 9 (O.S. III, 9, 6–13).
5. Ibid., (O.S. III, 9, 18–20).
6. Ibid. (O.S. 9, 16–17); italics added.
7. Ibid., 4 (O.S. III, 6, 18–25).
8. Haroutunian and Smith, *Calvin: Commentaries*, Library of Christian Classics 23, 38.

language; and in the French edition of 1560, he stated his purpose in composing the work: "First of all I put it into Latin so as to serve all men of learning, to whatever nation they belonged; then afterward, desiring to communicate what could bear fruit for our French nation, I have also translated it into our tongue."[9] The inclusive nature of his purpose becomes obvious when he states: "I can at least promise that it [the *Institutes*] can be a key to open a way for all children of God into a good and right understanding of Holy Scripture."[10]

Calvin's emphasis on the didactic element, however, should not be understood to mean that he has abandoned the apologetic purpose which he had outlined in the *Prefatory Address*. In spite of the death of King Francis I in 1547, the *Address* continued to be published with some revisions in subsequent editions of the *Institutes*. Moreover, the apologetic and polemic tones of the work itself cannot be overlooked. As we shall see later, Calvin's emphasis on certainty, which is a fundamental concept for the understanding of his doctrine of Scripture as well as his whole theology, was his response to the attack of the Roman Catholic Church against the "doubtful and uncertain" doctrine of the evangelicals.[11]

It is also very important for us to remember that faith is presupposed within the whole of the *Institutes*. Calvin was clearly conscious that he was approaching his task as both a believer and minister in the Church. Therefore he says:

> God has filled my mind with zeal to spread His Kingdom and to further the public good. I am also duly clear in my own conscience, and have God and the angels to witness, that since I undertook the office of teacher in the Church, I have had no other purpose than to benefit the Church by maintaining the pure doctrine of godliness.[12]

Thus far then, we have taken note of Calvin's intended audience. But it is also important to mention those whose ideas he was combating. His most obvious battle was with the Schoolmen of the Roman Church. But also, despite their many areas of agreement, Calvin found himself

---

9. *Inst.* 7, (O.S. III, 7, 40–8, 2).
10. Ibid. 7, (O.S. III, 8, 4–7).
11. Ibid. 16, (O.S. III, 15, 19).
12. Ibid. 4, (O.S. III, 5, 286, 5).

compelled to fight against the Anabaptists. And thirdly, though humanistic in outlook himself, he challenged the negative rationalist attacks of some humanists.

With these general remarks in mind we shall now pay particular attention to the problem of biblical authority in Calvin's theology. To do this, it is necessary to briefly remind ourselves of the problems that Luther faced in order to understand how the Reformation raised this issue. Then we shall briefly survey recent scholarly literature that has sought to interpret Calvin's teaching on this topic.

THE PROTESTANT PROBLEM

At the beginning of Luther's reforming career, he does not seem to have fully realized that he was dealing with the issue of authority. In 1517 he concluded his famous Ninety-five Theses with a statement of pious submission to the Church.[13] It was at the Leipzig debate of 1519 that Johann Eck made clear to Luther the implications of his protest; and it was here that Luther was forced to enunciate the principle of *sola Scriptura*. Thus he said, "No believing Christian can be coerced beyond holy writ. By divine law we are forbidden to believe anything which is not established by divine Scripture or manifest revelation."[14] Or again, "A simple layman armed with Scripture is to be believed above a pope or a council without it."[15] The revolutionary element in Luther's words is not his assertion of the authority of Scripture but his denial of the ultimate authority of the Roman Church and pope.[16]

Viewed from this perspective, Calvin's contribution can be considered identical to that of Luther. As Lehmann noted, "It is the emphasis upon the *sole* rather than the *supplementary* character of the ultimate Scriptural norm that distinguishes the Reformers from their predecessors."[17] Calvin was not concerned with establishing Scripture's authority. Rather, his main concern was to draw the line between the authority of the church and that of Scripture.

---

13. "Herewith we would say nothing and believe we have said nothing which does not harmonize with the Catholic Church and the Church teachers." Quoted by Reu, *Luther and the Scriptures*, 14. Cf. Luther, *First Principles of the Reformation*, 13–14.

14. Bainton, *Here I Stand*, 89.

15. Ibid., 90.

16. Gerrish, "Biblical Authority," 342.

17. Lehmann, "The Reformers' Use of the Bible," 333.

The latter part of the nineteenth century saw a revival of interest in this problem of authority. Theological views varied widely. At one end of the spectrum were the liberal theologians; at the other end were those who wanted to take the Scriptures more or less literally. Schleiermacher's great French disciple, August Sabatier,[18] is perhaps the best representative of a liberal theologian's interaction with Calvin's doctrine of authority. The subjectivism and romanticism of his day led him to distinguish between what he called "religions of authority" and the "religion of the spirit."[19] Sabatier thereby rejected both Roman Catholicism with its doctrine of papal infallibility and Protestant scholasticism with its doctrine of biblical inerrancy.[20] The religion of the spirit was then propounded as being in accordance with the teaching of the Reformers and especially with Calvin's doctrine of the "inner witness of the Holy Spirit."[21] Sabatier's emphasis is also found in the teaching of his disciple Jacques Pannier, who wrote the *Inner Witness of the Holy Spirit*[22] and a review article on the authority of the Holy Scriptures according to Calvin.[23] Both works bear the marks of romantic subjectivism. While Pannier's discussion of the authority of Scripture provides an adequate survey, he mentions the relation between Calvin's doctrine of Scripture and his doctrine of faith only in a brief manner.[24] His writings reveal little awareness of the problems that were later raised in connection with Calvin's doctrine of Scripture.

Closer still to the approach of Sabatier was that of one of his admirers and a theologian of the same school of thought, P. Lobstein. His article "La connaissance religieuse d'après Calvin"[25] makes a sharp distinction between Calvin's doctrine of authority and his doctrine of faith. The latter is seen as practical, moral, and religious, promoting liberty and action,[26] and is identified with Luther's insight. Lobstein then claims that Calvin "did not remain faithful" to his doctrine of faith, for in spite of it

18. Johnson, *Authority in Protestant Theology*, 74.
19. Sabatier, *Religions of Authority and the Religion of the Spirit*.
20. Ibid., 250–53.
21. Ibid., 160–62.
22. Pannier, *Témoignage du Saint-Esprit*.
23. Pannier, "L'autorité de l'é criture sainte,» 193–211; 367–81.
24. Ibid., 378. "*Pour Calvin, la chose importante essentielle, c'est la foi.*"
25. Lobstein, "Connaissance religieuse," 53–110.
26. Ibid., 60–62. Italics added.

and under the influence of the Middle Ages he established Scripture as an external legal authority and thus resorted to the domain of "theoretical reason."[27] Lobstein thus found Calvin's doctrines of faith and authority irreconcilable, and believed that a choice had to be made between the scholastic principle of authority and the evangelical spiritual principle.[28] Here one can see again Sabatier's distinction between religions of authority and the religion of the spirit. And once more like Sabatier, in typical romantic confidence, Lobstein says, "It should be affirmed without presumption that modern theology has made its choice."[29] It is the choice of the doctrine of faith over the doctrine of authority.

Those who viewed the Scriptures more authoritatively had to face the problems posed by Biblical criticism. In the course of their debate, the different parties sought to prove that the reformers were on their side. This discussion likewise revived an interest in Calvin's doctrine of authority. The discussion finds its clearest expression in the writings of B. B. Warfield and Charles A. Briggs. In 1881, A. A. Hodge and B. B. Warfield postulated a doctrine of inspiration that claimed inerrancy for the original autographs of the Scriptures.[30] Calvin's name was mentioned along with several others in an incidental manner.[31] In 1909, however, in his discussion of Calvin's doctrine of the knowledge of God, Warfield claimed that the doctrine of inspiration that he himself had taught twenty-eight years earlier was actually Calvin's.[32] Nonetheless, the biblical critic Briggs was also able to claim that the Genevan Reformer was on his side.[33]

Warfield's position has been held in varying degrees by extreme conservatives up to the present.[34] With the rise of fundamentalism, the

---

27. Ibid., 82–83. The distinction between practical and theoretical reason betrays a post-Kantian influence.

28. Ibid., 109.

29. Ibid.

30. Hodge and Warfield, "Inspiration," 226.

31. Ibid., 241.

32. Warfield, *Calvin and Calvinism*, 65.

33. Briggs, "Critical Theories of the Sacred Scriptures," 562–63; also *Bible, Church and Reason*, 110–12; 219–20.

34. Moore, "Calvin's Doctrine of Holy Scripture," 49–70; Hodge, "Witness of the Holy Spirit to the Bible," 41–84. Later publications include Kantzer, "Calvin and the Holy Scripture," 115–155; and Murray, *Calvin on Scripture and Divine Sovereignty*. It is interesting that Murray states his case repeatedly against C. A. Briggs (12, 20, 27). Yet Warfield, the arch opponent of Briggs's thesis, and to whom Murray is definitely

inerrancy of the Bible came to occupy a central place in Christian faith, at least among some Protestant groups. Several other studies of Calvin's views on inspiration arrived at similar conclusions to those of Warfield, though no reference is made to his concept of the original autographs. These writers considered that Calvin held a rigid, formal doctrine of biblical authority.[35] As we shall explore more fully in Chapter Five of the present work, the findings of this group have been contested by several Calvin scholars. Both parties, however, have placed the Bible at the center of discussions of Calvin's theology.[36]

With an eye on the findings of biblical criticism, and seeking to correct the mistakes of scholastic orthodoxy and fundamentalism, the proponents of so-called neo-orthodoxy declared that the Reformation teaching was christocentric rather than bibliocentric. Wilhelm Niesel presented this point of view in 1938,[37] claiming that the theology of Calvin was bound to the word of Scripture and was called to do nothing more than point to the end (*scopus*) of the Bible, Jesus Christ.[38] Throughout the discussion, Calvin's doctrine of Scripture is presented as christocentric. Accordingly, after some quotes from Calvin, Niesel declared:

> Here again we recognize the two factors: The theme of the Bible cannot be divorced from its letters and words, from the extant book. And yet this theme is not identifiable with these words. In themselves they are dead words. The theme alone to which they bear witness makes them live; and this theme is Jesus Christ. Jesus Christ is the soul of the law, the focal point of the whole of Scripture.[39]

---

indebted, is neither credited nor even mentioned. See also Runia, *Karl Barth's Doctrine of Holy Scripture*, especially 39–46.

35. Bauke, *Die Probleme der Theologie Calvins*; Davies, *Problem of Authority in the Continental Reformation*; Hunter, *Teaching of Calvin*; Lobstein, "Connaissance religieuse," 53–110; Seeberg, *Lehrbuch der Dogmengeschichte*, 2d ed., vol. 4, part 2; and Seeberg, *Revelation and Inspiration*.

36. Muller, *Post-reformation Reformed Dogmatics*, 244–45.

37. Niesel, *Theology of Calvin*; *Die Theologie Calvins*, 2d. ed. References will be made to the second edition.

38. Ibid., 30.

39. Ibid., 33; E.T., 32–33.

This view of Calvin's doctrine of Scripture was presented again and supported by T. H. L. Parker[40] and J. K. S. Reid.[41] A book on the same subject was published by Dowey[42] in the same year that Parker's book was released. Dowey considers knowledge to be "the fundamental and central category of Calvin's theological thought."[43] With this postulate in mind he presents his understanding of the structure of the *Institutes* as follows: "The really significant ordering principle of the *Institutes* in the 1559 edition is the *duplex cognitio Domini*, not the Apostles Creed."[44] He then concludes that "Calvin's final plan, which from the epistemological point of view follows the *duplex cognitio* and not the Creed, is simply the systematic arrangement most compatible with his concept of the knowledge of God."[45] Dowey admits that Köstlin[46] had proposed this ordering principle before him. He is, however, presenting it "in greater detail and with more emphasis upon its importance."[47]

In the new Chapter VI that Dowey added to the enlarged 1994 edition of his book, he mentions some distinguished Calvin scholars in support of his understanding, and goes on to say:

> Köstlin, Wendel and Gerrish all hold that the four-part division of the *Institutio* according to the four articles of the Apostles' Creed is less revealing of Calvin's actual disposition of the subject matter than a two-part division: first, the doctrine of the Creator and creation in Book I and second, salvation throughout Books II–IV.[48]

To further support this argument Dowey refers to the "approximately thirteen times in the *Institutio* of 1559 by which in explicit methodological statements Calvin recalls and clarifies this distinction."[49] Accordingly Dowey states, "The doctrines of scripture and faith are separated throughout Calvin's thought on the basis of the *duplex cognitio*

---

40. Parker, *Calvin's Doctrine of the Knowledge of God*.
41. Reid, *Authority of Scripture*.
42. Dowey, *Knowledge of God*, 1952 ed.
43. Ibid., 247, 1994 ed.
44. Ibid., 41–42 (1994).
45. Ibid., 49 (1994).
46. Köstlin, «Calvins Institutio nach Form und Inhalt.»
47. Dowey (1994), 49.
48. Ibid., (1994), 253.
49. Ibid.

Domini. Scripture is always used in support of knowledge of the Creator and faith in support of knowledge of the Redeemer."⁵⁰ He also says:

> . . . two 'interpretations' exist side by side in Calvin's theology concerning the object of the knowledge of faith. Because he [Calvin] never fully integrated and related systematically the faithful man's acceptance of the authority of the Bible *en bloc* with faith as directed exclusively toward Christ.⁵¹

Dowey considers this distinction to be a flaw in Calvin's theology; he describes it as a "discrepancy between the so-called formal and material principles of the Reformation: the authority of Scripture and justification by faith in Christ."⁵² Dowey therefore speaks of a real difficulty in Calvin's theology, namely "the incongruity between the doctrines of revelation and of faith. Calvin's doctrine of revelation concerns itself wholly with the recognition by the believer of the authority of Scripture, while his doctrine of faith concerns the believer's appropriation of Christ."⁵³ These same words of the first edition of Dowey's book in 1952 are repeated in the enlarged edition of 1994.⁵⁴

In the final chapter of the 1952 edition, Dowey suggests that a "dialectical relationship" is a solution to the problem.⁵⁵ Calvin's section on the knowledge of the Creator, within which he discusses the authority of Scripture, provides a "logical or conceptual presupposition" for the knowledge of the Redeemer—which according to Dowey is where Calvin places his doctrine of faith.⁵⁶ On the other hand, Dowey also says that "the knowledge of the Redeemer is an epistemological presupposition for the knowledge of the Creator."⁵⁷ Dowey again presents this dialectical relationship in the third enlarged edition⁵⁸ and repeats the same words in the chapter that was added to the third enlarged edition of his

---

50. Ibid., 255.
51. Ibid., 161–62 (1952, 1994).
52. Ibid., 161 (1952, 1994).
53. Ibid., 210.
54. Ibid, (1994), 89.
55. Ibid., 238–40.
56. Ibid., 238–39.
57. Ibid., 239.
58. Ibid., 238–40.

book.⁵⁹ Dowey explains what he means by the dialectical relationship as follows:

> There is, then, no continuum in Calvin's theology between the two orders of knowing and their parallel parts . . . . In terms of human reason, the relation of the two orders of knowledge can best be called a dialectical one—not a dialectic resolved within the thought system as in Hegel, but one in which the final unity lies in the transcendent God and is partially apprehended by faith as in Kierkegaard.⁶⁰

Now it is interesting that in the same enlarged third edition of his book, Dowey also says:

> Although many years have gone by, and much has been written on the subjects covered in this volume, the work as a whole does not seem to have been entirely superseded. It apparently brought to the fore certain subject matter in Calvin's writings that is still more comprehensively treated here than elsewhere. Also assessments of the structure of Calvin's *Institutes* of his thought in general as developed here, are both widely accepted and also widely debated today.⁶¹

In light of this statement, it becomes evident that there were those who supported Dowey's dialectical explanation as well as those who were critical of it. We have already quoted Dowey's references to some distinguished theologians who support his presentation. Gerrish, while admitting his indebtedness to Dowey, repeatedly emphasizes the supposed incongruity in Calvin's teaching. In 1957 he wrote that "we may say (as Edward Dowey says repeatedly) that Calvin did not adequately relate his doctrine of faith with his doctrine of authority."⁶² This same position was defended in 1993.⁶³ In 2004 Gerrish wrote yet again: "But it may still be argued, with Edward Dowey, that Calvin did not adequately relate the doctrine of faith and his doctrine of authority, for while his faith was strongly Christocentric, he continued to work with the Bible—in the medieval fashion—as an external and formal authority."⁶⁴

---

59. Ibid., 256.
60. Ibid., 241.
61. Dowey, *Knowledge of God*, ix (1994).
62. Gerrish, "Biblical Authority," 353.
63. Gerrish, *Grace and Gratitude*, 77–78.
64. Gerrish, *Old Protestantism and the New*, 62.

A few years after Gerrish's first reference to Dowey's thesis, Forstman expressed the same idea and tried to solve the problem by using a modified form of Dowey's concept of the double presupposition or the dialectical relationship. Forstman says, "Faith may fasten on the divine promises as distinguished from the rest of the Bible, but faith in the divine promises depends in turn on a certain persuasion of the truth-fullness of God."[65] Forstman does not express any indebtedness to Dowey for this "solution," though he praises his treatment of Calvin's doctrine of faith.[66]

The existence of what Dowey describes as a problem should not be overlooked. Calvin scholarship is certainly indebted to Dowey for raising the question and trying to provide an answer. The dialectical relationship that Dowey offers as the solution to the problem, however, is based on the supposition that Calvin "must be judged to have two not entirely reconcilable theological explanations of the faithful man's knowledge of God's special revelation."[67] Dowey's presentation was challenged by T. H. L. Parker in an appendix to the revised American edition of his book.[68] After praising Dowey for his wide and detailed knowledge of Calvin's writings, he went on to criticize his presentation for two reasons.

Parker first questioned Dowey's principles for interpreting Calvin's *Institutes*. He criticized him for altering the order of the *Institutes* by considering Book I to refer to the revelation and knowledge of the Creator and Books II through IV to discuss the revelation and knowledge of the Redeemer. Parker emphasized that we are not at liberty to change the *Institutes* into a completely different form and then analyze the result as if we were still discussing Calvin. Further, Parker emphasized Calvin's own insistence on the titles of Books I through III to show how the doctrine of the Trinity structures the whole of his Christian vision.

Second, Parker questioned Dowey's conclusions about Calvin's use of natural theology: while admitting that Dowey had quoted passages in which Calvin denied the validity of knowledge gained apart from the Scriptures, he nevertheless argues that Dowey himself gives natural theology too positive a role within Christian preaching. Parker claims that Dowey overlooked Calvin's teaching that the "utmost extent (of natural

---

65. Forstman, *Word and Spirit*, 44.
66. Ibid., 4.
67. Dowey, *Knowledge of God*, 161 (1952 and 1994).
68. Parker, *Calvin's Doctrine of the Knowledge of God*.

theology) is to make men inexcusable."⁶⁹ Dowey responded to Parker in a book review that appeared in *Theology Today*.⁷⁰ Later he also responded briefly in the preface to the second printing of his book (1964):

> The polemic of T. H. L. Parker . . . misses the mark. The claim that problems of the *duplex cognitio Domini* arise from my 'rearranging' of the *Institutes* is made so irresponsibly as to cast doubts on Parker's desire to be taken seriously. His second claim, concerning the treatment of 'inexcusability,' may have something in it. But I fail to see the difference between his summary on page 125 and my own expressed view. A glance at Mr. Parker's bibliography and text reveals a second-hand acquaintance with the continental debates from which his own case (and mine) derives.⁷¹

In 1966 David Willis⁷² criticized Dowey's presentation of Calvin's theology through a discussion of "*The Duplex cognitio Dei and the Doctrine of the Trinity*."⁷³ Willis convincingly presents two arguments. He begins by stating that the *duplex cognitio Domini* is one act of knowing in a twofold movement, even as *cognitio* is singular not only grammatically but also in the actual experience of the church. Willis then notes that since the one act of knowing, which can be analyzed in a twofold fashion, is given its unity by the unity of the one thus known, this knowledge of God is fully Trinitarian not only in presupposition but also in result.⁷⁴ Countering Dowey's restructuring of the *Institutes*, Willis goes on to say:

> Even if it be decided that the *duplex cognitio* scheme and not the three articles of the Creed provides the primary instrument for structuring the final edition of the *Institutes*, still the subject of Books III and IV is generally the work of the Holy Spirit, as the subject of Book I is generally God the Creator and of Book II generally the Redeemer. The Holy Spirit is not for Calvin only the means of our knowledge of God: he is also the subject of our knowledge of God, along with the Father and the Son. Books III and IV should be seen as serving in part to elaborate the con-

---

69. Ibid., 117–19.
70. Dowey, review of *Calvin's Doctrine of the Knowledge of God*, 115–17.
71. Dowey, *Knowledge of God* (1994), xvi.
72. Willis, *Calvin's Catholic Christology*.
73. Ibid., 120.
74. Ibid., 122.

tent of our knowledge of the Holy Spirit from a consideration of his offices."[75]

Willis acknowledges that Calvin does not discuss Christology proper in Book I, yet he finds that "Dowey extends himself a bit too much in claiming that the doctrine of the Trinity 'does not include Calvin's Christology.'"[76] In addition, Willis responded to Dowey's contrast between the knowledge of God the Creator with that of God the Redeemer and to his attempt to find a solution in the so-called dialectical relationship. "Calvin's delight in creation as a source confirming knowledge of God is missed too easily in a theology which sets Christological knowledge in virtual opposition to the knowledge of God from creation."[77] After further discussion Willis comes to the conclusion that "creation and redemption are not competing sources of revelation."[78]

Dowey responded to Willis's challenge in a lecture at the International Congress on Calvin Research in 1982[79] and again in the enlarged third edition of his book in 1994.[80] He conceded that the criticism of a dialectical relationship is well taken. He says:

> The criticism that this description although valid, appears to result in an exaggerated disparity within Calvin's thought structure, has been well taken in *Calvin's Catholic Christology* (1966) of David Willis, who offers through his study of Christology a fuller Trinitarian setting for the twofold knowledge as does Krusche. The danger, however, remains (especially in Krusche's presentation) that the proper dialectic may be lost.[81]

Then after a very brief discussion of Willis's Trinitarian presentation and in reference to the use of the so called *extra Calvinisticum*, Dowey goes on to say:

> My suggestion would be that the full Trinitarian setting as developed by Willis, entailing more adequate treatment of the Spirit and the Son in creation and providence is adequate to give the

---

75. Ibid., 123.
76. Ibid., 123–24, n.4.
77. Ibid., 127.
78. Ibid., 131.
79. Neuser, ed., *Calvinus Ecclesiae Genevensis Custos*, 145–46.
80. Ibid., 256–57.
81. Ibid., 256.

quietus to the old 'extra' formula, and that duplex twofoldness. Calvin's own characteristic expression better reflects the structure of his theology in Christology and throughout.[82]

In his 1985 doctoral dissertation dealing with the *duplex gratia Dei*,[83] Cornelis Venema considered the twofold grace of God in Calvin studies to represent a particular doctrinal theme within the broader framework of the knowledge of God as Creator and Redeemer. He noted that the history of Calvin studies has more often been marked by conflict than consensus.[84] Then he outlined three representative approaches to Calvin's theology

1. The so-called traditional approach, which finds the key to Calvin's theology in a dominant doctrine or in an idea considered to act as an organizing principle to interpreting Calvin's thought.[85]

2. Alternately, there are those who regard the key to interpreting Calvin's theology as lying in the form or method and not in its doctrinal content; i.e., its structure and method. One of the distinctive features of this approach is what Venema calls formal-dialectical rationalism.[86]

3. Those who attempt to relate more closely the content and form in the study of Calvin's theology. An outstanding representative of this approach is Wilhelm Niesel, for whom the self-revelation of God controls both the form and content of Calvin's theology.[87]

Venema believed that these approaches and the interpretive questions they raise to be intimately related to the interpretation of Calvin's doctrines of justification and sanctification. In considering the twofold grace of God, he looked at the secondary literature and found no consensus on the place, importance, or nature of the doctrines of justification

---

82. Ibid., 257, n.50.

83. Venema, *Twofold Nature of the Gospel in Calvin's Theology*. Mention of a dissertation (later published under a different title) here is to point out the sequence of the interaction in the matter under discussion. It is to Venema's credit that he directed attention to the twofold grace of God.

84. Ibid., 14.

85. Ibid., 14.

86. Ibid., 16–17.

87. Ibid., 18.

and sanctification in Calvin's thought.[88] He did see, however, an important connection between the issues raised by the general approaches to Calvin and those raised by interpretations of his doctrines of justification and sanctification.[89]

Venema noted five important questions that are raised in the secondary literature on the doctrine of justification and regeneration:[90]

1. The place and importance of the doctrines of justification and sanctification in Calvin's theology.
2. The precise relation between justification and sanctification.
3. The relation between Calvin's understanding of union with Christ and his forensic definition of justification and sanctification.[91]
4. The nature and relationship of law and gospel.
5. The so-called practical syllogism in Calvin's theology.

Venema then studied the interpretations of Calvin's twofold grace of God. He concluded that the interpretations of this doctrine had often been shaped by the general approach that his interpreters had adopted towards Calvin's theology.[92] Furthermore, he pointed out that the knowledge of God and ourselves comprises the whole subject matter of Calvin's theology.[93]

For this purpose, Venema considered Dowey and Parker's perspectives on the structure of Calvin's theology viewed from the perspective of the knowledge of God. After some discussion he went on to say that these two accounts of the structure of Calvin's theology represent important alternatives that have emerged in previous studies of Calvin's thought.[94] Venema then commenced a long explication of the reasons behind Calvin's arrangement of the material, and why he started with knowledge of God the Creator before speaking of knowledge of God the Redeemer. Venema suggested that Calvin's decision to order his material

---

88. Ibid., 21.
89. Ibid., 22.
90. Some of these questions will be dealt with in our study.
91. *Op. cit.*, 22.
92. Ibid., 29.
93. Ibid., 34.
94. Ibid., 42.

in this way was based in part upon his conviction that this arrangement constitutes an *ordo docendi* which serves a persuasive function consistent with his theological perspective. In this connection Venema refers to Calvin's use of rhetoric and the example of St. Paul.[95]

As we proceed in our study I think it will become evident that Calvin intentionally placed knowledge of the Creator in Book I before knowledge of the Redeemer in Book II and that there is no need to seek for such reasons. Nonetheless the debates have continued. In 1989 Brian Armstrong, in an essay titled "Duplex cognitio Domini, or?—The Problem and Relation of Structure, Form, and Purpose in Calvin's Theology," praises Dowey's work because it raised important questions concerning the structure of Calvin's thought:

> Perhaps more than anything else, the reason for the continuance of, and diversity of opinion in, the debate lies in the confusion which Calvin himself contributed to the matter of the nature, structure, and unity of his thought. That confusion may have its basis, *inter alia*, in findings such as that of William Bouwsma in his recent, fascinating *John Calvin: A Sixteenth-Century Portrait*, when he argues that, in fact, there are 'two Calvins, coexisting uncomfortably within the same historic personage.' While I have grave difficulty applying this idea to the problem of the nature and structure of Calvin's thought in the *Institutio*, Bouwsma has highlighted the fact that there are elements of Calvin's theology which are not easily integrated by the modern mind.[96]

Armstrong accordingly says that the *Institutes* "should be read not from the perspective of the topics which Calvin discusses, for these are arranged, he tells us, only according to an *ordo docendi*. Rather, the material should be read and evaluated on the basis of the large themes which run through all the material."[97] Furthermore, Armstrong states that the structure of Calvin's theology is based in "a broad, general philosophical dialectic between the ideal and the real."[98]

Armstrong next posits that the spiritual purpose of Calvin's theology is solely and exclusively aimed at believers, for the people of faith, as opposed to having systematic-theoretical purposes. Thwarted by the fall,

---

95. Ibid., 48.
96. Armstrong, "Duplex Cognitio Dei, or?," 135.
97. Ibid., 138.
98. Ibid.

there came to be a "constant tension, interplay, and interrelationship between the ideal world of God's goodness and the 'real' world where evil triumphs over good, which provides an important key to understanding the structure of Calvin's thought."[99] Armstrong sought to provide a new perspective on the structure of Calvin's thought:

> Calvin lived intimately in the two worlds of Renaissance and Reformation, and he never was able to resolve the conflicts of fundamentally different ideologies. Consequently, his theology was accommodated to conflicting ideologies in such a way that there will always be two poles, two aspects, two dialectical and conflicting elements in each theological topic which he discusses.[100]

This Renaissance/Reformation, ideal/real dialectic, Armstrong suggests, is the basis for the division of the *Institutes*, and permeates and informs every topic covered. Starting with Book I and its statement about "the primal or simple knowledge to which the very order of nature would have led us *if* Adam had remained upright (1.2.1), Armstrong points to the hypothetical or conditional structure of this book. He argues:

> What is to be carefully noted at this point is that this pattern which is established at the outset is the one which will be followed throughout; that is to say, Calvin always develops what might have been if sin had not occurred, of what God has perfectly done, as over against that disruption and distortion which has been brought about by sin.[101]

It is interesting that when Armstrong deals with Book III, he claims that the soteriological doctrines are likewise to be understood as conditional, and that "all the topics that follow and which 'depend' on faith are governed by the hypothetical motif."[102] Further, Armstrong states:

> The hypothetical and actual, the ideal and the real, structure which characterizes Calvin's theology is nowhere more clearly seen than in the discussion of the doctrine of justification . . . viewed from the perspective of justification (i.e., viewed in Christ) the individual is pure and holy, accepted and forgiven. On the other hand, viewed from the perspective of sanctification

---

99. Ibid., 142–44.
100. Ibid., 137.
101. Ibid., 143.
102. Ibid., 149.

(i.e., viewed in themselves and from the perspective of their actual condition and performance), all believers are still enmeshed in sin, impure, and in need of constant forgiveness.[103]

Despite the title and opening words of his essay, however, Armstrong fails to make any connection between the *duplex cognitio Domini* and the *duplex gratia* in his discussion of soteriology. Moreover, we agree with Garcia's remarks:

> . . . reduction of the justification/sanctification distinction to differing perspectives in light of which believers are, in the one case viewed in Christ (justification) and in the other viewed in themselves (sanctification) seems to obscure Calvin's regular insistence that *both* graces reflect on our union with Christ. Even more fundamentally, however, Armstrong's positing of a fundamental tension or conflict between Renaissance and Reformation can be criticized for separating unnecessarily what, perhaps especially in Calvin . . . certainly belong together.[104]

Concluding his essay, Armstrong says that "an indispensable element in ascertaining the structure of Calvin's thought in the *Institutes* is the hypothetical motif which one finds throughout the material."[105] As we carefully study the *Institutes* in the next chapters, however, it should become abundantly clear that far from being hypothetical, Calvin, even in Book I, is never interested in empty speculations.

In 1995, Butin also took up the dialectical presentation of the *Institutes* that Dowey and others had upheld.[106] He emphasized that the "dialectical interpretations . . . tend to underestimate the significance of Calvin's own explicit and persistent use of the trinitarian structure of the Apostles' Creed as the organizing paradigm for successive editions of the *Institutes*." He also pointed out that "the predominance of dialectical patterns of interpretation significantly distract Calvin scholarship from a proper appreciation of the prominence of the Trinity in Calvin's understanding of the divine-human relationship."[107] Moreover, he says, "even [Calvin's] discussion of the first article of the Creed (God the Father, including creation) fell within an overall context that assumed the noetic

103. McKee and Armstrong, *Probing the Reformed Tradition*, 149.
104. Garcia, *Life in Christ*, 23–24.
105. McKee and Armstrong, *Probing the Reformed Tradition*, 151.
106. Butin, *Revelation, Redemption, and Response*.
107. Ibid., 21.

priority of redemption in Christ for the true knowledge of God as either Creator or Redeemer."[108] In Butin's criticism of Dowey, he says, "the sharp conceptual distinction assumed in his use of the *duplex cognitio* as a comprehensive interpretive hypothesis for the *Institutes* makes inevitable an operative dichotomy between the two that is more imposed upon than drawn from Calvin."[109] In a further criticism he notes that "on Dowey's reading of Calvin, the essential unity of God's trinitarian nature and God's trinitarian economic activity for the accomplishment of human salvation is easily overlooked."[110] It is worth noting that in spite of Butin's criticism of Köstlin (and Dowey), Butin considered Book I of the *Institutes* to relate to fallen humanity.[111]

In a 2008 analysis of Calvin's theology, Charles Partie referred to four structural patterns that have been proposed for the *Institutes*

1. The four articles of the Apostles' Creed.
2. The twofold knowledge of God.
3. The Trinitarian nature of God.
4. The believer's union with Christ.

Quoting a statement from Institutes III, i, 1, Partie then wrote:

> This statement suggests that Calvin's previous exposition was concerned with what Christ does *for* us and the subsequent discussion will treat what Christ does *within* us. In this connection our union with Christ is powerfully affirmed. Since the incarnation, Christians are not allowed to think of themselves apart from Christ in whom by God's grace, they live. Using this statement as a pivot, the four books of the *Institutes* can be divided into equal parts: Part I, God *For* Us: Book I God the Creator, Book II God the Redeemer, Part II, God *Within* Us: Book III the faithful Person(s), Book IV The Faithful Community.[112]

Later, however, we will show that the twofold knowledge of God of Books I and II of the *Institutes* and the twofold grace of Book III are so related that they cannot be seen as God for us and God within us.

---

108. Ibid., 22.
109. Ibid., 24.
110. Ibid.
111. Ibid., 22.
112. Partie, *Theology of John Calvin*, 40.

xxxvi *Introduction*

Nonetheless, there is still room for further debate on Dowey's concept of two explanations and two orders of the knowledge of God. It is here that Dowey finds incongruity between the doctrines of revelation and of faith. I would suggest that what Dowey considered to be incongruity and discrepancy are in fact entirely reconcilable, and that the relationship between revelation and faith can be systematically explained. There is also no need to suggest a two-part division of the *Institutes*, with Book I concerning the knowledge of God the Creator and Books II through IV, the knowledge of God the Redeemer. Furthermore, a better understanding can be achieved when the twofold knowledge of God is seen in light of Calvin's treatment of the corresponding twofold knowledge of the *duplex gratia Christi*.[113] Although this topic will be explored more fully in the following two chapters, a brief summary follows.

Twofold Knowledge of God and Twofold Knowledge of Ourselves

I am fully aware that Calvin scholarship believes that the *duplex cognitio Domini* is either *a* or *the* controlling principle of the *Institutes*. Gamble expresses this position very clearly:

> The first and most important postulate of Calvin's thought is this twofold knowledge of God and of man. Calvin scholarship has shown increasing unanimity that this basic presupposition of Calvin must be reckoned with as either *a* controlling principle of his theology or *the* controlling principle. In addition to the earlier work of Ford Battles of Calvin Seminary, Tom Parker of Cambridge, Ed Dowey of Princeton, and J. Köstlin, we should note that very recently John Leith of Union Seminary in Virginia, Joseph McClelland of McGill University, and Fritz Büsser of Zürich have agreed that a twofold knowledge of God and man is *the* controlling structure of Calvin's theology. Echoing Augustine, the great theologian of Hippo Regius, Calvin was convinced that we cannot understand ourselves until we understand who God is.[114]

To take the *duplex cognitio Domini* as the exclusive framework for understanding the *Institutes* and Calvin's theology, as Dowey and some Calvin scholars do, is misleading, however. The starting point for Calvin is clearly stated in *Inst*.I.i.1: "True and sound wisdom consists *of two*

---

113. *Inst*. III, xi, 1.
114. Gamble, ed., *Articles on Calvin and Calvinism*, 180.

parts: the knowledge of God *and of ourselves.*" Regarding this opening sentence de Greef says: "The entire *Institutes* is written in the light of these opening lines."[115] The same is repeated in I, xv, 1; II, i, 1; and II, viii, 1. "Both are true simultaneously. There is no proper knowledge of God which does not involve self-understanding."[116] Parker agrees, saying: "The inter-relationship between the knowledge of God and the knowledge of ourselves is throughout the *Institutes* taken as the necessary epistemological presupposition to theology."[117]

It should be noted that regardless of the titles of Book I, *The Knowledge of God the Creator*, and Book II, *The Knowledge of God the Redeemer*, Calvin presents a twofold knowledge of ourselves in both books. In Book I he says:

> The knowledge of ourselves is twofold: Namely to know what we were like when we were first created and what our condition became after the fall of Adam. While it would be of little benefit to understand our creation unless we recognize in this sad ruin what our nature in its corruption and deformity is like, we shall nevertheless be content for the moment with the description of our originally upright nature. And to be sure, before we come up to the miserable condition of man to which he is now subjected, it is worthwhile to know what he was like when first created.[118]

In order to know what man was like when he was first created, Calvin says:

> That, indeed, can nowhere be better recognized than from the *restoration* of his corrupted nature . . . the beginning of our recovery of salvation in the *restoration* which we obtain through Christ, who also is called the Second Adam for the reason that he *restores* us to true and complete integrity.[119]

In Book II, which according to its title concerns the knowledge of God as Redeemer, Calvin again speaks about knowledge of ourselves:

> In our discussion of the knowledge of ourselves we have set forth this chief point: that empty of all opinion of our own virtue and

---

115. de Greef, *Writings of John Calvin*, 197.
116. George, *Theology of the Reformers*, 189.
117. Fisher, *History of Christian Doctrine*, 387–88.
118. *Inst.*, I, xv, 1.
119. *Inst.*, I, xv, 4; italics added.

shorn of all assurance of our own righteousness—in fact broken and crushed by the awareness of our own utter poverty—we may learn genuine humility and self-abasement.[120]

It is therefore evident that for Calvin the twofold knowledge of God has a corresponding twofold knowledge of ourselves. This parallel is spelled out repeatedly in accordance with his opening words of the *Institutes*. The knowledge of God the Creator in Book I corresponds to the knowledge of ourselves as we were originally created, or rather as we are being restored, since Calvin considers this to be the best way to recognize what we were like when we were first created. The knowledge of God the Redeemer in Book II corresponds to the knowledge of ourselves as sinners. Thus the first five chapters of Book II in fact belong where they are, and there is no need to say with Dowey that Book II really begins only in Chapter vi.[121]

Because of this correspondence, it is unnecessary to consider Dowey's reservations about relating the "knowledge of God and of ourselves" to the twofold knowledge of God. We can therefore ignore his protestations that:

> It would promote clarity and accuracy in Calvin scholarship generally if Calvin's own terminology of the 'twofold' knowledge were used exclusively as Calvin used it for the knowledge of God the Creator and redeemer. This technical term should not be carelessly applied to the 'knowledge of God and ourselves,' as often happens.[122]

Twofold Knowledge and Twofold Grace

In our consideration of the place of twofold grace within Calvin's theology, we have already explored Venema's contributions to the discussion at hand. He sought to determine the theological context within which Calvin broached the subject of the *duplex gratia Dei* and without which it remains unintelligible; and to clarify the connections between the *duplex gratia Dei*

---

120. *Inst.*, II, viii,1; this statement is looking back to *Inst*; II, i–vi.

121. Ibid., 45. It is worth nothing that Battles accepted Dowey's understanding; see 41, n.4.

122. Dowey; *Knowledge of God*, 1994, x; also 252, n.30. It should be noted that in spite of Dowey's extended presentation of the "Correlative Character of the Knowledge of God and Man," he ended by stating that "The knowledge of 'ourselves' is a term which Calvin uses by synecdoche for all man's knowledge of creation," 21.

with the preceding and subsequent material, as well as to understand it within the overall structure and movement of Calvin's theology. Venema found that the knowledge of God and of ourselves constitutes the larger context for the twofold grace of God in Calvin's thought.[123]

As will become clear throughout this book, the *duplex cognitio Domini* and the *duplex gratia* are in fact related in a very different fashion. In contrast to Venema's position, I maintain that the *duplex gratia dei* is the key to a better understanding of Calvin's twofold knowledge of God and his whole theology. Furthermore, the reader should note that the correspondence between the *duplex cognitio Domini* of I, ii,1 and the *duplex gratia* of III, xi, 1 provides us with a better understanding of the *Institutes*. Calvin writes:

> By partaking of Him (Christ) we principally receive a double grace (*duplex gratia*) namely, that being reconciled to God through Christ's blamelessness, we may have in Heaven instead of a Judge a gracious Father; and secondly, that sanctified by Christ's Spirit we may cultivate blamelessness and purity of life.[124]

Calvin explains that he is speaking of the twofold grace of justification and regeneration (sanctification). In this connection Antony Lane states: "The crucial element of Evangelical theology, the distinction between justification and sanctification slogan is not to be found in the medievals."[125] Instead, this concept was presented by Calvin. As Geoffrey Bromiley pointed out:

> The Reformers in general can hardly be said to have presented a comprehensive view of Christian salvation and the Christian life in a way which brings out the full relationship of justification and sanctification. This was to be the great achievement of Calvin.[126]

Throughout this book, I will seek to demonstrate clearly that the grace of sanctification corresponds to the knowledge of ourselves as we are being restored and to what we were before the fall (knowledge of God the Creator), while the grace of justification corresponds to the knowledge of God the Redeemer and the knowledge of ourselves as sinners. I believe that this distinction explains why Calvin teaches about

123. Venema, *Accepted and Renewed in Christ*, 52.
124. *Inst.* III. xi, 1.
125. Lane, *Calvin and Bernard of Clairvaux*, 56.
126. Bromiley, *Historical Theology*, 237.

sanctification first and only later discusses justification in conjunction with the concept of the *duplex gratia Dei*.[127] Consequently there is no need to rearrange the material of the *Institutes* nor to speak of incongruities and discrepancies in Calvin's theology. There is also no need to claim with Venema that the arrangement of the material of the *Institutes* depends partially upon rhetorical considerations.[128] This issue will be dealt with more fully in the first chapter of this book.

AN ECUMENICAL PERSPECTIVE

We have already noted that biblical criticism of the modern era has challenged the authority of Scripture. This development ensured that the issues of biblical criticism determined the course and form of the answer to a great extent. Biblical authority came to be linked to the doctrine of inspiration, and the church was forced more than ever before to formulate this doctrine fully and carefully.

The debate, however, was at first very much limited to Protestant circles. This result, of course, is due to the *sola Scriptura* principle upheld in Protestantism. Yet it is interesting that even among Roman Catholics the authority of Scripture was also discussed from the perspective of the doctrine of inspiration.[129] In 1893 Pope Leo XIII wrote in his encyclical letter *Providentissimus Deus*, "On the Study of Holy Scripture," that inspiration is incompatible with error:

> It follows that those who maintain that an error is possible in any genuine passage of the sacred writings either pervert the Catholic notion of inspiration or make God the author of such error. And so emphatically were all the Fathers and Doctors agreed that the divine writings, as left by the hagiographers, are free from all error, that they labored earnestly, with no less skill than reverence to reconcile with each other those numerous passages which seem at variance.[130]

The Second Vatican Council later issued a dogmatic constitution on divine revelation, *Dei Verbum*, which reflected the prominent place

---

127. *Inst.*, III, xi, 1.
128. Venema, *Accepted and Renewed in Christ*, 63.
129. *Rome and the Study of Scripture*, 5th ed., 48, 113.
130. Ibid., 25. See *Spiritus Paraclitus* of Pope Benedict XV, in which "Biblical inerrancy" is mentioned again in 1920. The phrase appeared later in the encyclical *Humani generis* of Pope Pius XII. Ibid., 48, 113.

given to the Bible at the council's meetings. Gabriel Daly, an Augustinian priest who teaches theology at Trinity College in Dublin and at the Irish School of Ecumenics, reported that:

> The privileged status of the Bible as mediator of divine revelation was safeguarded by *Dei Verbum*'s tacit, though immensely significant, abandoning of the two-source theology ('revelation is contained *partly* in Scripture and *partly* in Tradition'). Instead it teaches that 'tradition and scripture make up a single sacred deposit of the word of God, which is entrusted to the Church.'[131]

As far as Protestantism is concerned, however, it was only natural that a renewed investigation of the Reformation principle should lead to a revival of interest in the Reformers. Surveying the literature on Calvin's doctrine of authority, Forstman points out that "the question of Calvin's view of inspiration has become the focal point of debate in the various discussions of Calvin's view of the Scriptures."[132] Forstman accordingly found the secondary Calvin literature to fall into three categories with "the exposition of Calvin's view of inspiration" as "the key to the categorization."[133] The examination of this secondary literature will not be undertaken here. It will be considered in the last chapter of this work, which discusses the doctrine of inspiration. Yet the reader should remember that when Calvin's doctrine of Scripture is studied on the basis of his remarks on inspiration, his doctrine of authority will be approached from the wrong perspective. Nowhere in his writings did Calvin leave us a formulated doctrine of inspiration. Moreover, the teachings we have from his pen were not written with modern biblical criticism in mind. To call on Calvin for the support of one view or the other in the contemporary debate would be to drag him into an arena where he does not really belong. It is little wonder indeed that both sides of the argument could claim his thought as foundational to their own (as seen with Warfield, Briggs and others), and as we shall explore further in Chapter Five.

We shall likewise more fully address the context within which Calvin propounded his doctrine of the authority of Scripture. His battle

---

131. *Dei Verbum*, art. 11; cited by Daly in "Revelation in the Theology of the Roman Catholic Church," 37.

132. Forstman, *Word and Spirit*, 3. Cf. Reid, *Authority of Scripture*, "Supplementary Note," 54–55.

133. Ibid., 4.

was conducted on three fronts: against the Roman Catholics, the left-wing Anabaptists, and some humanist rationalists. As far as the latter, Calvin repeatedly maintained that arguments and disputations could not establish the authority of Scripture, for such authority could not be achieved except through faith.[134] Against the radical Anabaptists, he emphasized the "inviolable bond" between the Word and the Spirit, for he thought that the "fanatics, abandoning Scripture and flying over to revelation, cast down all the principles of godliness."[135]

Calvin, however, considered his most important adversary to be the Roman Catholic Church. Despite the Reformers' *sola Scriptura* principle, Calvin did not consider the church to be altogether without authority. His high doctrine of the church and its ministry makes this point quite evident. Thus in relation to the Roman Church, Calvin did not deny the authority of the church but rather tried to define its limits and draw a line between it and the authority of Scripture. Therefore, it seems more appropriate to study Calvin's doctrine of biblical authority from the perspective of his doctrine of the church and its ministry than to start with his views on inspiration.

Some expression of this approach can be found in books by Wallace[136] and Krusche.[137] These two books, however, are not primarily concerned with Calvin's doctrine of Biblical authority. Wallace states clearly that his work "is not a critical study of Calvin."[138] In fact, he is not involved in conversation with Calvin scholarship. Krusche's book is an excellent piece of work, yet he makes no reference to the problems that Dowey has raised concerning Calvin's doctrine of authority. Consequently he does not relate the twofold knowledge of God and the twofold knowledge of ourselves to the doctrine of Scripture—a relationship that is very important for the understanding of Calvin's doctrine of biblical authority, as we shall see.

A study of the authority of Scripture in Calvin's theology from the perspective of his teaching on the authority of the Church, rather than nineteenth-century concerns with inspiration, coincides with the present trend in ecumenical discussions. It is obvious that the doctrine of author-

---

134. See pages 137f below.
135. *Inst.*, I, ix.
136. Wallace, *Calvin's Doctrine of the Word and Sacrament*.
137. Krusche, *Das Wirken des Heiligen Geistes nach Calvin*.
138. Wallace, *Calvin's Doctrine of Word and Sacrament,* vi.

ity is of utmost importance in the contemporary ecumenical movement. Within the ecumenical context, the questions that are raised regarding biblical authority are no longer connected to the doctrine of inspiration. The phase of this problem is seen to be more or less over. The question has become how to understand the authority of Scripture vis-à-vis tradition and the authority of the Church. Thus in a paper produced by the World Council of Churches' Faith and Order Commission, the question is posed "how 'really and truly' ... do we relate our Church tradition to Holy Scripture ... now that the leadership of our Churches no longer maintains the inerrancy of Holy Scripture?"[139] Thus the questions that have rocked the church until recent years are left behind while other questions are gaining momentum.[140] The Commission on Tradition and Traditions of the World Council of Churches also bears witness to this fact.[141]

Moreover, a remarkable interest in Calvin's doctrine of the authority of Scripture is found today in Roman Catholic circles. The *sola Scriptura* principle of the Reformation as well as the pronouncements of the Council of Trent on Scripture is being restudied and reevaluated. The main concern of the discussion is to explain the relationship of tradition to Scripture or the authority of the church to biblical authority.[142] As shown above, the dogmatic constitution *Dei Verbum* of the Second Vatican Council settled this question for the Catholic Church.[143]

OVERVIEW OF THE BOOK

For a proper understanding of Calvin's doctrine of Biblical authority, it is necessary to consider the twofold knowledge of God and the twofold knowledge of ourselves as well as the twofold grace and its implications as expressed by Calvin and their relationship to Scripture. These subjects will be discussed in Chapters One and Two of this study. After this re-

---

139. World Council of Churches, Commission on Faith and Order. *Old and New in the Church*, 7–8; Cf. "Tradition as an Issue in Contemporary Theology," Ibid., 20–22.

140. Bakhuizen van den Brink, "La tradition dans l' église primitive et au xvie siècle," 271–81; see also "The Value of Tradition" *in Reformation and Catholicity*, edited jointly with Loos, 16–19.

141. Faith and Order Commission, *Old and New in the Church*, 12–14.

142. Horton, *Christian Theology*; John M. Todd ed., *Problèmes de l'autorité*, (London: Darton Longman and Todd, 1962), especially "L'autorité de l' Écriture et la Tradition,» 39-41 ; Ehrlich, «Papacy and Scripture,» 113–23.

143. See p. xli above.

lationship has been clarified, Calvin's doctrine of authority will then be viewed in the light of the correlation between word and Spirit that finds repeated expression in his writings.[144] Calvin looked at the relationship between word and Spirit from four different angles. First, and logically, Calvin considered the production of the sacred record; in this context, he touched on the doctrine of inspiration. Two further discourses on word and Spirit are considered in his discussion of faith. Calvin distinguishes between two operations of the Spirit that result in the miracle of faith. One is the enlightening of the mind, which Calvin terms "illumination of the mind," and the second is in the strengthening of the heart, or what Calvin calls "sealing of the heart." These two operations correspond to Calvin's division of the faculties of the human soul into understanding and will.[145] It is in connection with the latter operation that Calvin then speaks of the *testimonium internum Spiritus Sancti*. This internal testimony is closely related to his concept of certainty with its various applications. These two operations of the Spirit will be the subject matter of Chapters Three and Four.

Calvin also considered the operation of the Spirit as he combated the theology of the Anabaptist fanatics, who claimed to receive new revelations. Here Calvin utilized his concept of the correlation of Word and Spirit to emphasize that the Spirit cannot contradict himself: "He is the Author of the Scripture; he cannot vary and differ from himself."[146] This fourth dimension of Calvin's perspective on Word and Spirit will also be discussed in Chapter Four.

Although Calvin discussed inspiration in light of his teaching on the production of the word, we will defer its consideration until Chapter Five. This reservation will enable us to fully explore Calvin's explication of the correlation of the word and the Spirit, which will provide a foundation for better understanding his insights concerning inspiration.

---

144. Johnson in *Authority in Protestant Theology*, 48–50, presents Calvin's doctrine of authority under the correlation of word and Spirit, but because of the nature of his book the discussion is brief. Most of the space is given to the first noetic office of the Holy Spirit, or inspiration. Moreover, no distinction is made between the two operations of the Holy Spirit in faith—a distinction essential to understanding Calvin's doctrine of the *testimonium internum Spiritus Sancti*. This doctrine in turn is important for an adequate understanding of his doctrine of authority.

145. *Inst.*, I, xv, 6–8.

146. *Inst.*, I, ix, 2 (O. S. III 83, 33).

A further note: In this book reference is occasionally made to Rome, the Roman Catholic Church, the Anabaptists, the Schoolmen, and others about whom Calvin had much to say. The writer would like to make clear that whenever references are made to these institutions and persons, they are presented as Calvin saw, understood, and presented them. From our perspective his depictions are often less than charitable, but we must understand that Calvin was deeply affected by the debates of the sixteenth century and his writings reflect his period. We have made no effort to present the viewpoints of his opponents because these controversies lie outside the scope of this study.

PART ONE

Scripture and the Knowledge of God

1

Knowledge of God: The *Duplex Cognitio Domini*

CALVIN OPENED THE FIRST edition of the *Institutes* in 1536 with the following thought, "All sacred doctrine consists in two things: the knowledge of God and of ourselves."[1] Again in his *Instruction in Faith* of 1537, he began by pointing out that "we all are created in order that we may know the majesty of our Creator, that having known it, we may esteem it above all and honor it with all awe, love and reverence."[2] Later on, the first question that is asked in the Geneva Catechism is: "What is the chief end of human life?" The answer is: "To know God."[3] From its reprinting in 1539 until the definitive edition of 1559, the *Institutes* opened with the well-known words: "Nearly all the wisdom we possess, that is to say, true and sound wisdom, consists of two parts: the knowledge of God and of ourselves."[4] These references, as well as many others, show the prominence of the theme of the knowledge of God in Calvin's theology.

It should be noted at the outset that the knowledge of God for Calvin differs fundamentally from any other form of knowing because the object of this knowledge is God, who is unique;[5] and God comes to be the object of human knowledge only inasmuch as he objectifies himself and makes himself knowable in the act of self-revelation. Therefore, even when God becomes the object of human knowledge, he is known "not as he is in himself, but as he is toward us."[6] Moreover, the reception of this knowledge, for Calvin, is not an act of the mind alone, but

---

1. O.S. I, 37.
2. Translated by Fuhrmann, 17 (O.S. I, 378).
3. Translated by Torrance, *School of Faith*, 3 (C.O. VI, 9).
4. *Inst.* I, i, 1 (O.S. III, 31, 6–8).
5. Cf. Barth, Church Dogmatics, II:1, *Doctrine of God*, 14ff. Cf. Parker, *Knowledge of God*, 106.
6. *Inst.*, I, x, 2 (O.S. III, 86, 17ff.).

involves the heart as well. Such reception is what Calvin considered to be faith.

We have surveyed some important works in the introduction in order to clarify what the knowledge of God meant for Calvin and to situate this doctrine within his theology. We have seen that Lobstein in his article "La connaissance religieuse d'après Calvin" stated that religious knowledge for Calvin is practical, experimental, subjective, moral, and teleological.[7] He considered this knowledge to be Calvin's doctrine of faith. Yet Calvin is seen to have combined an objective factor with this subjective doctrine, the objective factor being his doctrine of Scripture.[8] Lobstein considered the doctrine of faith to be the real spiritual, liberal, and evangelical element in Reformation theology.[9] On the other hand, he identified the doctrine of authority as rigid, formal, scholastic, and medieval.[10] Lobstein then raised the question of how and why Calvin combined these two irreconcilable elements in his doctrine of the knowledge of God. Answering his own question, he suggested that Calvin was forced to formulate his doctrine of authority in the manner he did because of his struggle against the Roman Church on one side and the Anabaptists on the other.[11]

In the final analysis, as we have said before, Lobstein finds that we have to choose between Calvin's doctrine of authority and his doctrine of faith. He then very confidently states that the choice has already been made and that modern theologians have favored the liberal, spiritual, evangelical, and subjective doctrine of faith over the doctrine of authority.[12]

We have also seen that the same year Lobstein's article appeared, another article on Calvin's doctrine of the knowledge of God was published by B. B. Warfield.[13] This article is to a great extent an exposition of *Inst.*, I, i–x. Warfield discusses Calvin's doctrine of Scripture at length, and considers that the doctrine of inspiration is basic to an understanding of

---

7. Lobstein, "Connaissance religieuse," 58 ff.; italics added.
8. Ibid., 68ff.
9. Ibid., 58ff.
10. Ibid., 68ff.
11. Ibid., 83ff.
12. Ibid., 109ff.
13. Warfield, "Inspiration," 219–325. References in this essay are quoted from Warfield, *Calvin and Calvinism*, where this article was republished.

Calvin's doctrine of authority.[14] Warfield expresses disappointment that Calvin separated the discussion of the accreditation of the Scriptures from that of the "assimilation of its revelatory contents."[15] Yet he goes on to remind the reader that Calvin explicitly refers to his doctrine of faith as the context within which the doctrine of the testimony of the Spirit should be understood.[16] Warfield concludes accordingly that the testimony of the Spirit "is only one application of the general doctrine of faith."[17] This application is seen to be a "repairing operation on the souls of sinful men by which they are enabled to perceive light"[18] or regeneration.[19] As far as the authority of Scripture is concerned, Warfield maintains that "Calvin would certainly have said that our faith in Christ presupposes faith in the Scriptures, rather than that we believe in the Scriptures for Christ's sake."[20] Yet Warfield does not commit himself to a chronological sequence for the *ordo salutis*.[21] This same approach to Calvin was reiterated with some modification by Osterhaven.[22] Neither Lobstein nor Warfield, however, make any use of Calvin's concept of the twofold knowledge of God and the corresponding twofold knowledge of ourselves—a concept that is essential for an understanding of Calvin's doctrine of Scripture.

Parker[23] and Dowey,[24] as we have already noted, considered the knowledge of God in its twofold nature. As far as the former is concerned, he shows some interest in the nature and function of the Scriptures.[25] Little attention, however, is given to the question of biblical authority. Moreover, Parker does not relate the twofold knowledge of God at all to the twofold knowledge of ourselves except in passing,[26] and does not

14. Ibid., 60ff.
15. Ibid., 71.
16. Ibid., 71ff.
17. Ibid., 72.
18. Ibid., 32.
19. Ibid., 102ff.
20. Ibid., 107.
21. Ibid.
22. Osterhaven, "Our Knowledge of God."
23. Parker, *Doctrine of the Knowledge of God*.
24. Dowey, *Knowledge of God in Calvin's Theology* (1952).
25. Parker, *Doctrine of the Knowledge of God*, 42ff.
26. Ibid., 119.

clarify the relationship of Scripture to both. Dowey, on the other hand, shows great interest in Calvin's doctrine of authority. As we have already seen in the Introduction, he regards Calvin's division of the definitive edition of the *Institutes* as misleading. "From the point of view of the knowledge of God, which is the foundation of Calvin's theological writing, Calvin's *Institutes* of 1559 contains two, not four, divisions."[27] With regard to dividing the *Institutes* into two parts, Dowey goes on to say:

> This division corresponds to what Calvin conceived of as the two kinds of revelation: the revelation of God as Creator, and as Redeemer. The short Book I of the 1559 edition represents the former, and the whole remainder of the work represents the latter.[28]

Dowey then goes on to say, "The really significant ordering principle of the *Institutes* in the 1559 edition is the *duplex cognitio Domini*, not the Apostles' Creed."[29] Dowey accordingly makes a careful analysis of knowledge of God the Creator and knowledge of God the Redeemer. Then, like Lobstein, he finds discrepancies and dissonance between Calvin's doctrine of authority and his doctrine of faith.[30] And once again, like Lobstein, he suggests that Calvin was driven to a heteronomous formal doctrine of authority in spite of his doctrine of faith because of his struggle against the Roman Catholics on the one hand and the Anabaptists on the other.[31] Dowey, however, does not think that we have

---

27. Dowey, *Knowledge of God* (1994), 41.

28. Ibid. The same view, as Dowey tells us, is expressed by Köstlin, „Calvins Institutio nach Form und Inhalt," 57ff. ; and Wendel, *Calvin, Sources et évolution de sa pensée religieuse*, 87. The writer has also found the same division of the *Institutes* suggested by Dakin, *Calvinism*,15 and 247.

29. Dowey, *Knowledge of God* (1994), 41. Regarding the ordering of the material of the definitive edition of the *Institutes* according to what Calvin considered the "four parts" of the Apostles Creed, Dowey says, "Calvin not only follows this order but also specifically claims to be doing so in I. xvi. 18." Ibid., p. 41, n. 1. The reference that Dowey gives should be II, xvi,18. At this place, however, Calvin is not referring to the *Institutes* as a whole. He is referring only to the material in the chapter at hand. Whenever Calvin intended to follow the Apostles' Creed he stated this fact very clearly and explicitly, as he did in the Geneva Catechism and in all editions of the *Institutes* before 1559.

30. Ibid., 161 (1952 and 1994).

31. Ibid., 162 (1952 and 1994). It is interesting to note that the solution offered by Dowey after the words: "I offer the following suggestion . . . " is similar to Lobstein's in "Connaissance religieuse," 83ff.

to choose between Calvin's doctrine of authority and his doctrine of faith. He rather subsumes the first under the latter.[32]

Most of the writers we have dealt with who touched on biblical authority, especially Dowey, speak of the correlative character of the knowledge of God in Calvin. Yet to my knowledge, none has so far related the twofold knowledge of God in Calvin's theology to the twofold knowledge of ourselves in order to promote a fuller understanding of Calvin's theology and the *Institutes* in particular. We shall soon see that this correlation is important for a clear understanding of Calvin's doctrines of the knowledge of God and of biblical authority.

THE NATURE OF THE TWOFOLD KNOWLEDGE

Calvin expresses the twofold knowledge of God in these words: "First . . . the Lord shows himself to be the Creator. Then, he shows himself to be the Redeemer."[33] Calvin discusses the knowledge of God as Creator and then as Redeemer on the basis of this twofoldness in Books I and II respectively. We have already pointed out that the twofold knowledge of God implies a corresponding twofold knowledge of ourselves. Calvin presents his discussion of the twofold knowledge of God and of ourselves as we find it in the first two books of the *Institutes* as that of a believer speaking from his experience of faith. Yet he does not speak of his own experience in isolation. Therefore, he very often takes the reader along with him as if he were going through the same experience with the reader. On this basis he speaks in the plural, in terms of *we*, *us*, *our*, and the like. Furthermore, we should notice that Calvin speaks of himself as part of the human race. This knowledge of faith makes him see that God's plan and purpose go beyond himself to embrace humanity as a whole. The earlier editions of the *Institutes* demonstrate this fact quite clearly. Thus in the edition of 1536, after he had pointed out that sacred doctrine consists of the knowledge of God and of ourselves, Calvin opens a section on the knowledge of God saying,

> Now for the present we must learn these things about God. First, we must hold with firm conviction . . . that God is infinite wisdom, justice, goodness, mercy, truth, virtue, and life . . . . Second,

---

32. Ibid., vii (1952), xvii (1994).
33. *Inst.*, I, ii, 1 (O.S. III, 34, 21–24).

all things which are in heaven and earth were created for his glory.... In the third place, he himself is a just judge.... In the fourth place, he is compassionate and gentle.... He is ready to spare and forgive, if any ask pardon from him.[34]

Here we see Calvin speaking of the knowledge of God as God's relationship to human beings.

The same pattern is obvious when Calvin goes on to speak about the knowledge of ourselves. Here he says:

> In order that we may arrive at a sure knowledge of ourselves, we must hold this point first: that Adam, the parent of us all, was created in the image and likeness of God, that is, he was endowed with wisdom, righteousness, and holiness.... But as soon as he fell into sin (Gen 3) this image and likeness of God was erased and obliterated.... This calamity fell not only upon Adam, but also upon us who are his seed and posterity.[35]

From this point, Calvin goes on to speak about humankind as sinners, which is what he meant by the knowledge of ourselves. This same idea finds expression in the editions of the *Institutes* that appeared between 1539 and 1554, where we find the first chapter titled "On the Knowledge of God" and the second "On the Knowledge of Man." Once again we notice that Calvin speaks as a person of faith out of his own experience, though he is also addressing humanity as a whole. The discussion of the knowledge of ourselves in the second chapter makes this fact stand out very clearly. Here Calvin regards humanity in terms of Adam as created and as fallen. It is important for us to keep this whole approach in mind for a proper understanding of Books I and II of the 1559 *Institutes*.

Calvin added a new subtitle to the first chapter in the edition of 1543 and all later editions that describes the function of Scripture: "On the knowledge of God, which is the first fundamental of religion; and where its true norm is to be sought."[36] Here we see that Calvin is concerned about the *what* and the *where* of the knowledge of God, not about the way in which we arrive at that knowledge. Thus it will be sufficient to note here that the discussion of the authority of Scripture in I, vii–ix and

---

34. Hards, "Critical Translation and Evaluation," 68ff. (O.S. I, 37).

35. Ibid., 69ff. (O.S. I, 37ff.).

36. *De cognitione Dei: Quae primum est religionis fundamentum; et unde vera eius regula sit petenda* (C.O.I, 279ff.).

especially the inner witness of the Holy Spirit was not intended to be an epistemological introduction in which one finds the means of acquiring knowledge of God once it is known to be objectively found in Scripture. This will be seen more clearly as we consider Calvin's repeated references to faith as the only basis of the twofold knowledge.

FAITH: THE BASIS OF THE TWOFOLD KNOWLEDGE OF GOD

The discussion of the *duplex cognitio Domini* as we find it in the first two books of the *Institutes* was not intended by Calvin to show how we arrive at knowledge of God either as Creator or as Redeemer. Before introducing the concept of the twofold knowledge, Calvin clearly points out that, "In this ruin of mankind no one now experiences God either as Father or as Author of salvation, or favorable in any way, until Christ the Mediator comes forward to reconcile him to us."[37] Thus we can see that the twofold knowledge of God and of ourselves as discussed in Books I and II of the *Institutes* is intended to present the believer's view of God's nature in relationship to humankind as well as the nature of humankind in relationship to God. Butin states this pattern clearly as follows:

> In the 1536 edition, the catechetical structure of the *Institutes* highlighted Calvin's supposition that he was writing within a church context as a Christian teacher to the elect Christian believers who constitute the church. With regard to their knowledge of God, then, his assumed standpoint toward his readers was that they were already the beneficiaries of God's gracious redemption in Christ.[38]

This understanding appears in all subsequent editions of the *Institutes*. In both books in the 1559 edition, humankind is seen in Adam, first to show what he was like when he was first created, then to show his condition after the fall. In the course of the discussion, Calvin considers humanity's sinfulness and natural inability to arrive at this twofold knowledge. Yet the question of the individual's way to or means of arriving at this knowledge is not the focus of these two books. This restriction of focus applies to the knowledge of the Creator as well as knowledge of the Redeemer. Therefore, after Calvin had finished discussing the

---

37. *Inst.*, I, ii, 1 (O.S. III, 34, 15–17).
38. Butin, *Revelation, Redemption and Response*, 22.

knowledge of the Creator, he looks back and says, "since we have fallen from life into death, the whole knowledge of God the Creator that we have discussed would be useless unless faith also followed, setting forth for us God our Father in Christ."[39] Moreover, he goes on to say:

> God is comprehended in Christ alone. John's saying has always been true: "He that does not have the Son does not have the Father." For even if many men once boasted that they worshipped the Supreme Majesty, the Maker of heaven and earth, yet because they had no Mediator it was not possible for them truly to taste God's mercy, and thus be persuaded that he was their Father. Accordingly, because they did not hold Christ as their Head, they possessed only a fleeting knowledge of God. From this it also came about that they at last lapsed into crass and foul superstitions and betrayed their own ignorance. So today the Turks, although they proclaim at the top of their lungs that the Creator of heaven and earth is God, still, while repudiating Christ, substitute an idol in place of the true God.[40]

Thus we can see that Calvin presents the whole knowledge of God the Creator in Book I, with no intention at all of pointing out the way to arrive at this knowledge. Yet he also emphasizes two important facts that clearly mark the movement of his thought. They are closely related but we shall try to distinguish them for the sake of clarity.

On the one hand, Calvin observes that no one can have knowledge of God the Creator in isolation from knowledge of the Redeemer. For "John's saying has always been true: He that does not have the Son does not have the Father." Therefore, anyone who claims to know the Creator without the knowledge of the Redeemer possesses "only a fleeting knowledge of God," and "at last lapses into crass and foul superstition." Here we can see why Calvin must move from discussion of the knowledge of God the Creator to consideration of knowledge of God the Redeemer.

On the other hand, Calvin points out that faith is the only way to arrive at knowledge of the Creator, which when experienced cannot be held in isolation from knowledge of the Redeemer. The two points are brought out clearly and pointedly in the sentence previously quoted: "The whole knowledge of God the Creator . . . would be useless unless faith also followed setting forth for us God our Father [knowledge of

39. *Inst.* II, vi, 1 (O.S. III, 320, 10–12).
40. *Inst.* II, vi, 4 (O.S. III, 326, 6–18).

the Creator] in Christ [knowledge of the Redeemer]." Thus no one can have knowledge of God the Creator in isolation from knowledge of God the Redeemer; and neither can be appropriated except through faith.[41] This same thought is found in Calvin's remarks on "Ye know neither me" (John 8:19) where he says:

> God in Christ descended to the lowliness of men to stretch out His hand to them. So, do not those who reject God when He approaches them like this deserve to be excluded from heaven? Let us know that the same thing is addressed to us all. Whoever aspires to know God without beginning at Christ must wander in a labyrinth, so to say. . . . Again, because everyone is deprived of all right knowledge of God who leaves Christ and strives Titan-like after heaven, so whoever directs his mind and all his senses to Christ will be led straight to the Father. . . . And it is indeed an incomparable reward for the obedience of faith that he who humbles himself before Christ penetrates above all the heavens.[42]

Again, in discussing knowledge of God the Redeemer Calvin clearly points to faith as the only means for attaining this knowledge. Thus after some remarks about the knowledge of God the Creator, he says, "Surely, after the fall of the first man no knowledge of God apart from the Mediator has had power unto salvation."[43] Then he goes on to say: "No worship has ever pleased God except that which looked to Christ . . . . Now since John teaches that life was in Christ from the beginning (John 1:4), and all the world fell away from it (Cf. John 1:10), it is necessary to return to that source."[44]

---

41. The present writer is puzzled by a statement in Dowey's discussion of knowledge of God the Creator, in which he claims that "Calvin gives us God's attributes, holding that we are taught in Scripture *apart from Christ* the eternity and self-existence, clemency, goodness, mercy . . . of God." Dowey, *Knowledge of God*, 126 (1952) and 127 (1994); italics added. As a matter of fact, this was one of Calvin's major complaints against the Schoolmen, when he emphasizes the fact that there is no knowledge whatever of God "apart from Christ." In this connection Calvin says, "This evil . . . like innumerable others, must be attributed to the Schoolmen, who have, as it were, drawn a veil over Christ to hide him. Unless we look straight toward him, we shall wander through endless labyrinths." *Inst.* III, ii, 2 (O.S. IV, 10, 1- 4). This concern of the writer has been repeated by Willis and Butin as noted above.

42. *Com.* John 8:19 (C.O. XLVII, 194ff.); cf. *Com.* John 14:7, C.O. XLVII, 325).

43. *Inst.* II, vi, 1 (O.S. III, 320, 37–321, 1).

44. Ibid. (321, 18; 20–22).

At this point Calvin finds himself speaking briefly about faith. Therefore, to make sure that the plan of his work is clear to the reader he says, "But because it is not yet my purpose exhaustively to discuss faith in Christ, it will be sufficient to touch upon it in passing."[45] The same thought occurs again a few pages later. Here Calvin is emphasizing once more the fact that "God is comprehended in Christ alone,"[46] and that there is no knowledge of the Creator in isolation from knowledge of the Redeemer. Yet to show clearly that he is deferring discussion of the way to arrive at this twofold knowledge, he adds, "I am not yet discussing faith because there will be a more suitable place for it elsewhere."[47]

Thus we have seen that Calvin looked back at Book I concerning knowledge of God the Creator and indicated that this entire knowledge "would be useless unless faith also followed." Again, after he had discussed both aspects of the twofold knowledge of God, he returned again and made a similar remark. Here he says, "As long as Christ remains outside of us, and we are separated from him, all that he has suffered and done for the salvation of the human race remains useless and of no value for us."[48] Then, he pointed again to faith as the only means for turning a useless knowledge into benefits that we receive. Thus we can see that Calvin considers faith to be the only means to attain knowledge of God. When this role of faith is kept in mind, there will be no need to call the inner witness of the Holy Spirit as presented in Book I a repair operation; or to attribute regeneration to it as if it were in and by itself the means to come to know God. Otherwise, the relationship between Calvin's doctrine of the *testimonium internum Spiritus Sancti* and his doctrine of faith will be obscured. Warfield and several others, however, did precisely this.[49] They seem to have believed that the inner witness of

---

45. Ibid. (321, 28–30).
46. *Inst.*, II, vi, 4 (O.S. III, 326, 6ff.).
47. Ibid. (325, 34ff.).
48. *Inst.*, III, i, 1 (O.S. IV, 1, 10–13).
49. Warfield, *Calvin and Calvinism*, 32, 82ff., 120ff.; Gerrish, "Biblical Authority," 356; Osterhaven, "Our Knowledge of God," 189ff. Regarding the doctrine of the inner witness of the Holy Spirit in Calvin's theology, Warfield says "It is but one application of his general doctrine of faith; or to be more specific, one application of his general doctrine of the function of the Holy Spirit in the production of faith." *Calvin and Calvinism*, 72. Yet this is not clarified in terms of what Calvin calls the "two operations" of the Holy Spirit in faith, which we shall discuss in the third chapter of this book. The present writer thinks that if Warfield had continued writing articles on the *Institutes*, his discus-

Knowledge of God: The Duplex Cognitio Domini   13

the Holy Spirit accredits the authority of the Scriptures, thus supporting the claim that God the Creator has revealed Himself therein. They misunderstood Calvin's intent, however, when they correlated word and Spirit, or the Scripture and the *testimonium internum Spiritus Sancti*, thus making them incongruent with Christ and faith.[50]

Meanwhile, we should not overlook the clear insight of both Warfield and Dowey in this respect. At an early stage in his discussion of Calvin's doctrine of the knowledge of God, Warfield says about the inner witness of the Holy Spirit, "This whole subject is only one application of the general doctrine of faith."[51] The same thought is also expressed by Dowey in the concluding section of his book, where he says, "His [Calvin's] doctrine of Scripture is in fact not *sui generis*, but a derivative of his doctrine of faith."[52] Yet, in spite of this insight both scholars present Calvin's doctrine of Scripture by itself and before examining his doctrine of faith—which is the context within which one can gain a better understanding of the role that Calvin intended the former doctrine to play. What requires emphasis here is not merely a question of organization. It is obvious that Calvin presented his doctrine of the authority of Scripture (I, vii–ix) before his doctrine of faith (III, ii). To discuss his doctrine of authority, however, before examining his doctrine of faith on the basis of following his lead as Dowey suggests, does not help the situation here. Once we gain the insight that Calvin's doctrine of biblical authority is in one way or another part of his doctrine of faith, we must study it within this context or at least after his doctrine of faith has been considered. It is only in this way that we can hope to interpret such a doctrine in the manner in which Calvin wanted it to be understood. We shall now turn to discussion of the twofold knowledge of God.

THE *DUPLEX COGNITIO DOMINI*

The paragraph in which Calvin introduces the concept of the twofold knowledge of God is one of the hardest sections of the *Institutes* to understand. Therefore, it is wise to see how he sets the stage for this concept

---

sion of Calvin's doctrine of the *testimonium* would have clarified his understanding when he came to address Calvin's doctrine of faith.

50. Ibid., 150.
51. Warfield, *Calvin and Calvinism*, 72.
52. Dowey, *Knowledge of God*, 240 (1952, 1994).

by considering the correlative character of the knowledge of God in his theology.

The Correlative Character of Knowledge of God

Calvin pointed out in 1536 that "all sacred doctrine consists in two things: the knowledge of God and of ourselves."[53] The scope of this idea was expanded in the 1539 edition, and from that time until the final edition, he opened the *Institutes* with these words: "Nearly all the wisdom we possess, that is to say, true and sound wisdom, consists of two parts: the knowledge of God and of ourselves. But while joined by many bonds, which one precedes and brings forth the other is not easy to discern."[54] Thus we can see that knowledge of God and knowledge of ourselves are closely related in Calvin's thought. For him, "the knowledge of ourselves not only arouses us to seek God, but also, as it were, leads us by the hand to find him."[55] Meanwhile, "man never achieves a clear knowledge of himself unless he has first looked upon God's face."[56]

Now, in surveying the correlative character of *knowledge of God and of ourselves* as presented by Calvin, the correspondence between the twofoldness of knowledge of God and the twofoldness of knowledge of ourselves has to be kept clearly in mind. If these two are not seen in the way Calvin presents them there will be danger of misunderstanding his entire thought. We have already dealt briefly with this matter in the Introduction; now we must treat it in more detail.

As we consider the twofold knowledge of ourselves, we notice that Calvin insists on putting it in close correspondence with the twofold knowledge of God. Therefore he says, "We cannot have a clear and complete knowledge of God unless it is accompanied by a corresponding knowledge of ourselves. This knowledge of ourselves is twofold."[57] Before proceeding further, however, we should return at this point to the earlier editions of the *Institutes* to be able to fully appreciate Calvin's arrangement of the book in the 1559 edition.

---

53. *O.S.* I, 37.
54. *Inst.* I, i, 1 (O.S. III, 31, 6-10).
55. Ibid. (32, 7-9).
56. *Inst.* I, i, 2 (O.S. III, 32, 10ff).
57. *Inst.* I, xv, 1; Cf. II, I, 1; II, I, 3 (O. S. III, 173, 30–32; 228, 20–28; 231, 5–13).

Knowledge of God: The Duplex Cognitio Domini   15

It has been noted that the opening section in the *editio princeps* considered the knowledge of God. This section was followed by a discussion of the knowledge of ourselves in which humanity was seen to be in Adam both before and after the fall. These two sections were expanded in the editions of 1539 through 1554 into two chapters, "On the Knowledge of God," and "On the Knowledge of Man." One can clearly see the twofoldness of the knowledge of ourselves in the chapter titled "On the Knowledge of Man." Now it would be worthwhile to see whether the twofold knowledge of God is also present in the first chapter.

The chapter "On the Knowledge of God" as it appeared in the editions of the *Institutes* between 1539 and 1554 was incorporated in the 1559 edition with some modification in Book I to constitute Chapters i through x as part of the discussion of knowledge of God the Creator. It may appear at first glance that the earlier chapter was concerned exclusively with the knowledge of God as Creator. A careful examination, however, shows that Calvin had in mind both aspects of the twofold knowledge in his discussion of knowledge of God in this earlier chapter. This arrangement seems to have been underlying his presentation of Scripture as a source of this knowledge. Therefore, when he gave expression to the *duplex cognitio* in the definitive edition of the *Institutes*, he introduced Scripture by saying: "He added the light of his Word by which to become known unto salvation."[58] It is obvious that knowledge unto salvation is not just knowledge of God as Creator but rather knowledge of him as Creator and Redeemer. Therefore, referring to the patriarchs Calvin goes on to say, "For, that they might pass from death to life, it was necessary to recognize God not only as Creator but also as Redeemer."[59] Then he continues, "for undoubtedly they arrived at both from the Word."[60] At this point he explains that he will concern himself in Book I with knowledge of God as Creator, deferring the discussion of knowledge of God as Redeemer to Book II.

Along with the concept of the *duplex cognitio* in the definitive edition of the *Institutes*, Calvin also introduces two terms in connection with Scripture. He points out that Scripture contains general teaching, related to knowledge of God as Creator,[61] and special teaching, connected to

58. *Inst.*, I, vi, 1 (O.S. III, 60, 17ff.).
59. Ibid. (61, 11–13).
60. Ibid. (61, 13ff.).
61. *Inst.*, I, ii, 1; I, x, 3 (O.S. III, 34, 23; 87, 20).

knowledge of him as Redeemer.⁶² Calvin then states that he will deal with the first type of teaching in Book I and the second in Book II. Thus we can see that both aspects of the twofold knowledge were implied in the chapter "On the Knowledge of God" in the editions between 1539 and 1554. We also notice that between 1539 and 1554 Calvin always closes his chapter "On the Knowledge of God" with the following statement:

> Nevertheless, since God does not show himself rightly and to intimate contemplation except in the face of his Christ, which can be regarded only with the eyes of faith that which remains to be said of the knowledge of God can best be deferred to the place where we have to speak of the knowledge of faith.⁶³

Here Calvin refers the reader to his doctrine of faith, which is followed by the discussion of the Apostles' Creed. Yet we should remember that in this statement Calvin is not implying at all that the knowledge that he has discussed up to this point is less than knowledge of faith. He is only saying that what remains to be said can best be deferred. Calvin deferred his discussion of the first article of the Creed, which later came to be Chapters xiii through xviii in Book I of the definitive edition of the *Institutes*. When this explication was no longer deferred, the earlier statement had to be dropped.⁶⁴ It is clear that part of the material that was deferred is the discussion of the second article of the Creed, which later came to be Chapters xii through xvii in Book II of the 1559 edition, in which knowledge of the Redeemer is considered. Thus we can see that when Calvin closed his first chapter "On the Knowledge of God" as published in the editions between 1539 and 1554, which refers the reader to "that which remains to be said of the knowledge of God," he was pointing to both aspects of the twofold knowledge. Consequently, this earlier chapter was not concerned exclusively with the knowledge of the Creator, although the emphasis is definitely placed on this side

---

62. *Inst.,* I, vi, 2 (O.S. III, 62, 16ff.).

63. O.S. III, 87, 36–40.

64. This fact has to be taken seriously, especially in the light of McNeill's remark that "very few sentences of the 1536 text, or of any intervening edition, are omitted in that of 1559." Calvin, *On Christian Faith*, xiii. If the above-quoted statement refers to knowledge of the Redeemer as distinguished from knowledge of the Creator, as Dowey considers it to be, saying of Chapters xiii–xviii of Book I that "they concern solely the Creator and have essentially nothing to do with the work of the Redeemer" and "do not include Calvin's Christology" (Dowey, *Knowledge of God*, 1994, 47ff.), then we cannot explain the omission. It would have been mandatory for Calvin to retain it!

of the knowledge of God. One can observe a certain lack of clarity here. Nevertheless, this lack should not be surprising since Calvin did not give full expression to the *duplex cognitio Domini* before 1559.

Turning to the second chapter of the *Institutes* in the editions of 1539 through 1554, "On the Knowledge of Man," the twofold knowledge of ourselves can be seen very clearly. We have noted already that even as early as 1536, when Calvin turned to the discussion of *knowledge of ourselves*, he had a section on humankind as created followed by another section on humankind as fallen. In both cases, the human race is seen in the person of Adam. One does not really need to underscore the fact that as far as the twofold knowledge of ourselves is concerned, the motif was there in all editions of the *Institutes* from the very beginning. Because of this inclusion, the knowledge of ourselves does not present readers with the difficulties and problems that they encounter in trying to understand the twofoldness of the knowledge of God when the twofold concept is introduced in the definitive edition.

Thus we can see that the twofoldness of the knowledge of God and of ourselves was present in all editions of the *Institutes* before 1559. It should be remembered that Calvin emphasized from the very beginning the correspondence between knowledge of God and knowledge of ourselves, although he discussed each of these in a separate chapter in the editions between 1539 and 1554. The present writer contends that one of Calvin's dissatisfactions regarding the former editions was the fact that he had separated discussion of the knowledge of God from that of knowledge of ourselves. To eliminate this defect, Calvin introduced the concept of the *duplex cognitio Domini*. Thus he worked out a correspondence between knowledge of God the Creator and knowledge of ourselves as we were first created; and on the other hand between knowledge of God the Redeemer and knowledge of ourselves as fallen. As a result, after the twofold knowledge of God had been pointed out, and in introducing the first part of the knowledge of ourselves, Calvin says:

> . . . as we said at the beginning, we cannot have a clear and complete knowledge of God unless it is accompanied by a corresponding knowledge of ourselves. This knowledge of ourselves is twofold: namely, to know what we were like when we were first created and what our condition became after the fall of Adam.[65]

---

65. *Inst.*, I, xv, 1 (O.S. III, 173, 29–33).

With the introduction of the *duplex cognitio* in the edition of 1559, Calvin added several statements to show that the twofoldness pertains to knowledge of God as well as to knowledge of ourselves, that is, "joined by many bonds" (I, i, 1). The corresponding character was always there and many writers have indicated some awareness of it in Calvin's theology. Nevertheless, the present writer is not aware of any presentation that relates the twofold knowledge of God to the corresponding twofold knowledge of ourselves.[66]

The reader should recall what was said in the Introduction, that Calvin makes it quite evident that knowledge of God the Creator corresponds to knowledge of ourselves as we were first created, while knowledge of God the Redeemer corresponds to knowledge of ourselves as fallen in Adam.[67] With this correlation in mind we shall now consider more closely the twofold knowledge of God.

The Twofold Knowledge of God

The *locus classicus* of Calvin's doctrine of the twofold knowledge of God is found in the following words:

> First, as much in the fashioning of the universe, as in the general teaching of Scripture, the Lord shows himself to be the Creator.

---

66. I am aware of one writer who makes extensive use of the twofold knowledge of ourselves: Jean Boisset, *Sagesse et sainteté dans la pensée de Jean Calvin*, 15ff. The knowledge of ourselves as we were before the fall, which Calvin considered to correspond to the knowledge of the Creator, is, however, dispatched in seven pages; while the knowledge of ourselves after the fall is discussed in 116 pages. It is interesting that in Boisset's chapter on humankind after the fall, he discusses the economy of salvation, reprobation, election, justification, the present life and the life to come, and the doctrines of the Church and the sacraments. It is evident that for Boisset the knowledge of ourselves as we were first created is nothing more than speculative knowledge. We shall soon see that this is not what Calvin intended. It is also interesting to notice that Boisset has a very short chapter on the knowledge of God in which he makes no use of Calvin's concept of the *duplex cognitio Domini*. Consequently, he does not correlate the twofold knowledge of God with the twofold knowledge of ourselves.

67. Having seen the correlation and correspondence between the twofold knowledge of God and the twofold knowledge of ourselves as presented by Calvin, one cannot understand how Dowey can claim that "Book II really begins only in Chapter vi, after Calvin has completed his analysis of sin, which is the occasion for the redemptive revelation." Dowey, *Knowledge of God* (1994), 45, cf. 19. It would be correct to say that discussion of knowledge of the Redeemer begins at II, vi. Calvin, however, considers this knowledge to correspond to the knowledge of ourselves as sinners, which is the subject matter of II, i–v. Therefore, Book II *really* begins in Chapter I as Calvin intended.

Then in the face of Christ he shows himself to be the Redeemer. Of the resulting twofold knowledge of God we shall now discuss the first aspect; the second will be dealt with in its proper place.[68]

Calvin's phrasing, "as much . . . as," or *tam . . . quam* in the Latin text, must be taken seriously.[69] We shall soon see the meaning and importance of this statement. Yet before we go further, we shall have to consider the context of the *locus classicus* of the twofold knowledge of God very carefully because it is introduced within a difficult passage. At the very outset Calvin explains what he means by knowledge of God the Creator. Accordingly he says, "I speak only of the primal and simple knowledge to which the very order of nature would have led us if Adam had remained upright."[70] It is in the light of this statement that we should understand all that Calvin is going to say about the knowledge of God the Creator.

Immediately after Calvin had made this statement, however, he realized the difficulty of his project and the possibility of misunderstanding. Therefore we see him hastening to note that no one can arrive at knowledge of God whether as Creator or Redeemer after the fall, except on the basis of the work of Christ. Therefore Calvin says, "In this ruin of mankind no one now experiences God either as Father or as Author of salvation, or favorable in any way, until Christ the Mediator comes forward to reconcile him to us."[71] Calvin introduces the *locus classicus* of the twofold knowledge of God against the background provided by these two clarifying statements, and it is in this context that it should be understood and interpreted.

We are now ready to examine more closely the way Calvin presented this twofold knowledge of God. Here again are his words:

> First, as much in the fashioning of the universe as in the general teaching of Scripture, the Lord shows himself to be the Creator. Then in the face of Christ he shows himself to be the Redeemer.[72]

---

68. *Inst.* I.ii,1 (O.S. III, 34, 21–25); author's translation.

69. All English translations have used "both . . . and" (Allen), "as well . . . as" (Beveridge), and "in . . . and in" (Ford Battles). The present author corresponded with Battles, who conceded that the author's translation is an improvement.

70. Ibid., 34, 13ff.

71. Ibid., 34, 15–17.

72. Ibid., 34, 21–24.

First of all, we must clarify what Calvin meant by the term *general teaching of Scripture* (*generalis Scripturae doctrina*). The present writer contends that a proper understanding of this term will be helpful for the correct interpretation of Calvin's project. As we continue in our reading of the *Institutes* we discover, as was mentioned earlier in passing, that Calvin considered the Scriptures to contain general teaching as well as specific or proper teaching. He says:

> Yet I repeat once more: besides the specific doctrine of faith and repentance that sets forth Christ as Mediator, Scripture adorns with unmistakable marks and tokens the one true God, in that he has created and governs the universe, in order that he may not be mixed up with the throng of false gods.[73]

The meaning of this statement cannot be grasped unless it is understood as a direct reference to the term *general teaching of Scripture* which we have found in the *locus classicus* of the twofold knowledge of God.

Once more, before Calvin goes to speak about knowledge of the Creator from Scripture, he indicates that he will first discuss the general teaching of Scripture; he says, "Here I propose to summarize the general doctrine."[74] These references together with our former findings show that the *locus classicus* of the twofold knowledge of God should be understood in the following manner: The Lord shows himself to human beings, as much in creation as in the general teaching of Scripture, as the Creator. Then in Christ, who is set forth by the specific (proper) teaching of Scripture, he shows himself to be the Redeemer. We shall now consider the knowledge of God as Creator and as Redeemer separately.

Knowledge of God the Creator

In studying the concept of knowledge of God in Calvin's theology, our main concern has been to determine in particular what Calvin meant by knowledge of God the Creator. This determination will help us understand the meaning and significance of his discussion of the authority of Scripture in Book I, vii–ix. For this purpose, we shall briefly follow

---

73. *Inst.* I, vi, 2. "Iterum tamen repeto, praeter, doctrinam fidei et poenitentiae Propriam, quae Christum Mediatorem proponit, Scripturam unicum et verum Deum quatenus mundum creavit et gubernat, certis notis et insignibus ornare .... " (O.S. III, 62, 16–20).

74. *Inst.*, I, x, 3 (O.S. III, 87, 20).

Calvin's steps in the first book of the *Institutes*, avoiding any details that would take us beyond our goal.

The first chapter of Book I is introductory. This characteristic can be seen clearly from its title: "The Knowledge of God and That of Ourselves Are Connected. How They Are Interrelated." When we come to the second chapter, we reach the proper discussion of knowledge of God the Creator. Calvin defines this knowledge at the outset as "the primal and simple knowledge to which the very order of nature would have led us if Adam had remained upright."[75] It is obvious that the controlling thought here is *si integer stetisset Adam*. This qualification reminds us again of the fact that Calvin is addressing himself in Book I to the question of the *nature* of God as Creator in relationship to humankind as seen in Adam before the fall. This is the knowledge of ourselves as we were first created in relationship to God as our Creator.[76]

Immediately after his definition of *knowledge of God the Creator*, Calvin goes on to say, "In this ruin of mankind no one now experiences God either as Father (Creator) or as Author of salvation (Redeemer), or favorable in any way, until Christ the Mediator comes forward to reconcile him to us."[77] Now, if we had discovered in Book I the discussion of both the objective revelation and the subjective means of arriving at knowledge of God the Creator, then the book would be difficult to understand as a whole. For if Calvin says that the knowledge of God the Creator is not experienced "until Christ . . . comes forward," one would then wonder: How could he speak of the appropriation of this knowledge before speaking about Christ? Yet as we have pointed out before, Calvin is speaking in Book I of knowledge of God the Creator as the experience of the believer in faith, with discussion of faith itself intentionally postponed.

In his discussion of knowledge of God the Creator, Calvin describes the relationship that God wanted to establish and to continue between himself and humankind. This relationship is what Calvin calls knowledge of God the Creator. On the side of God this knowledge involves an act of self-revelation.

---

75. *Inst.*, I, ii, 1 (O.S. III, 34, 13ff.).
76. *Inst.*, I, xv, 1 (O.S. III, 173, 32).
77. *Inst.*, I, ii, 1 (O.S. III, 34, 15–17).

> For, to begin with, the pious mind does not dream up for itself any god it pleases, but contemplates the one and only true God. And it does not attach to him whatever it pleases, but is content to hold him to be as he manifests himself.[78]

God's revelation calls for a response from the side of humankind. This response involves trust and reverence. Therefore, as far as the *pious mind* is concerned,

> Because it is persuaded that he is good and merciful, it reposes in him with perfect trust (*fiducia*) and doubts not that in his loving-kindness a remedy will be provided for all its ills. Because it acknowledges him as Lord and Father, the pious mind also deems it meet and right to observe his authority in all things, reverence his majesty, take care to advance his glory, and obey his commandments.[79]

When these elements are found together then we have true and real religion or piety,[80] which is also true faith.[81] Calvin calls this faith knowledge of God the Creator or simply knowledge of God, because it is, as we have just said, the relationship that God wills to establish between people and himself. This relationship is the goal that, as far as God is concerned, even the fall could not frustrate. For "however much we have brought death upon ourselves yet He has created us unto life."[82] Before the fall, humankind's salvation consisted in such knowledge of God:

> The natural order was that the frame of the universe should be the school in which we were to learn piety, and from it passes over to eternal life and perfect felicity. But after man's rebellion, our eyes—wherever they turn—encounter God's curse. . . . For even if God wills to manifest his fatherly favor to us in many ways, yet we cannot by contemplating the universe infer that he is Father.[83]

---

78. *Inst.*, I, ii, 2 (O.S. III, 36, 5–8).
79. Ibid. (36, 14–20).
80. *Inst.*, I, ii, *passim*.
81. *Inst.*, I, xiv, 21 and 22 *passim*.
82. *Inst.*, II, xvi, 3 (O.S., III, 484, 29ff.).

83. *Inst.*, II, vi, 1. (O.S. III, 320,13-20) Cf. *Inst.*, I, xv, 8 (O.S. III, 186, 1–2). "In his integrity man by free will had the power, if he so willed, to attain eternal life. See also the Argument of Calvin's commentary on Genesis. "Man was endued with understanding and reason, that being distinguished from brute animals he might meditate on a better life, and might even tend directly towards God, whose image he bore engraven

Again, Calvin says, "Consequently, the beginning of our recovery of salvation is in that restoration which we obtain through Christ."[84] Thus in order that human beings might know their Creator again and recover their salvation, they must first come to know him on the basis of knowing him as their Redeemer. "Surely, after the fall of the first man no knowledge of God apart from the Mediator has had power unto salvation (Rom 1:16; 1 Cor 1:24). For Christ . . . comprehends all ages when he says: 'This is eternal life, to know the Father to be the one true God, and Jesus Christ whom he has sent (John 17:3).'"[85] Consequently, "unless God confronts us in Christ, we cannot come to know that we are saved."[86]

Calvin therefore places the fall as well as its remedy in Book II, where he discusses knowledge of God the Redeemer, while in Book I he points to the continuity of God's original plan. Here we can partially see the immediate reason behind Calvin's arrangement of his material in the definitive edition of the *Institutes*, although we shall not be able to appreciate it fully until a later stage.[87] Hence it will be sufficient for us to see at this point that Calvin intends to show in Book I that God, who revealed himself to Adam in creation, continues this revelation in exactly the same manner even after the fall. Humankind has changed; God, however, does not change his revelation. Therefore Calvin says, "As much in the fashioning of the universe as in the general teaching of Scripture the Lord shows himself to be the Creator."[88] Yet as far as humanity is concerned, the fall lies between this objective knowledge and the ability to obtain it. Again and again, Calvin points to faith as the only subjective path to this knowledge. We must therefore be satisfied at this stage with understanding this knowledge as an objective possibility that cannot be achieved because of the fall. The fall is presented in this way

---

on his own person. Afterwards followed the fall of Adam" (C.O. XXIII, 11). "Without controversy, just as man was made for meditation upon the heavenly life, so it is certain that the knowledge of it was engraved upon his soul" *Inst.*, I, xv, 6 (O.S. III, 183, 1–4). Cf. Wallace, *Calvin's Doctrine of the Christian Life*, 104ff.

84. *Inst.*, I, xv, 4 (O.S. III, 179, 11f.). Also Com. Gen 2:7 "Paul makes an antithesis between his living soul and the quickening spirit which Christ confers upon the faithful (1 Cor xv, 45), for no other purpose than to teach us that the state of man was not perfected in the person of Adam; but it is a peculiar state."

85. *Inst.*, II, vi, 1 (O.S. III, 320, 37–321, 4).

86. *Inst.*, II, vi, 4 (O.S. III, 325, 25ff.).

87. Cf. pages 77ff below.

88. *Inst.*, I, ii, 1 (O.S. III, 34, 21–23).

in both Books I and II of the *Institutes* to show the subjective inability of the unregenerate person to respond to God.

With this outline in mind we are enabled to read and understand both Chapters iii and iv in Book I of the *Institutes*. In Chapter iii Calvin refers to an "awareness of divinity" (*divinitatis sensum*) that exists "within the human mind, and indeed by natural instinct."[89] Then in Chapter iv he says, "Experience teaches that the seed of religion has been divinely planted in all men."[90] The word *conscience* is also mentioned twice in the course of the discussion, although in an incidental manner.[91] These two chapters then constitute more or less a unit with a particular purpose. The titles of these two chapters then make this point clear. Here we find Calvin showing that "The Knowledge of God Has Been Naturally Implanted in the Minds of Men;"[92] and secondly that "This Knowledge Is Either Smothered or Corrupted, Partly by Ignorance, Partly by Malice."[93] The whole point of these two chapters appears in the opening sentences: "Since, therefore, men one and all perceive that there is a God and that he is their Maker, they are condemned by their own testimony because they have failed to honor him and to consecrate their lives to his will."[94] The same idea is repeated in the final paragraph:

> From this, my present contention is brought out with greater certainty, that a sense of divinity is by nature engraved on human hearts. For necessity forces from the reprobate themselves a confession of it. . . . From this it is clear that they have not been utterly ignorant of God, but that what should have come forth sooner was held back by stubbornness.[95]

On this basis God has prevented "anyone from taking refuge in the pretense of ignorance."[96] People carry in themselves subjectively the sentence of their own condemnation. Therefore, the only role that Calvin would allow the *sensus divinitatis* to play is a negative one: people

---

89. *Inst.*, I, iii, 1 (O.S. III. 37, 16ff.).
90. *Inst.*, I, iv, 1 (O.S. III, 40, 31ff.).
91. *Inst.*, I, iii, 2 & 3 (O.S. III, 39, 9; 40, 2).
92. *Inst.*, I, iii, chapter title.
93. *Inst.*, I, iv, chapter title.
94. *Inst.*, I, iii, 1 (O.S. III, 37, 21–24).
95. *Inst.*, I, iv, 4 (O.S. III, 44, 19–27).
96. *Inst.*, I, iii, 1 (O.S. III, 37, 18).

are, considered subjectively, inexcusable. A knowledge of God built on such a weak foundation is not worthy of the name.

> This, however, is but a vain and false shadow of religion, scarcely even worth being called a shadow. From it one may easily grasp anew how much this confused knowledge of God differs from the piety from which religion takes its source, which is instilled in the breasts of believers only.[97]

Thus as Calvin concludes Chapter iv, he makes it clear that as far as humankind is concerned, the fall stands between the revelation of God in creation and people's actual appropriation of it. Because, however, God continues to reveal himself as Creator, inviting people to respond in reverence and trust, Calvin continues his discussion of this revelation.[98] This is the subject matter of the rest of Book I except for Chapters vii through ix, which deal with the authority of Scripture. Here Calvin consciously and intentionally turns aside from his line of thought to the consideration of this important subject. These three chapters are introduced in this manner: "Before I go any further, it is worthwhile to say something about the authority of Scripture."[99] Thus as Dowey points out,

> The three all-important chapters on Scripture (I, vii–ix) appear, so far as the drift of the argument of the *Institutes* is concerned, as an excursus or a footnote to Chapter vi. They could be dropped, assuming that the problem of the authority of Scripture was dealt with elsewhere, without affecting the course of the argument between vi and x.[100]

For this reason we shall consider these three chapters only after we have fully understood Calvin's doctrine of knowledge of God the Creator.[101]

In the *locus classicus* of the twofold knowledge of God we have seen that Calvin introduced knowledge of God the Creator in these words: "As much in the fashioning of the universe as in the general teaching of Scripture, the Lord shows himself to be the Creator."[102] Here we should

---

97. *Inst.*, I, iv, 4 (O.S. III, 43, 33–44, 3).
98. *Inst.*, I, x, 2 (O.S. III, 87, 14–19).
99. *Inst.*, I, vii, 1 (O.S. III, 65, 5ff.).
100. Dowey, *Knowledge of God* (1994), 86ff.
101. Cf. pages 125ff below.
102. *Inst.*, I, ii, 1 (O.S. III, 34, 21–23).

remind ourselves again that from Chapter v until the end of the book we are dealing with a knowledge that is considered equivalent to the knowledge that Adam had before the fall. Between this knowledge and its achievement there stands the fall, the discussion of which Calvin intentionally postponed to Book II. With this in mind we shall examine an overview of Calvin's line of thought in the remainder of Book I.

Calvin discusses revelation in creation in Chapter v. This topic is followed in Chapter vi by a discussion of revelation in the general teaching of Scripture. In Chapter x these two revelations are compared and found to be in agreement in content as well as in purpose. Chapters xi through xviii are commentary on the revelation in Scripture as discussed in Chapter vi. Calvin had no doubt in his mind that revelation in creation is known only through faith. He says, "It is therefore in vain that so many burning lamps shine for us in the workmanship of the universe to show forth the glory of its Author . . . we have not the eyes to see this unless they be illumined by the inner revelation of God through faith."[103] The reason why Calvin discusses this form of revelation in this passage, although he knows that one cannot arrive at it except through faith, is because he wants to deal first with God's relationship to humankind in general. Therefore he says: "Now I have only wanted to touch upon the fact that this way of seeking God is common both to strangers and to those of his household, if they trace the outlines that above and below sketch a living likeness of him."[104]

Yet as we proceed with Calvin we find out that his whole interest in these so-called strangers is just to point out that they are inexcusable. "But although we lack the natural ability to mount up unto the pure and clear knowledge of God, all excuse is cut off because the fault of dullness is within us."[105] The same thought is repeated when Calvin introduces revelation in Scripture. Here Calvin remarks:

> That brightness which is borne in upon the eyes of all men both in heaven and on earth is more than enough to withdraw all support from men's ingratitude—just as God, to involve the human race in the same guilt, sets forth to all without exception his presence portrayed in his creatures.[106]

103. *Inst.*, I, v, 14 (O.S. III, 58, 35ff.; 59, 7ff.).
104. *Inst.*, I, v, 6 (O.S. III, 51, 18–21).
105. *Inst.*, I, v, 15 (O.S. III, 59, 24–27).
106. *Inst.*, I, vi, 1 (O.S. III, 60, 11–15); italics added.

Therefore, as far as the strangers are concerned, the sole purpose of revelation in creation is to render them inexcusable. As we come to Chapter vi, however, we notice a narrowing in the scope of revelation of the Creator, whether in creation or the general teaching of Scripture. Both are now seen within the context of the church. Calvin says:

> This [Scripture], therefore, is a special gift, where God, to instruct the church, not merely uses mute teachers [creation] but also opens his own most hallowed lips in *Scripture*. Not only does he teach the elect to look upon a god, but also shows himself as the God upon whom they are to look. He has from the beginning maintained this plan for his church, so that besides these common proofs he also put forth his Word.[107]

The revelation in creation starts to play a new role within this new context. Its purpose is no longer only to make human beings inexcusable.

We now reach a crucial point in our understanding of Calvin's whole thought in Book I as we consider the content and purpose of revelation in creation. Here we find the statement, "As much in the fashioning of the universe as in the general teaching of Scripture, the Lord shows himself to be the Creator."[108] Calvin himself thought that revelation in creation and the general teaching of Scripture are identical in content as well as purpose. When comparing their content he says, "Now we hear the same powers enumerated there (in Scripture, i.e., Exod 34: 6–7) that we have noted as shining in heaven and earth: kindness, goodness, mercy, justice, judgment, and truth."[109] Once more, Calvin compares revelation in the general teaching of Scripture with that in creation, and concludes in the following manner: "Nothing is set down there (in Ps 145:5) that cannot be beheld in his creatures. Indeed, with experience as our teacher we find God just as he declares himself in his Word."[110] As far as the content of both revelations is concerned, we can now understand what Calvin means by "As much in the fashioning of the universe as in the general teaching of Scripture the Lord shows himself to be the Creator."[111]

---

107. Ibid. (60, 31–61, 6); bracketed words supplied.
108. *Inst.* I, ii, 1 (O.S. 34, 21ff).
109. *Inst.*, I, x, 2 (O.S. III, 86, 19–22).
110. Ibid. (86, 27–30).
111. *Inst.*, I, ii, 1 (O.S. III, 34, 21–23).

As we turn to the purpose or goal of both forms of revelation, we again find Calvin to be clear:

> Indeed, the knowledge of God set forth for us in Scripture is destined for the very same goal as the knowledge whose imprint shines in his creatures, in that it invites us first to fear God, then to trust in him. By this we can learn to worship him both with perfect innocence of life and with unfeigned obedience, then to depend wholly upon his goodness.[112]

It is important that we see more clearly the relationship between these two revelations as Calvin presents it. Chapter v clearly stated the content of the revelation within creation. Calvin states that this revelation can be received subjectively only in faith.[113] Yet from the objective point of view, this revelation is "common both to strangers and to those of His household."[114] Therefore, although it is people of faith who discuss this revelation, they are not discussing it from Scripture. Dowey correctly points out here that

> Every single Scriptural reference that Calvin uses in developing the theme "The knowledge of God Conspicuous in the Formation and Continual Government of the World" (I, v, 1–13) could be dropped out without in any way affecting the argument. Scripture, mostly from Psalms and the Acts, is not appealed to as the ground of the argument, but to show that what is written stands in confirmation of what all men should know of the revelation in creation by their own experience.[115]

Calvin as a person of faith is consistent here, teaching others to do likewise:

> Let all readers know that they have with true faith apprehended what it is for God to be Creator of heaven and earth, if they first of all follow the universal rule, not to pass over in ungrateful thoughtlessness or forgetfulness those conspicuous powers which

---

112. *Inst.*, I, x, 2 (O.S. III, 14–19).

113. *Inst.*, I, v, 14. "It is in vain that so many burning lamps shine for us in the workmanship of the universe to show forth the glory of its Author ... we have not the eyes to see this unless they be illumined by the inner revelation of God through faith." (O.S. III, 58, 35–59, 7ff.). Cf. also I, v, 11–13 *passim*.

114. *Inst.*, I, v, 6 (O.S. III, 51, 18ff.).

115. Dowey, *Knowledge of God* (1994), 73ff. It is surprising that in spite of the above, Dowey says in reference to this issue, "nor have we come to the knowledge of creation by the man who has faith," 74.

God shows forth in his creatures, and then learn so to apply it to themselves that their very hearts are touched.[116]

As we have noted, Calvin mentions revelation in Scripture in Chapter vi; and compares it with the revelation in creation in Chapter x in order to demonstrate the agreement between the two in content as well as purpose. Chapters xi through xviii then discuss scriptural revelation. It is therefore important to discover the exact relationship between revelation in Scripture as found in Chapter vi and that found in Chapters xi through xviii. It has often been suggested that Calvin presents a form of knowledge of God from Scripture in Chapter vi, a form of knowledge that is identical with knowledge from creation as presented in the preceding five chapters. This presentation was assumed in light of the statements that Calvin makes in the first two sections of Chapter x, in which he points out that knowledge of the Creator revealed in creation agrees with that revealed in Scripture. Some scholars maintain that Calvin pointed out the areas in which revelation from Scripture, as far as content is concerned, goes beyond what can be learned from creation since the fall in Chapters xi through xvii. In this connection Dowey says, "Scripture repeats . . . everything that creation teaches about the Creator, and then adds to it."[117] Again, after discussing the relationship between the first five chapters and Chapter vi with its spectacles metaphor, he goes on to say, "But *over and above this*, Scripture also presents a new knowledge content about the Creator in the doctrines of the Trinity, creation, and particular providence."[118]

We have seen that Calvin points out that the knowledge of God as Creator gained from creation is identical in content and goal with the knowledge obtained from the general teaching of Scripture. It is the contention of the present writer, as has been stated, that Chapters xi through xvi of Book I are no more than a commentary on the general teaching of Scripture. This characteristic should be clear in light of the fact that in the first two sections of Chapter x Calvin compares both the content and the goal of knowledge of God the Creator from creation and the general teaching of Scripture while maintaining the identities of both. Then in the third section of the chapter he explains his intention for the rest of

---

116. *Inst.*, I, xiv, 21 (O.S. III, 171, 34–172, 4).

117. Dowey, *Knowledge of God* (1994), 131; italics added. Here we can appreciate Parker's criticism of Dowey discussed above.

118. Ibid., 145; italics added.

Book I by saying, "But here I propose to summarize the general doctrine [the general teaching of Scripture.]"[119] The reader should remember that Calvin presented the contents and the goal of knowledge of the Creator from creation at considerable length in Chapter v of Book I. The general teaching of Scripture is considered in Chapter vi. Calvin, however, postpones discussion of the content of knowledge of the Creator from this source. It is in Chapters xi through xviii that we find Calvin's detailed presentation of knowledge of God the Creator from the general teaching of Scripture. The vast number of cross-references between the discussion of knowledge from creation as found in Chapter v and knowledge from the general teaching of Scripture in the later chapters makes it quite clear that the later chapters are not newly conceived or unrelated to prior content. This statement of course needs further clarification—which, however, cannot be done at this stage. One should remember, however, that when Calvin speaks of revelation from creation in Chapter v, he speaks only because his eyes are illumined by the inner revelation of God through faith. We cannot fully appreciate his point here until we have discussed what he means by illumination. We shall consider his definition in Chapter III below.

So far we have satisfied ourselves with observing that knowledge of God the Creator in its objective form is knowledge that "invites us first to fear God, then to trust in him."[120] This knowledge of God the Creator corresponds to the knowledge of ourselves "as we were first created."[121] It is the continuing revelation on God's part in spite of the fall, and to which human beings cannot yet respond because of the fall. Between what we were and what has become of us, there is a chasm fixed; and as far as we have gone in our discussion, a way has not yet been provided for crossing the gulf. In spite of continuing revelation from the side of God, we have not as yet seen a proper response from our side.

As we come to the fifteenth chapter of the book under consideration, new light is thrown on Calvin's understanding of knowledge of God as Creator. To get to this point we must consider briefly the twofold knowledge of ourselves. We have seen earlier that Calvin understood this knowledge to be "to know what we were like when we were first

---

119. *Inst.*, I, x, 3 (O.S. III, 87, 20ff.).
120. *Inst.*, I, x, 2 (O.S. III, 87, 16ff.).
121. *Inst.*, I, xv, 1 (O.S. III, 173, 32).

created and what our condition became after the fall of Adam."[122] At first glance, his analysis of human self-knowledge may appear incomplete because he seems to stop with the fall. As a matter of fact he explicitly says, "Whoever is utterly cast down and overwhelmed by the awareness of his calamity, poverty, nakedness, and disgrace has thus advanced furthest in knowledge of himself."[123] Careful study, however, shows that Calvin does not stop with knowledge of ourselves as fallen in Adam. We shall see in the following chapter that he did not intend the discussion of knowledge of ourselves as we were first created to be any other than the knowledge of ourselves as restored in Christ. For Calvin saw the work of Christ to be a work of restoration. Thus human knowledge of God the Creator is that knowledge of God that Adam had before the fall, considered not from a speculative point of view or merely as something that we could have had if Adam had not sinned. It is rather a living reality here and now in Christ; it is the knowledge that was lost and yet has been restored in Christ.

Thus in Book I, when humanity is considered in the person of Adam after the fall, its knowledge of the Creator is nothing more than a lost knowledge. For humanity in fallen Adam is unable to respond to God in trust and reverence. But this issue is not Calvin's major concern in Book I. Nor is he interested in presenting humanity merely in Adam's sinless state. Accordingly he presents knowledge of God the Creator from the point of view of the new humanity as found in the Second Adam and Christ's restoring work. This knowledge "allows nature to regain its revelatory function,"[124] wherein people are enabled to know their Creator and thus respond to him in trust and reverence.

As we shall point out more fully in Chapter 2 below, however, the situation of the believer is not as simple as this initial description may suggest. For, although believers are restored in Christ, they are still sinners. As restored, they know God as their Creator; but as sinners, they know Him as their Redeemer. Here we can tentatively see why Calvin insists on the impossibility of isolating the knowledge of God the Creator from that of the Redeemer.[125] From this perspective, the concept of twofold knowledge, whether of God or of ourselves, can be seen as

---

122. Ibid. (173, 31–33).
123. *Inst.*, II, ii, 10 (O.S. III, 252, 20–22).
124. Schreiner, *Theater of His Glory*, 106.
125. Cf. pages xxxvi ff above.

Calvin's ingenious expression of the tension in the life of the Christian whom Luther defined as *simul iustus et peccator*. Here we know God in a twofold way simultaneously: as our Creator and as our Redeemer. This twofold knowledge of God corresponds to simultaneous twofold knowledge of ourselves: "Namely to know what we were like when we were first created and what our condition became after the fall of Adam."[126] To Calvin, the believer is nothing but a restored sinner; moreover,

> Indeed, this restoration does not take place in one moment or one day or one year; but through continual and sometimes even slow advances God wipes out in his elect the corruptions of the flesh, cleanses them of guilt, consecrates them to himself as temples renewing all their minds to true purity *that they may practice repentance throughout their lives* and know that this warfare will end only at death.[127]

Thus in discussing knowledge of God the Creator, Calvin is not actually looking backward in speculation to the knowledge to which the very order of nature would have led us if Adam had remained upright. He is rather looking *forward* to the full restoration of this knowledge in Christ. The reason why Calvin presents this knowledge in terms of the possibility of Adam's having remained upright rather than the knowledge to which we are restored in Christ is that the latter would seem to overlook altogether the tension in the life of faith. It is true that believers are restored in Christ. Yet as we shall see more fully in the following chapter, the believer is still a sinner. Therefore Calvin presents knowledge of the Creator as the primal and simple knowledge to which the very order of nature would have led us if Adam had remained upright— to remind readers that although they are restored in Christ, yet they are also sinners because of the fall. Accordingly, full restoration of human nature does not take place in this life although it is the goal toward which believers must strive throughout their lives.

It is only with this point in mind that we can understand how Calvin expects the knowledge of God the Creator to arouse us to *meditatio futurae vitae*. "By this knowledge," Calvin says, "he [a person] should arouse himself to meditation upon divine worship and the future life."[128] Thus knowledge of God the Creator and knowledge of ourselves as we were

---

126. *Inst.*, I, xv, 1.
127. *Inst.*, III, iii, 9 (O.S. IV, 63, 25–65, 2); italics added.
128. I, v, 10; (O.S. III, 54, 1–3); II, i, 3.

first created are not presented by Calvin as forms of knowledge to which we look *back* with sorrow and despair. On the contrary, this knowledge should make us look *forward* with hope and aspiration. "Knowledge of this sort . . . ought not only to arouse us to the worship of God but also to awaken and encourage us to the hope of the future life."[129] Or again he says about the believer: "By this knowledge he should arouse himself to meditation upon divine worship and the future life."[130] So far we have tried to explain the reason why Calvin separated discussion of knowledge of the Creator from knowledge of the Redeemer. This issue will be clarified still further in the following chapter.

The question that arises now is why Calvin spoke of humanity as restored in Christ before his discussion of sin and redemption. This is almost the same question that Dowey, after Wernle, raises regarding Book I of the *Institutes*: "The Creator and Father, the Provider, the faithful and merciful One, who deserves our deepest trust. And all that in the beginning without a word about Jesus Christ . . . !"[131] Again Dowey says, "Why . . . was the Knowledge of the Creator always kept separate from that of the Redeemer? We may wish that he had not done these things, but we may not pretend that he did not do them."[132] It is because of this that Dowey sees inconsistencies in Calvin's theology and after an extended discussion of God the Creator and before the discussion of God the Redeemer, says:

> Even now we do not, within the realm of special revelation, ascend to infer or deduce the work of the Redeemer from what we know of the Creator. Instead, we take a new orientation. We jump to another starting point theologically.[133]

We shall show, however, that it is rather the genius of Calvin's method that is at work here and is responsible for the organization of the material, without having to speak of a dialectical relationship to resolve what some consider dissonance and discrepancies in Calvin's thought in the *Institutes*. This argument also will be clarified in the second chapter of this book.

---

129. II, i, 3 (O.S. III, 231, 7ff.).
130. *Inst.*, II, i, 3.
131. Dowey, *Knowledge of God* (1994), 47.
132. Ibid.,133, n. 414.
133. Ibid., 147.

Knowledge of God the Redeemer

Our whole concern so far in discussing the twofold knowledge of God has been to show that the authority of Scripture in Book I, vii–ix should not be considered a presentation of the subjective means to knowledge of God, or knowledge of God the Creator. We come now to Calvin's presentation of the knowledge of God the Redeemer. It is clear that Calvin is discussing this subject as a believer and even as a teacher in the church. And it is obvious that only the person of faith can speak properly about knowledge of the Redeemer. Thus Calvin points the reader to the discussion of faith as the basis for knowledge of God the Redeemer.[134]

Yet as far as the role of Scripture is concerned, we need to look again briefly at the *locus classicus* of the twofold knowledge of God. Here we find knowledge of God the Redeemer expressed in these words: "Then in the face of Christ (cf. 2 Cor 4:6) he [the Lord] shows himself to be the Redeemer."[135] We need to observe that the expression "in the face of Christ" here does not refer to the subjective experience of believers. What Calvin is discussing at this point is what God has done for human beings *in Christ*—an act that is set forth in the specific teaching of Scripture.[136] This point is evident in the title of Book II: "The knowledge of God the Redeemer in Christ, First Disclosed to the Fathers under the Law and Then to Us in the Gospel." The reader should recall that the general teaching of Scripture that we have encountered in our discussion of knowledge of God the Creator is not quantitatively larger than the proper or specific teaching that sets forth Christ. In both cases Calvin is speaking of Scripture as a whole.

As we speak of knowledge of God the Redeemer in Christ, we find Calvin reiterating that "the Scriptures are to be read with the purpose of finding Christ there."[137] Or again he says in a sentence that was added in 1543 to the Preface to Olivétan's New Testament:

> This is what we should in short seek in the whole of Scripture: truly to know Jesus Christ and the infinite riches that are comprised in him and are offered to us by him from God the Father. If one were to sift thoroughly the Law and the Prophets, he would

---

134. Cf. pages 7f above, fn. 33, 34.
135. *Inst.*, I, ii, 1 (O.S. III, 34, 23 ff.).
136. *Inst.*, I, vi, 2 (O.S. III, 62, 16 ff.).
137. *Com.* John 5:39 C.O. XLVII, 125.

not find a single word which would not draw and bring us to him.¹³⁸

With this point in mind we can understand Calvin's whole approach in Book II and especially his understanding of the Old Testament and its relationship to Christ. He says in Book II:

> . . . apart from the Mediator, God never showed favor toward the ancient people, nor ever gave hope of grace to them. I pass over the sacrifices of the law, which plainly and openly taught believers to seek salvation nowhere else than in the atonement that Christ alone carries out. I am only saying that the blessed and happy state of the church always had its foundation in the person of Christ.¹³⁹

Discussion of the material of Book II would take us beyond the purpose of the present work. Therefore we shall limit ourselves to a brief statement of its contents as well as the goal of knowledge of God the Redeemer. We have seen that Calvin points to Christ who was revealed to the people of the Old Testament under the law and then at length clearly revealed in the Gospel.¹⁴⁰ This is the content of the knowledge of God the Redeemer. The difference that Calvin can see between the old covenant and the new is a difference in the manner of dispensation rather than the substance. Thus he says, "There will be nothing to hinder the promises of the Old and New Testaments from remaining the same, nor from having the same foundation of these very promises, Christ!"¹⁴¹ As we turn to the goal or purpose of knowledge of God the Redeemer, we find it clearly stated by Calvin in these words: "What the Mediator was to accomplish was no common thing. His task was so to *restore* us to God's grace as to make of the children of men children of God."¹⁴² Again he says, "We shall know why Christ was promised from the beginning: to *restore* the fallen world and to succor lost men."¹⁴³ The key word here is *restoration*.¹⁴⁴

---

138. Haroutunian, *Calvin: Commentaries*, 70; C.O. IX, 815.
139. *Inst.*, II, vi, 2 (O.S. III, 321, 31–37).
140. *Inst.*, II, ix *passim*.
141. *Inst.*, II, xi, 1 (O.S. III, 423, 13–15).
142. *Inst.*, II, xii, 2 (O.S. III, 438, 21–24); italics added.
143. *Inst.*, II, xii, 4 (O.S. III, 440, 28–31); italics added.
144. Cf. Wallace, *Calvin's Doctrine of the Christian Life*, 106ff.

We have seen that Calvin considered this knowledge of God as Redeemer to correspond to knowledge of ourselves as fallen in Adam and as sinners. We then find the discussion of this topic in the first five chapters of Book II. It is knowledge of God as our Redeemer that makes us truly know ourselves in our sinfulness. Yet this knowledge of the Redeemer and knowledge of ourselves as sinners *restores* us to knowledge of the Creator and knowledge of ourselves as *restored* in Christ to what Adam was before the fall. It is in this area of knowledge that humankind is enabled again to respond to God in trust and reverence.

Thus we have seen the twofold knowledge of God as Calvin presents it in Books I and II, and we have noted its correspondence with the twofold knowledge of ourselves. The discussion of faith, which is the basis of this twofold knowledge, is intentionally postponed until Book III, in which the objectivity of the previous two books, as Parker points out, "is transmitted into subjectivity, *Christus pro nobis* into *Christus in nobis* through His Holy Spirit. Epistemologically, this book deals with man's knowledge of God the Creator and Redeemer in Christ through the enlightening of the Holy Spirit."[145]

When we turn to Calvin's doctrine of faith, we see clearly the function that Calvin considered Scripture to serve. This doctrine will clarify the problem of Biblical authority in his theology, and to it we shall now turn.

---

145. Parker, *Calvin's Doctrine of the Knowledge of God*, 120.

2

Knowledge of God: The *Duplex Gratia Dei*

Calvin found the twofold knowledge of God summarized in John 17:3: "This is eternal life: to know you the only true God, and Jesus Christ whom you have sent" (NRSV). In Book I he opened his discussion of human knowledge of God the Creator through creation in this manner: "The final goal of the blessed life . . . rests in the knowledge of God (cf. John 17:3)."[1] As we continue reading Book I of the *Institutes*, we discover that the whole book is concerned with the concept of "the only true God."[2] Later, in Book II when Calvin comes to discussion of knowledge of God the Redeemer, he again states:

> Surely, after the fall of the first man no knowledge of God apart from the Mediator has had power unto salvation (cf. Rom 1:16; 1 Cor 1:24). For Christ not only speaks of his own age, but comprehends all ages when he says: This is eternal life, to know the Father to be the one true God, and Jesus Christ whom he has sent (John 17: 3).[3]

Calvin then goes on to note that "no worship has ever pleased God except that which looked to Christ."[4] After this statement he concludes in the following manner: "Now since John teaches that life was in Christ from the beginning (John 1:4), and that all the world fell away from it (cf. John 1:10), it is necessary to return to that source."[5] Therefore both Book I and Book II of the *Institutes* can be considered, in one sense, a commentary on the two parts of (John 17:3) with its twofold knowledge.

1. *Inst.*, I, v, 1 (O. S. III, 44, 30ff).
2. Cf. pages 115ff below.
3. *Inst.*, II, vi, 1 (O.S. III, 320, 37–321, 4).
4. Ibid. (321, 17ff).
5. Ibid. (321, 20–22).

The relationship between these two books can be seen in the following words:

> Christ himself bade his disciples believe in him, that they might clearly and perfectly believe in God: 'You believe in God; believe also in me.' (John 14:1) . . . although faith rests in God, it will gradually disappear unless he who retains it in perfect firmness intercedes as Mediator. . . .
>
> God is comprehended in Christ alone. John's saying has always been true: 'He that does not have the Son does not have the Father.'[6]

After discussing knowledge of the Creator in Book I and knowledge of the Redeemer in Book II, and at the beginning of his discussion of the faith through which the twofold knowledge becomes the living experience of the believer, Calvin says: "Indeed, it is true that faith looks to one God. But this must also be added, 'To know Jesus Christ whom he has sent' (John 17:3)."[7] Then he repeats, "Faith consists in the knowledge of God and Christ (John 17:3)."[8] The importance of this verse from the Fourth Gospel for an understanding of Calvin's project should not be overlooked; it is not by accident that he cites it in these three strategic passages. We shall discuss its importance later, but for now it is sufficient to note that this concept of knowledge of God was carried over from book to book in the *Institutes*.

INTRODUCTORY REMARKS ON FAITH

As we come to Calvin's doctrine of faith, the reader should remember that he considers faith the basis for experiencing knowledge of God, as discussed in both Book I and II. In Book II, Calvin looked back at Book I in saying: "The whole knowledge of God the Creator that we have discussed would be useless unless faith also followed."[9] Again, after he had discussed knowledge of God the Redeemer, he goes on to say, "As long as Christ remains outside of us, and we are separated from him, all that he has suffered and done for the salvation of the human race remains use-

---

6. *Inst.*, II, vi, 4 (O.S. III, 325, 14–16; 18–20; 14–16; 18–20; 326, 6–8). Cf. *Com.* Gen 2:9: "Let us know, therefore, that when we have departed from Christ, nothing remains for us but death" (C.O. XXIII, 39).

7. *Inst.*, III, ii, 1 (O.S. IV, 8, 9–11).

8. *Inst.*, III, ii, 3 (O.S. IV, 11, 9ff).

9. *Inst.*, II, vi, 1 (O.S. III, 320, 10–12).

less and of no value for us."[10] With this understanding he then went on to speak of faith. Calvin introduces his discussion of faith with a practical purpose in mind. He says:

> Now we ought to examine what this faith ought to be like, through which those adopted by God as his children come to possess the Heavenly Kingdom, since it is certain that no mere opinion or even persuasion is capable of bringing so great a thing to pass. And we must scrutinize and investigate the true character of faith with greater care and zeal because many are dangerously deluded today in this respect.[11]

Having stated his purpose in this manner, Calvin attacks the Schoolmen and their teaching about faith:

> Indeed, most people, when they hear this term [faith], understand nothing deeper than a common assent to the gospel history. In fact, when faith is discussed in the schools, they call God simply the object of faith, and by fleeting speculations . . . lead miserable souls astray rather than direct them to a definite goal.[12]

Here we see Calvin attacking two scholastic concepts that have a single root;[13] however, we need to discuss them separately for the sake of clarification. On the one hand, Calvin opposes the notion of calling God the object of faith when this usage is not closely associated with knowledge of Christ. He thus insists on the twofoldness of knowledge of God. On the other hand, he also rejects the idea of faith as merely assent.

Faith and Twofold Knowledge

In Calvin's discussion of knowledge of God the Creator in Book I, he attacks the "idle speculations" of the Schoolmen.[14] He contends that when the Schoolmen call God the object of faith, they claim for themselves that knowledge of God which he calls knowledge of the Creator. In the face of this claim, as we have already seen, he insists on the impossibility of arriving at knowledge of God as Creator in isolation from knowledge of him as Redeemer. He restates this point emphatically at the beginning

---

10. *Inst.*, III, I, 1 (O.S. IV, 1, 10–13).
11. *Inst.*, III, ii, 1 (O.S. IV, 7, 9–16).
12. Ibid. (7, 16–21).
13. Cf. p. 60 below.
14. Cf. *Inst.*, I, ii, 2; I, v, 9 (O.S. III, 35, 11–14; 53, 10–14).

of his chapter on faith. Immediately after criticizing the Schoolmen for calling God "simply the object of faith," he goes on to say:

> Since 'God dwells in inaccessible light' (1 Tim 6:16), Christ must become our intermediary. Hence, he calls himself 'the light of the world' (John 8:12), and elsewhere, 'the way, the truth, and the life'; for no one comes to the Father, who is the 'fountain of life' (Ps 36:9), except through him (John 14:6) because he alone knows the Father, and afterward the believers to whom he wishes to reveal him (Luke 10:22).[15]

Then he adds:

> Indeed, it is true that faith looks to one God. But this must also be added, 'To know Jesus Christ whom he has sent' (John 17:3). For God would have remained hidden afar off if Christ's splendor had not beamed upon us . . . While Paul proclaims faith in God, he does not have in mind to overturn what he so often emphasizes concerning faith: namely, that all its stability rests in Christ. Peter indeed most effectively connects both, saying that through him we believe in God.[16]

It is obvious that Calvin is referring here to the relationship which must be recognized between knowledge of God as Creator and knowledge of him as Redeemer. This same idea is also found in a statement that we have quoted before but need to reiterate.

> Christ himself bade his disciples believe in him, that they might clearly and perfectly believe in God: 'You believe in God; believe also in me' (John 14:1). For even if properly speaking, faith mounts up from Christ to the Father, yet . . . although faith rests in God, it will gradually disappear unless he who retains it in perfect firmness intercedes as Mediator. . . . I subscribe to the common saying that God is the object of faith, yet it requires qualification . . . [For] unless God confronts us in Christ, we cannot come to know that we are saved.[17]

There should be no doubt that Calvin is referring here to the relationship of knowledge of God as Creator to knowledge of him as Redeemer. In fact, the whole chapter was written in its entirety for the edition of 1559 in order to clarify this relationship. Calvin goes on to say:

---

15. *Inst.*, III, ii, 1(O.S. IV, 7, 21–8, 1).
16. Ibid. (8, 9–12; 9, 9–13).
17. *Inst.*, II, vi, 4 (O.S. III, 325, 14, 26).

God is comprehended in Christ alone.... 'He that does not have the Son does not have the Father.' For even if many men once boasted that they worshipped the Supreme Majesty, the Maker of heaven and earth, yet because they had no Mediator it was not possible for them truly to taste God's mercy, and thus be persuaded that he was their Father.[18]

Thus it becomes obvious that Calvin is emphasizing in this passage as well as at the beginning of his discussion of faith that there can never be knowledge of God the Creator without knowledge of the Redeemer. For this reason he believes that when the Schoolmen call God the object of faith without giving attention to Christ the Redeemer, they are only toying with fleeting speculations that lead people astray rather than direct them to a definite goal. He concludes his attack by saying: "This evil, then, like innumerable others, must be attributed to the Schoolmen, who have, as it were, drawn a veil over Christ to hide him. Unless we look straight toward him, we shall wander through endless labyrinths."[19]

Faith as Knowledge

Calvin also attacks the Schoolmen's concept of implicit faith. In this connection he says,

Besides wearing down the whole force of faith and almost annihilating it by their obscure definition [i.e. God is the object of faith], they have fabricated the fiction of 'implicit faith.' Bedecking the grossest ignorance with this term, they ruinously delude poor, miserable folk.[20]

Here Calvin rejects the Roman doctrine of *fides implicita* because he considers it to imply ignorance, whereas he considers faith to rest on knowledge. He goes on to say:

To state truly and frankly the real fact of the matter, this fiction not only buries but utterly destroys true faith. Is this what believing means—to understand nothing, provided only that you submit your feeling obediently to the Church? Faith rests not on ignorance, but knowledge... We... obtain salvation... when we

---

18. Ibid. (326, 6–12).
19. *Inst.*, III, ii, 2 (O.S. IV, 10, 1–4).
20. Ibid. (10, 4–8).

know that God is our merciful Father, because of reconciliation effected through Christ.[21]

We meet this concept repeatedly in Calvin's writings. Commenting on the words, "and the knowledge of that truth," he says:

> Faith is called knowledge, not as against opinion, but as against the hazy affair invented by the papists: for they have contrived an 'implicit faith' with no understanding in it. But when Paul makes this knowledge of truth a proper function of faith, he makes it clear that there is no such thing as faith without knowledge.[22]

One should remember, however, that Calvin does not naively consider faith to be mere knowledge. For, while emphasizing the fact that faith is knowledge, he also says, "Such is the ignorance with which we are surrounded—that most things are now implicit for us ... until ... we come nearer to the presence of God."[23] Or again:

> We certainly admit that so long as we dwell as strangers in the world there is such a thing as implicit faith; not only because many things are as yet hidden from us, but because surrounded by many clouds of errors we do not comprehend everything.[24]

Allowing for all this, Calvin nonetheless insists that "it would be the height of absurdity to label ignorance tempered by humility 'faith!' For faith consists in the knowledge of God and Christ (John 17:3), not in reverence for the Church."[25]

Here we can see the tension that Calvin knows to exist in the life of the believer. For this reason he rejects the Roman doctrine of implicit faith and insists that faith is a form of knowledge, while vigorously emphasizing that as long as believers are "burdened with the weight of the flesh," most things are implied, and "unbelief is ... always mixed with faith."[26]

This theme of tension and struggle in the believer's life occurs repeatedly in Calvin's discussion of faith. And it is this that we need to examine more closely because the present writer considers it to be the

---

21. Ibid. (10:8–18).
22. Haroutunian, *Commentaries, Com.* Titus 1:1, 237 (C.O. LII, 404).
23. *Inst.*, III, ii, 3 (O.S. IV, 11, 3–6).
24. *Inst.*, III, ii, 4 (O.S. IV, 11, 28–31).
25. *Inst.*, III, ii, 3 (O.S. IV, 11, 8–11).
26. *Inst.*, III, ii, 4 (O.S. IV, 12, 20–22).

clue to a proper understanding of the entire chapter. In commenting on the words "sure and firm" in his definition of faith,[27] Calvin says:

> We add the words 'sure and firm' in order to express a more solid constancy of persuasion. For, as faith is not content with a doubtful and changeable opinion, so it is not content with an obscure and confused conception; but requires full and fixed certainty, such as men are wont to have from things experienced and proved. For unbelief is so deeply rooted in our hearts, and we are so inclined to it, that not without hard struggle is each one able to persuade himself of what all confess with the mouth: namely, that God is faithful. Especially when it comes to reality itself, every man's wavering uncovers hidden weakness.[28]

The same thought occurs in his answer to an attack upon his doctrine of certainty:

> Still, someone will say: 'Believers experience something far different: In recognizing the grace of God toward themselves they are not only tried by disquiet, which often comes upon them, but they are repeatedly shaken by gravest terrors. For so violent are the temptations that trouble their minds as not to seem quite compatible with that certainty of faith.' Accordingly, we shall have to solve this difficulty if we wish the above-stated doctrine to stand. Surely, while we teach faith ought to be certain and assured, we cannot imagine any certainty that is not tinged with doubt, or any assurance that is not assailed by some anxiety. On the other hand, we say that believers are in perpetual conflict with their own unbelief. Far, indeed, are we from putting their consciences in any peaceful repose, undisturbed by any tumult at all. Yet, once again, we deny that, in whatever way they are afflicted, they fall away and depart from the certain assurance (*fiducia*) received from God's mercy.[29]

We find the same thought repeated throughout the whole chapter. We shall satisfy ourselves however, with two more statements:

> The godly heart feels in itself a division because it is partly imbued with sweetness from its recognition of the divine goodness, partly grieves in bitterness from an awareness of its calamity; partly . . . partly. . . . This variation arises from imperfection of

---

27. *Inst.*, III, ii, 7 (O.S. IV, 16, 31–35).
28. *Inst.*, III, ii, 15 (O.S. IV, 25, 24–32).
29. *Inst.*, III, ii, 17 (O.S. IV, 27, 19–34; Latin supplied).

faith, since in the course of the present life it never goes well with us that we are wholly cured of the disease of unbelief and calamity filled and possessed by faith.[30]

"Faith is tossed about by various doubts, so that the minds of the godly are rarely at peace—at least they do not always enjoy a peaceful state."[31] Regarding this last statement Calvin says of this fact that it is "repeatedly renewed by experience."[32] The tension and conflict that take place in the life of the believer find repeated expression in the chapters that follow the discussion of faith. Stuermann points out some of these tensions.[33] Indeed, one can easily see that Calvin never tired of emphasizing that even believers "as long as they dwell as strangers in the world," experience knowledge and ignorance, faith and unbelief, certainty and doubt, because although they are restored yet they are still sinners. Calvin clearly expressed this tension in his chapter on "Our Regeneration by Faith: Repentance."[34] Here he taught that "repentance not only constantly follows faith, but is also born of faith."[35] Or again, "I interpret repentance as regeneration, whose sole end is to restore in us the image of God that had been disfigured and all but obliterated through Adam's transgression."[36]

The most emphatic remarks in the *Institutes* regarding the tension in the life of faith can be found where Calvin clearly states that believers are still sinners:

> Thus, then, are the children of God freed through regeneration from bondage to sin. Yet they do not obtain full possession of freedom so as to feel no more annoyance from their flesh, but there still remains in them a continuing occasion for struggle whereby they may be exercised, and not only be exercised, but also better learn their own weakness. In this matter all writers of sounder judgment agree that there remains in a regenerate man

---

30. *Inst.*, III, ii, 18 (O.S. IV, 29, 7–15).

31. *Inst.*, III, ii, 37 (O.S. IV, 47, 16–18).

32. Ibid. (47, 15ff).

33. Stuermann, *Critical Study*, 234–58. Cf. also Dowey, *Knowledge of God*, 192ff. (1952 and 1994).

34. *Inst.*, III, iii, chapter title.

35. *Inst.*, III, iii, 1 (O.S. IV, 55, 16ff).

36. *Inst.*, III, iii, 9 (O.S. IV, 63, 11–14).

Knowledge of God: The Duplex Gratia Dei 45

a smoldering cinder of evil, for which desires continually leap forth to allure and spur him to commit sin.[37]

Calvin notes here a difference between Augustine and himself; although Augustine dealt with the same problem, "yet he dare not call this disease 'sin.'"[38] Calvin disagrees:

> We, on the other hand, deem it sin when man is tickled by any desire at all against the law of God.... We accordingly teach that in the saints, until they are divested of mortal bodies, there is always sin; for in their flesh there resides that depravity of inordinate desiring which contends against righteousness.[39]

It is in this context that Calvin writes of the believer as *simul iustus et peccator*.[40] This concept provides the clue to understanding the twofold nature of knowledge in Calvin's theology—which, I suggest, is essential for a proper interpretation of his doctrine of faith. It is to this duality that we now need to turn.

TWOFOLD KNOWLEDGE AND TENSION IN THE LIFE OF FAITH

Calvin taught that believers have a twofold knowledge of God as well as a corresponding twofold knowledge of themselves. They know God as their Creator, and this knowledge corresponds to their knowledge of themselves as they were first created. On the other hand they also know God as their Redeemer, which corresponds to their knowledge of themselves as sinners. Our analysis has shown that Calvin considered the life of faith to be a life of continuing struggle. The believer is restored, but believers are still sinners. As redeemed they are in continuous need of knowledge of God as Redeemer, but they have that "primal and simple knowledge to which the very order of nature would have led us if Adam had remained upright."[41] This latter knowledge enables believers to know

---

37. *Inst.*, III, iii, 10 (O.S. IV, 65, 12–20).
38. Ibid. (66, 3ff.)
39. Ibid. (66, 7–13).
40. We shall soon see that Calvin was not interested in this formula in itself. He went beyond it to its practical application in the life of the believer in relationship to God. See pages 000–000 below.
41. *Inst.*, I, ii, 1 (O.S. III, 34,13ff).

God as their Creator. It is only within the context of this knowledge that they can respond to God in trust and reverence.[42]

The reader should recall that the whole of believers' lives center around this twofold knowledge, which is experienced simultaneously. To borrow an expression from the christological formula of Chalcedon, as long as believers are in the flesh, their experience of the twofold knowledge is "without confusion, without change, without division, without separation." They know God as their Creator and Redeemer in the act of knowing themselves as restored and yet sinners. Likewise, the experience of believers might throw some light on the mystery of the incarnation. Baillie expresses this mystery as follows:

> If we try to isolate absolutely the mystery of the incarnation failing to connect it with the all-round paradox of our Christian faith and experience, we shall end by having on our hands a mystery which is not a religious mystery at all and has no bearing on our religious life.[43]

At this point we need to keep clearly in mind the correspondence between each side of the twofold knowledge of God and its proper counterpart in the twofold knowledge of ourselves.

Knowledge of God the Creator

We have seen that Calvin juxtaposed knowledge of God as Creator with knowledge of "what we were like when we were first created."[44] The understanding of this knowledge was meant to guard against any impious attempt to find some excuse for sin. Therefore Calvin says,

> We must guard against singling out only those natural evils of man, lest we seem to attribute them to the Author of nature. For in this excuse, impiety thinks it has sufficient defense, if it is able to claim that whatever defects it possesses have in some way proceeded from God.... And those who wish to seem to speak more reverently of the Godhead still willingly blame their depravity on nature, not realizing that they also, although more obscurely, insult God. For if any defect were proved to inhere in nature, this would bring reproach upon him.

---

42. *Inst.* I, ii, 2 *passim*; I, x, 2 (O.S. III, 87, 14–19); I, xiv, 22 *passim*.
43. Cf. Baillie, *God Was in Christ*, 106–32.
44. *Inst.*, I, xv, 1 (O.S. III, 173, 32).

> Since, then, we see the flesh panting for every subterfuge by which it thinks that the blame for its own evils may in any way be diverted from itself to another, we must diligently oppose this evil intent. Therefore we must so deal with the calamity of mankind that we may cut off every shift, and may vindicate God's justice from every accusation.[45]

In our study of the knowledge of God as Creator, it is important to notice that in Calvin's picture of "what we were like when we were first created," he has intentionally turned away from referring to the first Adam to speak of the Second Adam, who is Christ.[46] For Calvin's real interest in Book I is not to present the image of God in humanity as something that has been lost but rather as the image that is restored in Christ.[47] Therefore he says:

> It seems that we do not have a full definition of 'image' if we do not see more plainly those faculties in which man excels, and in which he ought to be thought the reflection of God's glory. That, indeed, can be nowhere better recognized than from the restoration of his corrupted nature. There is no doubt that Adam, when he fell from his state, was by this defection alienated from God. Therefore, even though we grant that God's image was not totally annihilated and destroyed in him, yet it was so corrupted that whatever remains is a frightful deformity. Consequently, the beginning of our recovery of salvation is in that restoration which we obtain through Christ, who also is called the Second Adam for the reason that he restores us to true and complete integrity.[48]

We are now ready to grasp the scope of Book I of the *Institutes* with its description of knowledge of God the Creator. We have seen God in his act of revealing himself to humankind. The same revelation that was offered to Adam continues in spite of the fall. Both before and after the

---

45. *Inst.*, I, xv, 1 (O.S. III, 174, 2, 17); cf. *Inst.*, II, 1, 10 *passim*.

46. This same intent is found in Calvin's comments on Gen. 1:26. Here he says "Since the image of God has been destroyed in us by the fall, we may judge from its restoration what it originally had been." (C.O. XXIII, 26). Cf. Krusche, *Das Wirken*, 44ff.

47. Berkouwer points out that in Calvin's doctrine of the image of God in human beings, "the stress on renewal . . . is predominant." *Man: The Image of God*, 89. Our point above is stressed by Niesel, *Theology of Calvin*, 69ff. While he uses it to point out the christocentricity of Calvin's theology, we are using it to clarify the twofold knowledge of God and consequently the relationship between Books I and II of the *Institutes*.

48. *Inst.*, I, xv, 4 (O.S. III, 179, 3–14).

fall, God offers the same invitation to all, that they might "repose in Him with perfect trust (*certa fiducia*)" and "revere Him as Father."[49]

From the perspective of humankind, however, the situation is not the same: the fall stands between God's continuing revelation and people's response. Nevertheless, God in his mercy did not allow the fall to frustrate his purpose. Fallen humanity is restored in Christ; and through the work of the Holy Spirit, the process of restoration becomes the believer's continuing experience in faith. From this point of view, when we know "what we were like when we were first created," this knowledge does not serve the purpose of satisfying our curiosity about a lost image, but rather induces us to press forward. After Calvin has spoken of the restoration of the image of God in believers through Christ, he goes on to say, "Now we see how Christ is the most perfect image of God; if we are conformed to it, we are so restored that with true piety, righteousness, purity, and intelligence we bear God's image."[50]

Thus the knowledge of "what we were like when we were first created" should lead us to worship God. Moreover, "knowledge of this sort ... ought not only to arouse us to the worship of God but also to awaken and encourage us to the hope of future life."[51] Regarding the image of God in humanity, Calvin says:

> Now God's image is the perfect excellence of human nature which alone shone in Adam before his defection, but was subsequently so vitiated and almost blotted out that nothing remains after the ruin except what is confused, mutilated, and disease-ridden. Therefore in some part it now is manifest in the elect, in so far as they have been reborn in the spirit; but it will attain its full splendor in heaven.[52]

It is as we "meditate on the future life"[53] and see the struggle towards full restoration that we can understand the full meaning of Book I of the *Institutes*. These joint concepts inform our interpretation of Calvin's doctrine of creation and providence. These should not be read as metaphysical treatises but rather as statements of faith. Calvin as believer

---

49. *Inst.*, I, ii, 2 (O.S. III, 36, 15; 37, 5 and *passim*); *Inst.* I, x, 2 (O.S. III, 87, 14–19).
50. *Inst.*, I, xv, 4 (O.S. III, 180, 3–5).
51. *Inst.*, I, v, 10 (O.S. III, 54, 1–3); cf. II, I, 3 (O.S. III, 231, 7ff).
52. *Inst.*, I, xv, 4 (O.S. III, 180, 19–24).
53. Chapter title of III, ix.

looks at the whole creation, and out of his own experience of restoration sees his Father the Creator at work.

Commenting on the words "The kingdom of God will not come with observation (Luke 17:20)," Calvin says:

> They are greatly mistaken who seek with the eyes of the flesh the kingdom of God, which is in no respect carnal or earthly, for it is nothing else than the inward and spiritual renewal of the soul. . . . It must be observed, however, that Christ speaks only of the beginnings of the kingdom of God; for we now begin to be formed anew by the Spirit after the image of God, in order that our entire renovation, *and that of the whole world*, may afterward follow in due time.[54]

The same approach that we have seen in the *Institutes* concerning the knowledge of ourselves as we were first created is also found in Calvin's argument to his commentary on Genesis. Once more we see that Calvin's doctrine of creation directs the attention of the reader to restoration:

> And, in fact, though Moses begins, in this Book, with the Creation of the World, he nevertheless does not confine us to this subject. For these things ought to be connected together, that the world was founded by God, and that man, after he had been endued with the light of intelligence, and adorned with so many privileges, fell by his own fault, and was thus deprived of all the benefits he had obtained; afterwards, by the compassion of God, he was restored to the life he had forfeited, and this through the loving kindness of Christ. . . . The end to which the whole scope of the history tends is to this point, that the human race has been preserved by God in such a manner as to manifest his special care for his Church.[55]

After these remarks, Calvin gives a summary of the "Argument of the Book." Here again his emphasis on restoration is unmistakable. Having referred to the fall, he goes on to say,

> Thus, Moses represents man as devoid of all good, blinded in understanding, perverse in heart, vitiated in every part, and under sentence of eternal death; but he soon adds the history

---

54. *Com.* Luke 17:20 (C.O. XLV, 424ff.); italics added.
55. *Com. On Genesis*, Argument, E.T., 64 (C.O. XXIII,11ff).

of his restoration, where Christ shines forth with the benefit of redemption.[56]

Calvin's interest is also clear in his comments on Paul's words, "And that ye put on the new man (Eph 4:24)," where he says,

> What is added about the creation may refer either to the first creation of man, or to the second creation, which is effected by the grace of Christ. Both expositions will be true. Adam was at first created after the image of God, and reflected, as in a mirror, the Divine righteousness; but that image, having been defaced by sin, must now be restored in Christ. The regeneration of the godly is indeed . . . nothing else than the formation anew of the image of God in them. There is, no doubt, a far more rich and powerful manifestation of Divine grace in this second creation than in the first; but our highest perfection is uniformly represented in Scripture as consisting in our conformity and resemblance to God. Adam lost the image which he had originally received, and therefore it becomes necessary that it shall be restored to us by Christ. The design contemplated by regeneration is to recall us from our wanderings to that end for which we were created.[57]

Knowledge of God the Redeemer

It is evident that Calvin purposely correlates the knowledge of God the Redeemer with the knowledge of ourselves as fallen; Book II of the *Institutes* clearly establishes this fact. Yet it seems that the framework of Book I with its emphasis on restoration is not as evident to the reader. Thus many readers seek to work out a correlation between knowledge of God the Redeemer and knowledge of ourselves as redeemed, with the latter then regarded as described in Book III. But if Calvin's work is understood in this way, Book I must then be understood solely as a hypothetical discussion or mere speculation regarding what human beings would have known about God and themselves had it not been for the fall. Yet, if there is a single evil that Calvin has charged to the Schoolmen's account, it would be their flimsy and idle speculation by which they "lead miserable souls astray rather than to a definite goal."[58] One can hardly expect Calvin to offer his readers a book of specula-

---

56. Ibid. E.T., 65 (C.O. XXIII, 11ff).
57. Com. Eph 4:24 (C.O. LI, 208ff).
58. *Inst.*, III, ii, 1 (O.S. IV, 7, 20 f). Cf. I, ii, 2; I, v, 9 (O.S. III, 35, 11ff.; 53, 12).

tions. Rather, we have seen that Calvin's interest in Book I is to point to knowledge of ourselves in our original state—not for itself, but rather to depict what we should seek after as sinners who have been restored. Thus knowledge of God the Creator is not merely that knowledge which we once had and have now lost, but rather the knowledge we can attain in Christ. Calvin is not interested in feeding speculation but rather in leading the reader to salvation. The whole discussion in Book I, as we shall clearly see, centers on Christ's words, "This is eternal life: to know you the only true God."[59]

When Calvin's true purpose in Book I is not understood in this way, problems also develop in understanding Book II. It then becomes difficult to see the correlation between knowledge of the Redeemer and knowledge of ourselves as sinners. One would then be tempted to see a new correlation in which knowledge of the Redeemer corresponds to knowledge of ourselves as redeemed. On preliminary investigation, this correlation might appear to be logical; however, it would make knowledge of ourselves threefold rather than twofold as presented by Calvin, which in turn would destroy the correlative character of knowledge of God and of ourselves. It might be for this very reason that many Calvin scholars have failed to emphasize the twofold knowledge of ourselves in spite of their insistence that Calvin taught the correlative character of the knowledge of God. It has also meant that discussion of knowledge of the Redeemer in Book II has been linked to the doctrine of faith in Book III. When interpreters link Book II to Book III in this way, it is impossible to know what to do with the first five chapters of Book II concerning the knowledge of ourselves as sinners. For example, this is what happened in Dowey's presentation. In discussing the content of knowledge of God the Redeemer, he says, "These two words [gratuitous mercy] represent the

---

59. Cf. 110 ff. below. For Dowey, Book I of the *Institutes* is hypothetical in nature. Summarizing its contents he says, "All these elements together and in this relationship comprise the knowledge of God the Creator in Calvin's theology, as assembled in Book I of the *Institutes* of 1559. *They constitute what men would have known* of God the Father, Son, and Spirit in his creating and preserving work, and all they would have needed to know to glorify him, but for the Fall." *Knowledge of God*, 147; italics added. This theme is certainly found in Book I, yet we have seen that the discussion of knowledge of God the Creator for Calvin has a far more important purpose than a mere hypothetical speculation. Parker seems to agree with Dowey on this point. *Knowledge of God*, 27. Wendel, whom we have seen to agree with Dowey in his division of the *Institutes* (see p. 23, n. 28 above), discusses the entire twofold knowledge of ourselves under the knowledge of God the Redeemer. Wendel, *Sources et é volution*.

two poles of saving knowledge 'of God' as Redeemer and 'of ourselves' *as redeemed*.[60] Conversely, our interpretation of Calvin shows that he puts knowledge of God as Redeemer in correspondence with knowledge of ourselves as sinners, while the knowledge of ourselves as redeemed corresponds to knowledge of God as Creator. Calvin's project will be easily grasped when we remember that for him the work of redemption is a work of restoration.

Note on Methodology

Having explored the twofold knowledge of God and of ourselves, we shall now try to understand what Calvin meant by both the general and special[61] teachings of Scripture. The reader should remember that Calvin found that knowledge of God the Creator, which corresponds to knowledge of ourselves as restored in Christ, is offered by the general teaching of Scripture. Meanwhile, he considered knowledge of God as Redeemer and knowledge of ourselves as sinners to be found in the special teaching. His discussion of knowledge of the Creator before knowledge of the Redeemer has a methodological significance that we shall encounter repeatedly. We have already pointed out that Calvin held together both sides of the twofold knowledge. Believers know God as their Creator and Redeemer as they know themselves *simultaneously* as restored and yet sinners.[62] Without losing sight of this unity we can still say that Calvin did not consider knowledge of the Creator to be the foundation for knowledge of the Redeemer. On the contrary, we have seen him repeatedly pointing out that knowledge of the Creator must be founded on knowledge of the Redeemer. Calvin did not intend his discussion of the general teaching of Scripture in Book I to be a general background or a foundation for discussion of the special teaching of Scripture as presented in Book II. Indeed the general teaching cannot be grasped except on the basis of the special teaching. Thus Calvin's movement from Book I to Book II of the *Institutes* cannot be called a progression in the strict sense of the term, for the foundation that one would have expected to be given prior consideration is not discussed first.[63] Instead, Calvin pres-

---

60. Ibid., .206; italics added.
61. Synonymous with this are the terms *proper*, *particular*, and *specific*.
62. Cf. pages 45ff above.
63. Hunter finds two methods operating in Calvin's doctrine of God and says, "There were two lines in his [Calvin's] thinking about Him [God]. In the one he descended upon

ents humanity as restored in Christ and knowledge of God the Creator *before* his discussion of humanity as fallen and Christ's work of redemption and restoration. Calvin's remarks on John 17:3 throw much light on the point that we are considering here. Explaining the relationship of knowledge of the Creator to knowledge of the Redeemer, he says:

> Because God is known only in the face of Jesus Christ, who is His living and express image, He says: *That they should know thee, and him whom thou didst send, even Christ.* That he puts the Father first does not refer to the order of faith, as if our minds descend from the knowledge of God to Christ; but the meaning is that God is known by the intervention of the Mediator.[64]

The same ordering is also found in Calvin's comments on the words, "Ye believe in God, believe also in me (John 14:1)." Here he says:

> He [John] points out the way to stand fast—by our faith resting on Christ . . . But it is surprising that faith in the Father is here put first. For He ought rather to have told His disciples that they should believe in God because they had believed in Christ. For, since Christ is the express image of the Father, we ought first to look to Him . . . But Christ had a different object. All acknowledge that we should believe in God . . . But there is scarcely one in a hundred who really believes . . . . Our faith, seeking God in His heavenly glory and inaccessible light, comes to nothing . . . . Therefore, Christ holds out Himself as the object to which our faith, if it is directed, will easily find where it may rest . . . . Faith will never reach heaven unless it submits to Christ.[65]

---

the world from a conception of God which might find support in Christ but which did not start from Him; in the other he ascended from Christ to God or rather with Christ to God. It is the dominance of the former way that shapes his whole system." *Teaching of Calvin,* 46. Hunter neither clarifies nor elaborates on this statement. We can find here, however, a striking resemblance between this remark and what Dowey calls the "double presupposition" or the "dialectical relationship." Calvin's method, as we have seen, is what Hunter considers to be the first line of thought. Yet we have to say that the fact that Calvin did not discuss knowledge of the Redeemer before his discussion of knowledge of the Creator should not be interpreted to mean that he does not start from Christ. We shall soon see that the twofold knowledge of God is nothing but the result of what Calvin calls the "twofold grace of Christ," which the believer receives through the work of the Holy Spirit in faith. Therefore, even in his discussion of knowledge of the Creator, Calvin is starting from Christ in whom humanity is restored.

64. Com. John 17:3 (C.O. XLVII, 376).

65. Com. John 14:1 (C.O. XLVII, 32lff). Cf. also *Inst.*, II, vi, 4: "Properly speaking, faith mounts up from Christ to the Father. . . . Although faith rests in God, it will gradu-

TOWARD A DEFINITION OF FAITH

So far we have seen that Calvin attacks the Schoolmen's doctrine of implicit faith because he considers it to promote ignorance while he thinks of faith as knowledge. Yet his concept of knowledge is not naïve but rather existential. It expresses the tension that believers experience "as long as they are in the flesh."

We have also seen that Calvin rejects the Schoolmen's way of thinking in which "they call God simply the object of faith, and by fleeting speculations . . . lead miserable souls astray."[66] We have noted that he has nothing against calling God the object of faith; he can see in this statement, if properly interpreted, an equivalent to what he calls knowledge of God the Creator. Yet he maintains that the Schoolmen claim a form of knowledge of God the Creator that is not based on Christ—an idea that Calvin strenuously rejected. Arguing against them, Calvin emphasizes that "God is comprehended in Christ alone."[67] The Schoolmen cannot claim a knowledge of Him since they have "as it were, drawn a veil over Christ to hide him."[68] For, "unless God confronts us in Christ, we cannot come to know that we are saved."[69]

As we examine the twofold knowledge yet again, it is important to remember that for Calvin knowledge of God the Redeemer corresponds to knowledge of ourselves as sinners. Here it becomes obvious that Calvin's complaint against the Schoolmen centers on the fact that they do not take human sinfulness seriously. Instead, they teach works-righteousness, a doctrine that makes them lose sight of the "freely given promise in Christ." It is against this background of the scholastic definitions as well as the needs of his readers that the whole chapter on faith should be interpreted. This is the key to understanding Calvin's approach. To be sure, Calvin makes his intention clear when he says, "Now, what is our purpose in discussing faith? Is it not that we may grasp the way of salvation?"[70] It is obvious that Calvin is interested in a doctrine of faith that takes sin seriously. For him, as we have seen, even believers are still

---

ally disappear unless he who retains it in perfect firmness intercedes as Mediator." (O.S. III, 325, 17–20).

66. *Inst.*, III, ii, 1 (O.S. III, iv, 7, 19–21).
67. *Inst.*, II, vi, 4 (O.S. III, 326, 6ff).
68. *Inst.*, III, ii, 2 (O.S. IV, 10, 1–4).
69. *Inst.*, II, vi, 4 (O.S. III, 325, 25ff).
70. *Inst.*, III, ii, 30 (O.S. IV, 40, 12ff).

sinners. Although they are restored, and although they have knowledge of the Creator and respond to him in trust and reverence, and thus their faith is not devoid of good works, yet at the same time they are still sinners and still in need of knowledge of God the Redeemer. Moreover, it is only on the basis of knowledge of themselves as sinners and the corresponding knowledge of God as their Redeemer that the image of God is restored in them. Likewise it is only on the basis of knowing themselves as restored that they can have the corresponding knowledge of God as their Creator. These two sides of the twofold knowledge correspond to Calvin's two definitions of faith.

First Definition of Faith

Calvin's first definition of faith is found in Book III, ii, 6: "We hold faith to be a knowledge of God's will toward us, perceived from his Word."[71] The language used here is identical with that of the description in Book I of knowledge of God the Creator. Calvin called this first description of faith general, in contrast to the second, which he called particular. This differentiation should bring to mind Calvin's distinction between the general teaching of Scripture, related to the knowledge of God the Creator;[72] and the specific, or proper, teaching that sets forth Christ.[73]

Once more, Calvin reminds us of knowledge of God the Creator by pointing out that: "In understanding faith it is not merely a question of knowing that God exists, but also—and this especially—of knowing what is his will toward us. For it is not so much our concern to know who he is in himself, as what he wills to be toward us."[74] The language he is using here is identical with the language that we have seen earlier: "What is God? Men who pose this question are merely toying with idle speculations. It is far better for us to inquire, 'What is his nature?' and to know what is consistent with his nature."[75] Or again: "He is shown to us not as he is in himself, but as he is toward us: so that . . . recognition

---

71. *Inst.*, III, ii, 6 (O.S. IV, 15, 10ff).
72. *Inst.*, I, ii, 1; I, x, 3 (O.S. III, 34, 23; 87, 20).
73. *Inst.*, I, vi, 2 (O.S. III, 62, 16ff).
74. *Inst.*, III, ii, 6 (O.S. IV, 15, 6–9).
75. *Inst.*, I, ii, 1 (O.S. III, 35, 11–14).

of him consists more in living experience than in vain and high-flown speculation."[76]

One should recall that Calvin points out repeatedly that this knowledge of God's will requires a response of trust and reverence from humankind.[77] Yet it must be founded on a "preconceived conviction of God's truth."[78] He goes on to say:

> As for its certainty, as long as your mind is at war with itself, the Word will be of doubtful and weak authority, or rather of none. And it is not even enough to believe that God is trustworthy (cf. Rom 3:3), who can neither deceive nor lie (cf. Titus 1:2), unless you hold to be beyond doubt that whatever proceeds from him is sacred and inviolable truth.[79]

Second Definition of Faith

We must carefully study the movement of Calvin's thought to see how he leads his readers from the first definition of faith to the second. In doing so, we find the same logical progression as is found between Books I and II. One should recall that having finished his discussion of knowledge of God the Creator, Calvin taught that this knowledge could have been enough to lead humanity to eternal life and salvation had it not been for the fall.[80] He showed that this renewing knowledge must be founded on the knowledge of the Redeemer. Here again, after presenting the first definition of faith, he says, "But since man's heart is not aroused to faith at every word of God, we must find out at this point what, strictly speaking, faith looks to in the Word."[81]

The difficulty in calling faith "a knowledge of God's will perceived from his Word" does not lie in the Word of God or God's truth but rather in the human heart because of sin. Calvin then goes on to say:

> God's word to Adam was, 'You shall surely die' (Gen 2:17). God's word to Cain was, 'The blood of your brother cries out to me from the earth' (Gen 4:10). But these words are so far from be-

---

76. *Inst.*, I, x, 2 (O.S. III, 86, 17–19).
77. *Inst.*, I, ii, 2: *passim*; I, x, 2 (O.S. III, 87, 16ff).
78. *Inst.*, III, ii, 6 (O.S. IV, 15, 12ff).
79. Ibid. (15, 13–18).
80. See pages 22f above.
81. *Inst.*, III, ii, 7 (O.S. IV, 15, 19–21).

ing capable of establishing faith that they can of themselves do nothing but shake it. In the meantime, we do not deny that it is the function of faith to subscribe to God's truth whenever and whatever and however it speaks. But we ask only what faith finds in the Word of the Lord upon which to lean and rest.[82]

Answering this question, Calvin teaches that "We need the promise of grace, which can testify to us that the Father is merciful; since we can approach him in no other way, and upon grace alone the heart of man can rest."[83]

Calvin has distinguished in these various quotes between "God's truth," "God's will" or "the word," and "the promise of grace." He does so while also making it clear that he is looking for a fuller definition of faith because of human sin. It is essential for us to discover Calvin's purpose. In this connection, Forstman reminds us, "It would be improper to conclude . . . that Calvin considered one part of the Scripture (that dealing especially with the promises of divine mercy) of greater importance than the rest. For one thing, that has not been the point of the discussion."[84] Moreover, we should not fail to notice that immediately after Calvin made this distinction, he went on to emphasize the mutual connection between God's mercy and his truth.[85] Never for a moment was Calvin willing to separate faith from the Word as a whole. He says, "There is a permanent relationship between faith and the Word. We could not separate one from the other any more than we could separate the rays from the sun from which they come."[86] Or again, "The same Word is the basis whereby faith is supported and sustained; if it turns away from the Word, it falls. Therefore, take away the Word and no faith will then remain."[87] This same thought appears repeatedly in the same chapter: "Believers embrace and grasp the Word of God in every respect,"[88] and "Faith needs the Word as much as fruit needs the living root of a tree."[89]

---

82. Ibid. (15, 21–28).
83. Ibid. (16, 1–4).
84. Forstman, *Word and Spirit*, 43.
85. *Inst.*, III, ii, 7 (O.S. IV, 16, 4–16).
86. *Inst.*, III, ii, 6 (O.S. IV, 14, 7–9).
87. Ibid. (14, 26 ff).
88. *Inst.*, III, ii, 7 (O.S. IV, 15, 31–33).
89. *Inst.*, III, ii, 31 (O.S. IV, 40, 22ff).

Calvin's real purpose in distinguishing between the word as a whole and the freely given promise cannot be fully grasped unless we understand the context of his chapter on faith. It is obvious that he is fighting against the Scholastic concept of faith as assent. Therefore he deals with the Schoolmen's view at the beginning of his chapter and comes back to it after he had given his fuller definition of faith.[90] Yet one can easily notice that his first definition of faith could be interpreted as equivalent to the Scholastic definition of assent. It is for this reason that he says, "It is plain then, that we do not yet have a full definition of faith, inasmuch as merely to know something of God's will is not to be accounted faith."[91]

The trouble with the notion of assent as Calvin sees it is not with the claimed content of such so-called knowledge. Calvin sees a relationship between faith and God's word or his will. He opposes the concept of assent, however, because it assumes a knowledge that it does not really possess. He considered that assent led to insubstantial speculations rather than knowledge because it failed to take sin seriously. This consideration can be seen clearly in Calvin's discussion of the Roman Church's concepts of formed and unformed faith, where he says:

> We must refute that worthless distinction between formed and unformed faith which is tossed about in the schools. For they imagine that people who are touched by no fear of God, no sense of piety, nevertheless believe whatever it is necessary to know for salvation . . . . They presumptuously dignify that persuasion, devoid of the fear of God, with the name 'faith.'[92]

Calvin's complaint here is that "[the Schoolmen] would have faith to be an assent by which any despiser of God may receive what is offered from Scripture."[93] Here we again see that Calvin is not rejecting the Roman Catholic doctrine of assent because of its content but rather because the notion of assent does not face sin seriously, and would open the door for "wicked" people and even devils to be considered to have faith. Against this potential distortion he says,

> We seek a faith that distinguishes the children of God from the wicked, and believers from unbelievers. If someone believes

---

90. *Inst.*, III, ii, 1 *passim*; III, ii, 8–10 *passim*.
91. *Inst.*, III, ii, 7 (O.S. IV, 15, 31–33).
92. *Inst.*, III, ii, 8 (O.S. IV, 16, 38–17, 7).
93. Ibid. (17, 13ff).

that God both justly commands all that he commands and truly threatens, shall he therefore be called a believer? By no means![94]

In light of this statement we can understand Calvin's repeated complaint against the Schoolmen, that their speculations lead miserable souls astray rather than direct them to a definite end. Having such a definite goal in mind, he says: "Now, what is our purpose in discussing faith? Is it not that we may grasp the way of salvation?"[95]

It becomes evident that Calvin is distinguishing between the word of God or truth on one hand and the freely given promise in Christ on the other, in order to combat the Roman doctrine of assent with its failure to differentiate between believers and unbelievers. He says,

> First they ought to have seen whether every man attains faith by his own effort, or whether through it the Holy Spirit is witness of his adoption. Therefore they babble childishly in asking whether faith is the same faith when it has been formed by a superadded quality; or whether it be a new and different thing. From such chatter it certainly looks as if they never thought about the unique gift of the Spirit. For the beginning of believing already contains within itself the reconciliation whereby man approached God.[96]

Calvin's case against the concept of assent can be seen in the following manner. He thinks that the Roman Church is working towards the right goal: its teachers want to embrace God's word and his truth. To this he has no objection. The difference between the Schoolmen and Calvin, however, concerns the road one must take to arrive at this goal. The Schoolmen claimed that when a pious inclination is added to assent, unformed faith becomes formed faith. Calvin, on the other hand, sees that sin stands between human beings and their ability to embrace God's word and truth in a direct and immediate fashion. Humanity must first arrive at the freely given promise before being able to assent to God's word. Thus Calvin considers the Schoolmen's approach backward in that assent to God's word and truth is the result rather than the beginning of faith. For this reason he says:

> If we possessed only this one reason, it would have been sufficient to end the dispute: that very assent itself—as I have already partially

---

94. *Inst.*, III, ii, 30 (O.S. IV, 40, 8–11).
95. Ibid. (40, 12ff).
96. *Inst.*, III, ii, 8 (O.S. IV, 17, 14–21).

> suggested, and will reiterate more fully—is more of the heart than of the brain, and more of the disposition than of the understanding. For this reason, it is called obedience of faith (Rom 1:8), and the Lord prefers no other obedience to it—and justly, since nothing is more precious to him than his truth. To this truth believers set their seal as if they have affixed their signature, as John the Baptist testifies (John 3: 33). Since there is no doubt about the matter, we establish in one word that they are speaking foolishly when they say that faith is 'formed' when pious inclination is added to assent. For even assent rests upon such pious inclination—at least such assent as is revealed in the Scriptures![97]

Here we see Calvin accepting the doctrine of assent, but in doing so he fills it with a new meaning.

We have noted earlier a similar approach, in which Calvin accepted the scholastic doctrine of God as the object of faith, yet made it clear that it is on the basis of the knowledge of Christ that we can know God. For knowledge of God as Creator has to be founded upon knowledge of him as Redeemer. We can now see that the two objections that Calvin had against the Schoolmen are actually one at root.[98] His entire point is that faith can never have regard for the word of God and God's truth unless it is established on the freely given promise in Christ. Moreover, since even believers are still sinners as long as they are in the flesh, then faith is in constant need of this freely given promise in Christ.

Now we can see more clearly that Calvin's battle against the Schoolmen focused on the objection that they did not take sin seriously. With their emphasis on works-righteousness they seemed to overlook that even believers are still sinners. It is interesting in this respect to note that Calvin closes his chapter on faith in the following manner:

> For our part, when we as sinners see that we are commanded by the oracles of God to conceive of hope of salvation, let us so willingly presume upon his truth that, relying upon his mercy alone, abandoning reliance (*fiducia*) upon works, we dare to have good hope.[99]

All through this chapter on faith, Calvin seeks to reiterate one objection to the Schoolmen: We are sinners who cannot rely upon works.

---

97. Ibid. (17, 23–18, 8).
98. Cf. page 39 above.
99. *Inst.*, III, ii, 43 (O.S. IV, 54, 28–31; Latin supplied).

Because of our condition we can never assent to God's truth nor bring forth good works unless we hold to the "freely given promise in Christ"; and by the same token, we can never have knowledge of God as Creator unless it is founded upon knowledge of him as Redeemer.

Now we can understand why Calvin was looking for something in the Word upon which faith can lean and rest. For the Scholastic concept of assent has no firm foundation because it does not understand the extent or depth of human sinfulness. Calvin says about it:

> But this shadow or image of faith, as it is of no importance, does not deserve to be called faith.... What ever sort of assent that is, it does not at all penetrate to the heart itself, there to remain fixed. And although it seems sometimes to put down roots, they are not living roots. The human heart has so many crannies where vanity hides, so many holes where falsehood lurks, is so decked out with deceiving hypocrisy, that it often dupes itself. Yet let those who boast of such shadow-shapes of faith understand that in this respect they are no better than the devils![100]

Only knowledge of the freely given promise in Christ can provide the proper foundation for knowledge of God's will and truth.

> Far indeed is the mind of man, blind and darkened as it is, from penetrating and attaining even to perception of the will of God! And the heart, too, wavering as it is in perpetual hesitation, is far from resting secure in that conviction! Therefore our mind must be otherwise illumined and our heart strengthened, that the Word of God may obtain full faith among us. Now we shall possess a right definition of faith if we call it a firm and certain knowledge of God's benevolence toward us, founded upon the truth of the freely given promise in Christ, both revealed to our minds and sealed upon our hearts through the Holy Spirit.[101]

It should be clear at this point that Calvin is not at all suggesting that faith in the word of God and the knowledge of his will is the *basis* for acceptance of the freely given promise in Christ. He is rather pointing out that the first has to be founded on the second. For, as the preceding passage states, "our mind must be otherwise illumined and our heart strengthened, that the Word of God may obtain full faith among us."

---

100. *Inst.*, III, ii, 10 (O.S. IV, 19, 29ff.; 20, 15–21).
101. *Inst.*, III, ii, 7 (O.S., IV, 16, 26–35).

Once more we encounter Calvin's methodology of reversing the order. For although the first definition of faith is given prior consideration, Calvin clearly points out that it has to be founded on the second. The acceptance of the freely given promise is the basis for faith in the Word of God. This same thought is also found in Calvin's comments on the words, "By faith Noah . . . moved with fear, prepared an ark" (Heb 11:7). Here he says:

> It seems . . . to have been improperly stated, that Noah was by faith led to fear. To this I reply that faith indeed properly springs from promises; it is founded on them, it rests on them. We hence say that Christ is the real object of faith, for through him our heavenly Father is reconciled to us, and by him all the promises of salvation are sealed and confirmed. Yet there is no reason why faith should not look to God and reverently receive whatever he may say; or if you prefer another way of stating the subject, it rightly belongs to faith to hear God whenever he speaks, and unhesitatingly to embrace whatsoever may proceed from his sacred mouth. Thus far it has regard to commands and threatenings, as well as to gratuitous promises. But as no man is moved as he ought and as much as is needful, to obey God's commands, nor is sufficiently stirred up to deprecate his wrath, unless he has already laid hold on the promises of grace, so as to acknowledge him as a kind Father, and the author of salvation,—hence the Gospel is called the word of faith, the principal part being stated for the whole; and thus is set forth the mutual relation that there is between them both. Faith, then, though its most direct regard is to God's promises, yet looks on his threatenings so far as it is necessary for it to be taught to fear and obey God.[102]

Here we see again the relationship between human knowledge of God as Creator and knowledge of him as Redeemer, which is also the relationship between the general teaching and the specific or proper teaching of Scripture. It is the same twofold knowledge in which believers as sinners are always in need of the knowledge of God as their Redeemer. Their whole faith has to be founded upon the freely given promise in Christ. On the other hand, they are restored, and as such they know God as their Creator. From this point of view they need the word of God as a whole and need to know his will in order to respond to

---

102. *Com.* Heb. 11:7 (C.O. LV, 150ff).

him in trust and reverence. With this in mind, we can understand what Calvin means when he says:

> We make the freely given promise of God the foundation of faith because upon it faith properly rests. Faith is certain that God is true in all things whether he command or forbid, whether he promise or threaten; and it also obediently receives his commandments, observes his prohibitions, heeds his threats. Nevertheless, faith properly begins with the promise, rests in it, and ends in it . . . .
>
> When we say that faith must rest upon a freely given promise, we do not deny that believers embrace and grasp the Word of God in every respect: but we point out the promise of mercy as the proper goal of faith. As on the one hand believers ought to recognize God to be Judge and Avenger of wicked deeds, yet on the other hand they properly contemplate his kindness, since he is so described to them as to be considered 'one who is kind (cf. Ps 86:5), 'and merciful.'[103]

Calvin made such remarks to ensure that he would not be misunderstood. Against the controversialists of his day he says:

> I admit, as I have already said, that God's truth is, as they call it, the common object of faith, whether he threaten or hold out hope of grace . . . . But our slanderers (Pighius and others) unjustly charge us with denying, as it were, that faith has regard to all parts of the Word of God. It is our intention to make only these two points: first, that faith does not stand firm until a man attains to the freely given promise; second, that it does not reconcile us to God at all unless it joins us to Christ.[104]

We have already seen how Calvin accepted "the common saying that God is the object of faith."[105] Yet he insisted that this faith must be founded on knowledge of Christ. Here again, he accepted the saying that God's truth is the common object of faith. Yet he insisted that it must be founded on knowledge of the freely given promise. In both cases, it is the twofold knowledge that expresses the tension in the life of faith.

---

103. *Inst.*, III, ii, 29 (O.S. IV, 39, 1–6; 25–34).

104. *Inst.*, III, ii, 30 (O.S. IV, 39, 37–39; 40, 2–7) "Calvin's definition of faith (in the 1539 *Institutio*, ch. iv) was assailed by Albert Pighius, archdeacon of Utrecht, as "indefinite," "confused," and tending to promote "a false security." (In Battles' translation of the *Institutes*, I, 576).

105. *Inst.*, II, vi, 4 (O.S. III, 325, 22ff.); cf. 57ff. above.

Dowey makes a careful study of Calvin's two emphases: the freely given promise and Scripture as a whole. Then he goes on to say:

> We must conclude, in fact, that two 'interpretations' exist side by side in Calvin's theology concerning the object of the knowledge of faith, because he never fully integrated and related systematically the faithful man's acceptance of the authority of the Bible *en bloc* with faith as directed exclusively toward Christ.[106]

It is in this connection that Dowey thinks that "Calvin points in two different ways at once."[107] And it is here that he finds Calvin's theology to be "dissonant"[108] and to contain "a discrepancy between the so-called formal and material principles of the Reformation: the authority of Scripture and justification by faith in Christ."[109] This same view finds milder expression in Forstman's presentation on Calvin when he says:

> Calvin operated with two distinct epistemologies, which, although they cannot be radically separated from one another, do submit to study in isolation from one another . . . . On the one hand, there is one epistemology for faith, and on the other hand, there is another for what may be called the wider knowledge, or, to use Calvin's words, for anything 'that has proceeded from God's sacred mouth.'[110]

With this pattern in mind, Forstman concludes: "In effect, then, there are two principles governing the *Institutes*, not entirely distinct, not entirely dissimilar, yet possessing different characters and operating on the basis of different presuppositions."[111]

Yet as we have pointed out, Calvin was not operating with two distinct epistemologies, nor did he fail to systematically relate the believer's acceptance of the authority of Scripture as a whole with faith which is directed towards the freely given promise in Christ. We do not need to say with Armstrong that "his theology was accommodated to conflicting ideologies in such a way that there will always be two poles, two aspects, two dialectical and conflicting elements in each theological topic which

---

106. Dowey, *Knowledge of God*, 161ff.
107. Ibid., 163, n. 67.
108. Ibid., 161.
109. Ibid.
110. Forstman, *Word and Spirit*, 38.
111. Ibid., 74.

he discusses."[112] Rather Calvin was only giving expression to the tension in the life of faith. As we continue our study of the relationship between the twofold knowledge of God and Calvin's doctrine of faith, we will clarify this point further.

THE *DUPLEX COGNITIO DOMINI* AND THE *DUPLEX GRATIA DEI*

We have seen that according to Calvin, people's salvation before the fall consisted in knowledge of God the Creator.[113] Because of human rebellion against God, however, this knowledge was lost; but God in his mercy restored and recovered this lost salvation in Christ. Now human beings can know their Creator only on the basis of knowledge of the Redeemer. Complete salvation consists in this twofold knowledge: to know the Father to be the one true God and to know Jesus Christ whom he has sent. Yet believers cannot know God or themselves except in faith through the work of the Holy Spirit and as a result of their reception of the grace of Christ. It is on this basis that the twofold knowledge of God and of ourselves becomes the simultaneous everyday experience of believers. God relates himself to humanity, and humanity relates itself to God in a twofold way. Believers come to know God as their Creator in knowing themselves as restored in Christ. This knowledge means that they respond to God in an active way by expressing trust and reverence toward their Creator. Likewise believers also know God as their Redeemer in knowing themselves as sinners. From this point of view the whole response to God is that of one who freely receives *sola gratia*, by grace alone.

We shall soon see that the *duplex cognitio* is nothing but the result of the believer's appropriation of the *duplex gratia*. As believers receive the grace of sanctification they come to know God as Creator and themselves as restored in Christ. On the other hand, when they receive the grace of justification they come to know God as their Redeemer and themselves as sinners. From this perspective it is evident that justification is by faith alone. To clarify this thesis we shall briefly study Calvin's doctrine of the *duplex gratia* and then relate it to the *duplex cognitio*.

---

112. Armstrong, "Duplex Cognitio Dei," 137.
113. Cf. pages 21f above.

The Duplex Gratia Dei

Calvin repeatedly emphasizes that faith means union with Christ:

> As long as Christ remains outside of us, and we are separated from him, all that he has suffered and done for the salvation of the human race remains useless and of no value for us. Therefore, to share with us what he has received from the Father, he had to become ours and to dwell within us . . . . For . . . all that he possesses is nothing to us until we grow into one body with him.[114]

A study of Calvin's teaching regarding the believer's union with Christ especially in connection with justification, important as it is, takes us beyond our purpose here.[115] It is sufficient to observe that as early as the 1539 *Institutes* Calvin pointed out that believers receive a twofold grace through union with Christ. The same statement containing Calvin's understanding of the *duplex gratia Dei* was retained in the following manner until the definitive edition:

> Christ was given to us by God's generosity, to be grasped and possessed by us in faith. By partaking of him, we principally receive a double grace: (*cuius participatione duplicem potissimum gratiam recipiamus*) namely, that being reconciled to God through Christ's blamelessness, we may have in heaven instead of a Judge a gracious Father; and secondly, that sanctified by Christ's spirit we may cultivate blamelessness and purity of life.[116]

Calvin introduced his discussion of this twofold grace immediately after he had presented his doctrine of faith. Thus at the beginning of his chapter on repentance he says,

> Even though we have taught in part how faith possesses Christ, and how through it we enjoy his benefits, this would still remain obscure if we did not add an explanation of the effects we feel. With good reason, the sum of the gospel is held to consist in repentance and forgiveness of sins (Luke 24:47; Acts 5:31). Any discussion of faith, therefore, that omitted these two topics would

---

114. *Inst.* III, I, 1 (O. S. iv, 1–2).

115. For a full discussion of union with Christ, especially the discussion of whether saving grace is forensic or personal, imputed, or imparted, see Garcia, *Life in Christ*, 11ff; Gaffin, "Justification and Union," 252ff.; Dowey, *Knowledge of God* (1994), 196 ff.; Krusche, *Das Wirken*, 265 ff.; Van Buren, *Christ in Our Place*, 95ff.; Partie, *Theology of John Calvin*, 40ff. For the present writer's point of view, see n. 184 below.

116. *Inst.*, III, xi, 1 (O.S. IV, 182, 3–8); Latin supplied.

be barren.... Now, both repentance and forgiveness of sins—that is, newness of life and free reconciliation—are conferred on us by Christ, and both are attained by us through faith.[117]

Calvin then indicated that he would discuss the second part of the twofold grace first. This discussion forms the subject matter of *Institutes* III, iii–x, while the first part is then taken up in *Institutes* III, xi. Calvin taught this concept of the twofold grace repeatedly in both his commentaries and his sermons.[118] Commenting on the words, "That he might present us holy (Eph 5:27)," he says: "For the entire blessing of redemption consist mainly in these two things, remission of sins, and spiritual regeneration."[119] The same thought is also found in his remarks on "For you are not under the law, but under grace (Rom 6:14)." Here he says: "By the word *grace* we understand both parts of redemption, i.e., the forgiveness of sins, by which God imputes righteousness to us, and the sanctification of the Spirit, by whom He forms us anew to good works."[120]

Calvin calls the bestowal of this twofold grace the "two offices of Christ."[121] Jansen highlights this nomenclature, noting that "whenever the office of the Redeemer appears it continues to be characterized by a two-fold chàracter—regal and priestly."[122] It is interesting that Christ's office as king corresponds to the grace of sanctification while his office as priest corresponds to the grace of justification.[123] This concept can be seen clearly in the *Mutual Consent* between the ministers of the church of Zürich and Calvin in the article on «Christ as Priest and King.» The article says:

117. *Inst.*, III, iii, 1 (O.S. IV, 55, 1–11).

118. Van Buren, *Christ in Our Place*, 107 ff.; Wallace, *Calvin's Doctrine of the Christian Life*, 23 ff.

119. *Com.* Col 1:22 (C.O. LII, 90).

120. *Com.* Rom. 6:14 (C.O. XLIX, 113).

121. *Com.* 1 Cor 1:30 (C.O. XLIX, 331).

122. Jansen, *Calvin's Doctrine of the Work of Christ*, 53. One should remember that in *Inst.* II, xv Calvin speaks of the three offices of Christ as prophet, priest, and king. After an interesting study of the offices of Christ in Calvin's theology, Jansen says, "The real question, however, is whether this revelatory (i.e. the prophetic) aspect of Christ's mission is for Calvin best understood in terms of a formula of offices which would place it alongside the kingly and priestly offices. This is precisely what later theology does, but apparently Calvin does not do this. If we read carefully, we find that the revelatory character of Christ's work does not receive a separate messianic or 'typical' treatment—rather, it belongs to His *de persona*, it permeates His kingly and priestly work," 58.

123. Cf. Krusche, *Das Wirken*, 277ff.

> Christ, in his human nature, is to be considered as our priest, who expiated our sins by the one sacrifice of his death, put away all our transgressions by his obedience, provided a perfect righteousness for us, and now intercedes for us, that we may have access to God.... He is to be considered as a King, who enriches us with all kinds of blessings, governs and defends us by his power, provides us with spiritual weapons, delivers us from all harm, and rules and guides us by the scepter of his mouth. And he is to be considered, that he may raise us to himself, the true God, and to the Father, until the fulfillment of what is finally to take place, viz., God be all in all.[124]

Calvin employs several different terms to express the concept of sanctification, referring to it as *repentance, restoration, renewal, rebirth, conversion,* and *regeneration*.[125] Commenting on Christ's words, "Sanctify them (John 17:17)," he says, "This sanctification comprehends God's kingdom and righteousness. That is, when God renews us by His Spirit, and confirms in us the grace of renewal and continues it to the end."[126] The same thought is found in Calvin's definition of repentance when he says:

> The meaning is that, departing from ourselves, we turn to God, and having taken off our former mind, we put on a new. On this account ... repentance ... is the true turning of our life to God, a turning that arises from a pure and earnest fear of him; and it consists in the mortification of our flesh and of the old man, and in the vivification of the Spirit.[127]

In this connection Parker remarks, "We are immediately in the sphere of repentance and sanctification, a sphere of quite special importance to the Reformers in that they were engaged *in correcting a long*-established doctrine of grace and the penitential practice joined to it."[128] Calvin defines justification in the following manner: "We explain justification simply as the acceptance with which God receives us into

---

124. Calvin, *Tracts and Treatises*, II, 213 (C.O. VII, 736).

125. Niesel, *Theology of Calvin,* 128; Wallace, *Calvin's Doctrine of the Christian Life,* 25. Cf. also Van Buren, *Christ in our Place,* 110ff.

126. *Com.* John 17:17 (C.O. XLVII, 384).

127. *Inst.*, III, iii, 5 (O.S. IV, 59, 31–60, 5).

128. Parker, "John Calvin," 395.

his favor as righteous men. And we say that it consists in the remission of sins and the imputation of Christ's righteousness."[129]

The relationship between the *duplex cognitio* and the *duplex gratia* is clearly stated by Calvin in his discussion of the late medieval Roman Catholic doctrines of assent and formed and unformed faith.[130] One should remember that Calvin had rejected such teaching because "they [the Schoolmen] presumptuously dignify . . . persuasion, devoid of the fear of God, with the name 'faith.'"[131] Over against this Roman concept of assent Calvin taught that true assent is "more of the heart than of the brain, and more of the disposition than of the understanding. For this reason it is called 'obedience of faith' (Rom 1:5)."[132] It is obvious that what Calvin considers here to be true assent is what he calls knowledge of God the Creator. Given his definition, he goes on to say, "They are speaking foolishly when they say that faith is *formed* when pious inclination is added to assent. For even assent rests upon such pious inclination—at least such assent as is revealed in the Scriptures."[133]

Calvin says immediately after this statement, "But another much clearer argument now offers itself."[134] He then speaks of the believer's experience of the twofold grace of Christ. He also equates scriptural assent, which we have seen to be nothing but the knowledge of God the Creator, with the believer's experience of the grace of sanctification. On the other hand he equates the grace of justification with the knowledge of Christ as Redeemer.

> Since faith embraces Christ, as offered to us by the Father (cf. John 6:29)—that is, since he is offered not only for righteousness, forgiveness of sins, and peace, but also for sanctification (cf. 1 Cor 1:30) and the fountain of the water of life (John 7:38; cf. 4:14)—without a doubt, no one can duly know him without at the same time apprehending the sanctification of the Spirit. Or, if anyone desires some plainer statement, faith rests upon the knowledge of Christ. And Christ cannot be known apart from

---

129. *Inst.*, III, xi, 2 (O.S. IV, 183, 7–10).
130. *Inst.*, III, ii, 8–10 *passim*.
131. *Inst.*, III, ii, 8 (O.S. IV, 17, 5–7).
132. Ibid. (17, 25–18, 1).
133. Ibid. (18, 5–8).
134. Ibid. (18, 8ff).

the sanctification of his Spirit. It follows that faith can in no wise be separated from a devout disposition.[135]

With this equation established, we shall now try to clarify the relationship between the *duplex cognitio* and the *duplex gratia*.

The Grace of Sanctification and Knowledge of God the Creator

We have just said that when believers receive the grace of sanctification through the work of the Holy Spirit in faith, they accordingly arrive at knowledge of God the Creator. This statement, however, requires clarification. Examining Calvin's doctrine of sanctification as we find it in *Institutes* III, iii, x we immediately notice many parallels between this doctrine and his teaching on knowledge of God the Creator. He states at the outset that repentance is equivalent to newness of life.[136] Thus "repentance not only constantly follows faith, but is also born of faith."[137] Furthermore, "repentance proceeds from an earnest fear of God,"[138] to which a person's mind is aroused "by thinking upon divine judgment," and on the fact that "God will someday mount his judgment seat."[139] This whole section is identical with Calvin's description of knowledge of God the Creator wherein he speaks of the relationship of the "pious mind" to God saying, "Because it sees him to be a righteous judge . . . it ever holds his judgment seat before its gaze, and through fear of him restrains itself from provoking his anger."[140]

Discussing repentance still further, Calvin says "I interpret repentance as regeneration, whose sole end is to restore in us the image of God that had been disfigured and all but obliterated through Adam's transgression."[141] Then, as we have seen before, he declares that

> This restoration does not take place in one moment or one day or one year; but through continual and sometimes even slow advances God wipes out in his elect the corruptions of the flesh

---

135. Ibid. (18, 9–17).
136. *Inst.*, III, iii, 1 (O.S. IV, 55, 9).
137. Ibid. (O.S. IV, 55, 16).
138. *Inst.*, III, iii, 7 (O.S. IV, 61, 10ff).
139. Ibid. (O.S. IV, 61, 12–14).
140. *Inst.*, I, ii, 2 (O.S. III, 36, 20–23).
141. *Inst.*, III, iii, 9 (O.S. IV, 63, 11–14).

> ... that they may practice repentance throughout their lives and know that this warfare will end only at death.[142]

Again the discussion here brings to mind the knowledge of God the Creator that we have seen to correspond to knowledge of ourselves as restored in Christ—knowledge of which Calvin says, "Therefore in some part it now is manifest in the elect, in so far as they have been reborn in the spirit; but it will attain its full splendor in heaven."[143]

This subject of renewal and restoration is again resumed by Calvin in his discussion of "The Life of the Christian Man."[144] Here he says:

> Scripture shows that God the Father, as he has reconciled us to himself in his Christ (cf. 2 Cor 5:18), has in him stamped for us the likeness (cf. Heb 1:3) to which he would have us conform.... It not only enjoins us to refer our life to God, its author, to whom it is bound; but after it has taught that we have degenerated from the true origin and condition of our creation, it also adds that Christ, through whom we return into favor with God, has been set before us as an example, whose pattern we ought to express in our life.[145]

This same thought is again found in Calvin's discussion of knowledge of God the Creator. "Now we see how Christ is the most perfect image of God; if we are conformed to it, we are so restored that with true piety, righteousness, purity, and intelligence we bear God's image."[146]

This concern for piety, righteousness, worship of God, and the believer's relationship of trust and reverence toward God is the dominant note in both Calvin's discussion of knowledge of the Creator and in his doctrine of sanctification. This emphasis is demonstrated clearly when Calvin says:

> For we have been adopted as sons by the Lord with this one condition: that our life express Christ, the bond of our adoption. Accordingly, unless we give and devote ourselves to righteous-

---

142. Ibid. (O.S. IV, 63, 25–65, 2).
143. *Inst.*, I, xv, 4 (O.S. III, 180, 22–24).
144. *Inst.*, III, vi, chapter title. It should be noted that Chapters iv & v contain Calvin's attack on Roman concepts of repentance.
145. *Inst.*, III, vi, 3 (O. S. III, 148,11–23).
146. *Inst.*, I, xv, 4 (O. S. III, 180, 3–5).

ness, we not only revolt from our Creator with wicked perfidy but we also abjure our Savior himself.[147]

Once more Calvin establishes the relationship between knowledge of God the Creator and the grace of sanctification in his discussion of "The Sum of the Christian Life."[148] Here he teaches that "the Christian must surely be so disposed and minded that he feels within himself it is with God he has to deal throughout his life,"[149] for such an attitude leads the Christian to a life of reverence toward God. This same thought is expressed yet again in his discussion of knowledge of the Creator in the following manner:

> No one will weigh God's providence properly and profitably but him who considers that his business is with his Maker and the Framer of the universe, and with becoming humility submits himself to fear and reverence.[150]

Likewise, this same idea is found repeatedly in Calvin's discussion of repentance.[151]

Even a cursory reading of the *Institutes* indicates that Calvin saw a correlation between his doctrine of providence, which is part of knowledge of God the Creator,[152] and his doctrine of sanctification, especially as found in his chapters on "The Sum of the Christian Life: The Denial of Ourselves,"[153] and "Bearing the Cross, a Part of Self-Denial."[154] It is interesting that in both places Calvin drew a sharp contrast between the Christian doctrine of providence and the "pagan" idea of fortune, as shown in the references in the footnote below.[155]

As we continue our study, it will become increasingly clear that Calvin's doctrine of sanctification is tied to knowledge of the Creator—which knowledge also corresponds to the knowledge of ourselves as we

---

147. *Inst.*, I, vi, 3 (O. S. IV, 148, 25–29).
148. *Inst.*, III, vii, chapter title.
149. *Inst.*, III, vii, 2 (O. S. IV, 152, 15–17).
150. *Inst.*, I, xvii, 2 (O. S. III, 203, 18–21).
151. *Inst.*, III, iii, 6; 16 (O. S. IV, 61, 2–3; 73, 5).
152. *Inst.*, I, xvi–xviii.
153. *Inst.*, III, vii.
154. *Inst.*, III, viii

155. *Inst.*, I, v, 11; I, xvi, 2; 8; 9; xvii, 1; III, vii, 10 (O. S. III, 55, 3–56, 5; 188, 31–190, 13; 198, 17–201, 30; 202, 3–203, 17; IV, 161, 6–15).

were first created. Human beings are seen in Adam as they were before the fall, or rather in the Second Adam in whom humans are restored to what they were before the fall. It is essential for us to notice that salvation for Calvin is never static. As we pointed out earlier, even Adam before the fall needed to relate himself to God continually in trust and reverence. Through this relationship he knew God as his Creator, and in this knowledge he worshipped him and meditated on a better future life. Such knowledge is necessary for human blessedness, happiness, eternal life, and salvation. This necessity applies to Adam before the fall as well as to humanity restored in Christ.

In Calvin's discussion of knowledge of God the Creator, he observes that "knowledge of this sort, then ought not only to arouse us to the worship of God but also to awaken and encourage us to the hope of the future life."[156] Or again, "By this knowledge he [man] should arouse himself to meditation upon divine worship and the future life."[157] In fact, we note that Calvin devotes a whole section in his doctrine of sanctification to the subject of "Meditation on the Future Life."[158] The entire chapter abounds with an emphasis on the trust and reverence that Calvin says is the goal of knowledge of the Creator.

Our thesis becomes clearer still when we come to Calvin's chapter on "How We Must Use the Present Life and Its Helps."[159] Here he says, "Let this be our principle: that the use of God's gifts is not wrongly directed when it is referred to that end to which the Author himself created and destined them for us, since he created them for our good, not for our ruin."[160] Throughout the chapter Calvin repeatedly directs the reader's attention to knowledge of God the Creator. It becomes obvious that Calvin

---

156. *Inst.*, I, v, 10 (O. S. III, 54, 1–3).

157. *Inst.*, II, i, 3 (O. S. III, 321, 7ff).

158. *Inst.*, III, ix. An interesting and clear parallel to this is to be found in Calvin's discussion of the kingly office of Christ. Here he says, "Now with regard to the special application of this to each one of us the same 'eternity' ought to inspire us to hope for blessed immortality. For we see that whatever is earthly is of the world and of time, and is indeed fleeting. Therefore Christ, to lift our hope to heaven, declares that his 'kingship is not of this world' (John 18: 36). In short, when any one of us hears that Christ's kingship is spiritual, aroused by this word let him attain to the hope of a better life; and since it is now protected by Christ's hand, let him await the full fruit of this grace in the age to come." *Inst.*, II, xv, 3 (O. S. III, 475, 21–29).

159. *Inst.*, III, x, chapter title.

160. *Inst.*, III, x, 2 (O. S. IV, 178, 11–14).

considers that the grace of sanctification which the Holy Spirit bestows upon us while uniting us with Christ in faith leads us to the knowledge of God the Creator as discussed in Book I of the *Institutes*.

The Grace of Justification and Knowledge of God the Redeemer

We now turn to the issue of justification. Speaking of the grace of justification Calvin says: "Being reconciled to God through Christ's blamelessness, we may have in heaven instead of a judge a gracious Father."[161] This statement brings to mind Calvin's discussion of knowledge of God the Redeemer, where he says of Christ, "His task was so to restore us to God's grace as to make of the children of men, children of God."[162] Discussing justification still further, Calvin says:

> I gather that Christ was made righteousness when 'he took upon him the form of a servant' (Phil 2:7); secondly, that he justified us in that he has shown himself obedient to the Father (Phil 2:8). Therefore he does this for us not according to his divine nature but in accordance with the dispensation enjoined upon him. For even though God alone is the source of righteousness, and we are righteous only by participation in him, yet, because we have been estranged from his righteousness by unhappy disagreement, we must have recourse to this lower remedy that Christ may justify us by the power of his death and resurrection.[163]

This thought is found repeatedly in Calvin's discussion of knowledge of the Redeemer. For example, in one place he says, "Relying on this pledge, we trust that we are sons of God, for God's natural son fashioned for himself a body from our body, flesh from our flesh, bones from our bones, that he might be one with us."[164] Or again:

> Our Lord came forth as true man and took the person and the name of Adam in order to take Adam's place in obeying the Father, to present our flesh as the price of satisfaction to God's righteous judgment, and, in the same flesh, to pay the penalty that we had deserved....
>
> Our common nature with Christ is the pledge of our fellowship with the Son of God; and clothed with our flesh he vanquished

---

161. *Inst.*, III, vi, I (. S. IV, 182, 6ff).
162. *Inst.*, II, xii, 2 (O. S. III, 438, 22–24).
163. *Inst.*, III, xi, 8 (O. S. IV, 190, 8–16).
164. *Inst.*, II, xii, 2 (O. S. III, 438, 27–439, 1).

death and sin together that the victory and triumph might be ours.[165]

All through Calvin's discussion of the grace of justification as well as knowledge of God the Redeemer, he speaks of the work of Christ as Mediator. In both places Christ is seen in his priestly office, expiating our sins.[166]

We have shown that Calvin considered knowledge of God the Redeemer to correspond to knowledge of ourselves as sinners. This same idea is also repeatedly presented in his discussion of the grace of justification. Calvin presents both doctrines with the same governing principle in mind. Knowledge of ourselves as sinners is thus presented in the light of the fact that "nothing, however slight, can be credited to man without depriving God of his honor, and without man himself falling into ruin through brazen confidence."[167] This same thought governs the discussion of the grace of justification. Writing on "Two Things to Be Noted in Free Justification,"[168] Calvin states: "The Lord's glory should stand undiminished and, so to speak, in good repair, and . . . our conscience in the presence of his judgment should have peaceful rest and serene tranquility."[169]

Moreover, throughout his discussion of justification, Calvin emphasizes that we should know ourselves as sinners. It is only with this knowledge in mind that justification can be seen as *sola gratia*. Therefore he says:

> Do you see that the righteousness of God is not sufficiently set forth unless he alone be esteemed righteous, and communicate the free gift of righteousness to the undeserving? For this reason he wills that 'every mouth be stopped and all the world be rendered accountable to him' (Rom 3:19). For, so long as man has anything to say in his own defense, he detracts somewhat from God's glory. Thus in Ezekiel, God teaches how much we glorify his name by recognizing our iniquity. 'You shall remember,' he says, 'your ways and all the crimes with which you have polluted

---

165. *Inst.*, II, xii, 3 (O. S III, 439, 24–28; 440, 14–16).

166. *Inst.*, III, xi, 6; 8; 9 (O. S. IV, 187, 14; 189, 11; 190, 22); cf. *Inst.*, II, xv, 6 (O. S. III, 480, 1–481, 19).

167. *Inst.*, II, ii, 1 (O. S. III, 241, 15–17).

168. *Inst.*, III, xiii, chapter title.

169. *Inst.*, III, xiii, 1 (O. S. IV, 215, 21–23).

yourselves, and you shall loathe yourselves in your own sight for all the evils you have committed' (Ezek 20:43). 'And you shall know that I am the Lord when I shall have bestowed benefits upon you for my name's sake, and not . . . according to your wicked offences.' (Ezek 20:44).[170]

Then he goes on to say:

> If these things are parts of the true knowledge of God—to be stricken by the awareness of our own iniquity and to reflect that he benefits us, unworthy as we are—why do we attempt, to our great harm, to filch from the Lord, even a particle of the thanks we owe his free kindness?[171]

It is evident then that Calvin considers that justification by grace alone and knowledge of ourselves as sinners go together. This association explains why, in his discussion of knowledge of God the Redeemer, he says:

> Whoever is utterly cast down and overwhelmed by the awareness of his calamity, poverty, nakedness, and disgrace has thus advanced farthest in knowledge of himself. For there is no danger of man's depriving himself of too much as long as he learns that in God must be recouped what he himself lacks. Yet he cannot claim for himself ever so little beyond what is rightfully his without losing himself in vain confidence and without usurping God's honor.[172]

As the Holy Spirit bestows on believers the grace of justification they come to know themselves as sinners and God as their Redeemer.

Methodological Remarks

So far we have demonstrated the relationship between the *duplex gratia* and the *duplex cognitio*. Now we need to briefly examine Calvin's understanding of the twofold grace, which will help clarify our understanding of his concept of the twofold knowledge of God. To understand Calvin's doctrine of the *duplex gratia Dei* we must keep two things in mind: first, Calvin insists on a distinction between sanctification and justification; and second, he also insists on the unity of the two. For example, com-

---

170. *Inst.*, III, xiii, 1 (O. S. IV, 215, 29–216, 4).
171. Ibid., (O. S. IV, 216, 4–8).
172. *Inst.*, II, ii, 10 (O. S. III, 252, 20–26).

menting on the words "Who was made unto us wisdom from God (1 Cor 1:30)," he says:

> We cannot be justified freely by faith alone, if we do not at the same time live in holiness: For those gifts of grace go together as if tied by an inseparable bond, so that if anyone tries to separate them, he is, in a sense, tearing Christ to pieces. . . . On the other hand notice that while those two offices of Christ are united, they are yet distinguishable from each other. Therefore we are not at liberty, indeed it would be wrong, to confuse what Paul expressly separates.[173]

Two major factors caused Calvin to distinguish between sanctification and justification: one was Roman Catholic theology, especially in light of the long-established doctrine of grace and the penitential practices joined to it; the other was the teachings of Andreas Osiander (1498–1552). Writing on the "Acts of the Council of Trent with the Antidote," Calvin referred to the sixth session with its decrees on justification in the following manner:[174]

> Under the eighth head, when they come to define, set out with cautioning us against supposing that the justification of man consists in faith alone. The verbal question is what is Justification? They deny that it is merely the forgiveness of sins, and insist that it includes both renovation and sanctification.[175]

Having stated the problem in this manner Calvin went on to say:

> When Christ is declared by Paul to be our righteousness and sanctification, a distinction is certainly drawn between these two things, though the Fathers of Trent confound them. For if there is a twofold grace, inasmuch as Christ both justifies and sanctifies us, righteousness does not include under it renovation of life. When it is said, 'Who shall lay anything to the charge of God's elect?—It is God that justifieth'—it is impossible to understand anything else than gratuitous acceptance.[176]

The whole point is then summed up in one statement. "It is not to be denied . . . that the two things, Justification and Sanctification, are

---

173. *Com*, 1 Cor. 1:30 (C. O. XLIX, 331).
174. Parker, "John Calvin," 395.
175. *Tracts and Treatises*, III, 114 (C. O. VII, 447).
176. Ibid., 115 (VII, 448).

constantly conjoined and cohere, but from this it is erroneously inferred that they are one and the same."[177]

The same Roman error was also found by Calvin in the teachings of Osiander. In this connection he said: "Osiander mixes that gift of regeneration with this free acceptance and contends that they are one and the same. Yet Scripture, even though it joins them, still lists them separately in order that God's manifold grace may better appear to us."[178]

Calvin insists on making a distinction between justification and sanctification in order to ensure that God's glory and honor will "stand undiminished" and believers be sure and certain of their salvation with their consciences at "peaceful rest and serene tranquility."[179] To the Roman Catholics he says:

> The whole dispute is as to The Cause of Justification. The Fathers of Trent pretend that it is twofold, as if we were justified partly by forgiveness of sins and partly by spiritual regeneration; or, to express their view in other words, as if our righteousness were composed partly of imputation, partly of quality. I maintain that it is one, and simple, and is wholly included in the gratuitous acceptance of God. I besides hold that it is without us, because we are righteous in Christ only.[180]

Calvin's interest becomes clear when he says:

> I would be unwilling to dispute about a word, did not the whole case depend upon it. But when they say that a man is justified, when he is again formed for the obedience of God, they subvert the whole argument of Paul, 'If righteousness is by the law, faith is nullified, and the promise abolished' (Rom 4:14). For he means, that not an individual among mankind will be found in whom the promise of salvation may be accomplished, if it involves the condition of innocence; and that faith, if it is propped up by works, will instantly fall. This is true; because, so long as we look at what we are in ourselves, we must tremble in the sight of God, so far from having a firm and unshaken confidence of eternal life.

---

177. Ibid., 115ff. (VII, 448).

178. *Inst.*, III, xi, 6 (O. S. IV, 187, 31–36). Calvin defended the doctrine of justification by faith against Andreas Osiander, an opponent of Philipp Melanchthon, whose conception of infused righteousness played havoc with the doctrine of justification by faith alone.

179. *Inst.*, III, xiii, 1 (O. S. IV, 215, 20–23).

180. *Tracts and Treatises*, III, 116 (C. O. VII, 448).

> I speak of the regenerate; for how far from righteousness is that newness of life which is begun here below?[181]

Calvin never tires of pointing out that "if we ask in what way the conscience can be made quiet before God, we shall find the only way to be that unmerited righteousness be conferred upon us as a gift of God."[182]

Writing against Osiander Calvin emphasizes, as we have seen, the distinction between justification and sanctification. He maintains that with his doctrine of essential righteousness, Osiander has failed to understand the work of Christ as Mediator.[183] Moreover, Osiander's doctrine, like that of the Roman Catholics, leaves no room for the certainty and assurance believers need regarding their salvation. Arguing against Osiander, Calvin says:

> The grace of justification is not separated from regeneration, although they are things distinct. But because it is very well known by experience that the traces of sin always remain in the righteous, their justification must be very different from reformation into newness of life (cf. Rom 6:4). For God so begins this second point in his elect, and progresses in it gradually, and sometimes slowly, throughout life, that they are always liable to the judgment of death before his tribunal. But he does not justify in part but liberally, so that they may appear in heaven as if endowed with the purity of Christ. No portion of righteousness sets our consciences at peace until it has been determined that we are pleasing to God, because we are entirely righteous before him. From this it follows that the doctrine of justification is perverted and utterly overthrown when doubt is thrust into men's minds, when the assurance of salvation is shaken and the free and fearless calling upon God suffers hindrance—nay, when peace and tranquility with spiritual joy are not established.[184]

Now we can see why Calvin insisted on distinguishing between sanctification and justification: The Holy Spirit confers on the believer a twofold grace that results in a twofold relationship between God and the person. This is what Calvin calls the twofold knowledge of God and the twofold knowledge of ourselves, wherein believers know God as their

---

181. Ibid., 115.
182. *Inst.*, III, xiii, 3 (O. S. IV, 217, 12–14).
183. *Inst.*, III, xiv, 9 *passim*.
184. *Inst.*, III, xi, 11 (O. S. IV, 193, 29–194, 8).

Creator in knowing themselves as restored in Christ, and they know God as their Redeemer in knowing themselves as sinners.[185] Both sides of this twofold knowledge are based on union with Christ who is both king and priest.[186]

With regard to justification, which is connected with the priestly office of Christ, the emphasis is on Christ's human nature. Calvin says:

> Even though Christ if he had not been true God could not cleanse our souls by his blood, nor appease his Father by his sacrifice, nor absolve us from guilt, nor, in sum, fulfill the office of priest, yet it is certain that he carried out all these acts according to his nature. . . . Paul has established the source of righteousness in the flesh of Christ alone. . . .
> We are justified in Christ, in so far as he was made an atoning sacrifice for us: something that does not comport with his divine nature.[187]

On the other hand, Calvin emphasizes the divine nature of Christ in regard to sanctification, which is connected with his kingly office. His kingship is spiritual, and he rules in the hearts of his people through the Holy Spirit.[188]

> Christ lives in us in two ways. The one life consists in governing us by his Spirit and directing all our actions; the other, in making us partakers of his righteousness; so that, while we can do nothing of ourselves, we are accepted in the sight of God. The first relates to regeneration, the second to justification by free grace.[189]

It should be noted that when Calvin speaks of justification and the knowledge of the Redeemer, he refers more frequently to Christ; in the course of his discussion of sanctification and knowledge of the Creator,

---

185. Here we find the answer to Dowey's question, "Why . . . was the knowledge of the Creator always kept separate from that of the Redeemer?" *Knowledge of God* (1994), 133, n. 414. It is obvious that we do not need to say with Dowey, "We may wish that he [Calvin] had not done [this thing]." Ibid.

186. With this twofold relationship in mind, Calvin's concept of union with Christ is both clarified and qualified. Christ is *in nobis* and yet he is at the same time *extra nos* where we need to be united to him again and again. Cf. *Inst.*, III, xi, 10 *passim*; see also Krusche, *Das Wirken*, 274.

187. *Inst.*, III, xi, 9 (O. S. IV, 190, 19–24; 30; 191, 6–8); cf. III, xi, 8 (O. S. IV, 189, 10–190, 16).

188. *Inst.*, II, xv, 3 (O. S. III, 474, 20).

189. *Com.* Gal 2:20 (C. O. L, 199).

he refers more often to the Holy Spirit. Commenting on "That he might present us holy (Eph 5:27)," Calvin says:

> The entire blessing of redemption consists mainly in these two things, remission of sins, and spiritual regeneration. (Jer 31:33). What he has already spoken of was a great matter that righteousness has been procured for us through the death of Christ, so that, our sins being remitted, we are acceptable to God. Now, however, he teaches us, that there is in addition to this another benefit equally distinguished—the gift of the Holy Spirit, by which we are renewed in the image of God.... Gratuitous righteousness is not conferred upon us in Christ, without one being at the same time regenerated by the Spirit to the obedience of righteousness.... The *former* we obtain by a gratuitous acceptance; and the *latter* by the gift of the Holy Spirit, when we are made new creatures.[190]

A similar thought is found in Calvin's reply to Cardinal Sadoleto, where he says:

> Wherever, therefore, that righteousness of faith, which we maintain to be gratuitous, is, there too Christ is, and where Christ is, there too is the Spirit of holiness, who regenerates the soul to newness of life. On the contrary, where zeal for integrity and holiness is not in vigor there, neither is the Spirit of Christ nor Christ himself; and wherever Christ is not, there is no righteousness, nay, there is no faith; for faith cannot apprehend Christ for righteousness without the Spirit of sanctification.[191]

Again, in his remarks on "But if any man hath not the Spirit of Christ (Rom 8:9)," Calvin says:

> The kingdom of the Spirit is the abolition of the flesh. Those in whom the Spirit does not reign do not belong to Christ; therefore those who separate Christ from His Spirit make Him like a dead image or a corpse. We must always bear in mind the counsel of the apostle, that free remission of sin cannot be separated from the Spirit of regeneration. This would be, as it were, to rend Christ asunder.[192]

This passage explains why Calvin discusses the person and work of Christ as Mediator in Book II of the *Institutes* while the doctrine of the

---

190. *Com.* Col 1:22 (C. O. LII, 90ff).
191. *Tracts and Treatises*, I, 43 (O. S. I, 470).
192. *Com.* Rom 8:9 (C. O. XLIX, 114).

Trinity is considered in Book I. It is with this in mind that we should read his doctrines of the inner witness of the Holy Spirit and the authority of Scripture.[193] For the Holy Spirit here is none other than the Spirit of adoption, who is also the Spirit of Christ living in the believers, governing and directing them. This direction is, as we have seen, knowledge of God the Creator.

Thus far we have seen why Calvin distinguished between sanctification and justification, which serves in turn to clarify why Calvin distinguished between knowledge of the Creator and knowledge of the Redeemer. Now we need to discover the reasons behind his discussion of knowledge of the Creator *before* that of knowledge of the Redeemer. Here again the *duplex gratia* sheds light on the *duplex cognitio*. The doctrine of justification by faith was given primary importance by the Reformers, and Calvin considered it to be the main hinge on which religion turns.[194] Discussing the twofold grace of Christ, that is, justification and sanctification, he calls the latter the "second gift."[195] Yet when he comes to discuss this *duplex gratia*, he intentionally postpones consideration of justification until he has presented the grace of sanctification. He considers this order to be the best way to show that justification is by faith alone. He says:

> Now, both repentance and forgiveness of sins—that is, newness of life and free-reconciliation—are conferred on us by Christ, and both are attained by us through faith. As a consequence, reason and the order of teaching demand that I begin to discuss both at this point. However, our immediate transition will be from faith to repentance. For when this topic is rightly understood it will better appear how man is justified by faith alone, and simple pardon.[196]

Then, pointing out that there should be no separation between justification and sanctification, Calvin continues, "Nevertheless actual holiness of life, so to speak, is not separated from imputation of

---

193. Thus we shall not need to say with Dowey, "Even the doctrine of the 'internal testimony of the Holy Spirit' is presented with no reference to Christ and Faith." *Knowledge of God* (1994), 47.

194. *Inst.*, III, xi, 1 (O. S. IV, 182, 15ff).

195. Ibid. (O. S. IV, 182, 9).

196. *Inst.*, III, iii, 1 (O. S. IV, 55, 8–14); cf. *Inst.*, III, xi, 1 (O. S. IV, 182, 10–14).

righteousness."[197] Therefore we do not need to distinguish between justification and sanctification in the manner presented by Armstrong.[198]

The reader should recall that the Reformation emphasis on justification by faith *alone* was criticized by the Roman Catholic Church. The Roman theologians claimed that this doctrine does away with good works,[199] stifles zeal for the same,[200] and invites humans to sin.[201] It is obvious that the teachings of the fanatical antinomians of Calvin's day lent considerable support to the Roman charges. To defend the Reformation doctrine Calvin continually reiterated that although justification is to be distinguished from sanctification on the conceptual level, yet they should never be separated in day-to-day Christian living. Commenting on Paul's words, "who was made unto us wisdom from God," he says:

> Paul calls Him our *Sanctification*. He means by that, that we, who are in ourselves unholy by nature, are born again by His spirit into holiness that we may serve God. From this we also gather that we cannot be justified freely by faith alone, if we do not at the same time live in holiness. For those gifts of grace go together as if tied by an inseparable bond, so that if anyone tries to separate them, he is, in a sense, tearing Christ to pieces. Accordingly, let the man who aims at being justified by God's free goodness through Christ take note that this cannot possibly be done, unless at the same time he lays hold of Him for sanctification; in other words, he must be born anew by His Spirit to blamelessness and purity of life. Men find fault with us, because in preaching the free righteousness of faith, we seem to be calling men away from good works. But this passage clearly refutes them, by showing that faith lays hold of regeneration just as much as forgiveness of sins in Christ.[202]

The same thought is found in Calvin's remarks on the words, "For if ye live after the flesh ye must die (Rom 8:13)." Here he says:

> [Paul] adds a warning in order to shake off their sluggishness with greater severity. This also provides a useful refutation of those who boast of justification by faith without the Spirit of Christ.

---

197. Ibid. (O. S. IV, 55, 14ff).
198. Cf. page xxxiii above.
199. *Inst.*, III, xvi, 1 (O. S. IV, 248, 15ff).
200. *Inst.*, III, xvi, 2 (O. S. IV, 249, 23ff).
201. *Inst.*, III, xvi, 4 (O. S. IV, 252, 16ff).
202. *Com.* 1 Cor. 1:30 (C.O. XLIX, 331).

Their own conscience, however, more than sufficiently convicts them, since there is no confidence in God where there is no love of righteousness. It is indeed true that we are justified in Christ by the mercy of God alone, but it is equally true and certain, that all who are justified are called by the Lord to live worthy of their vocation. Let believers, therefore, learn to embrace Him, not only for justification, but also for sanctification, as He has been given to us for both these purposes, that they may not rend Him asunder by their own mutilated faith.[203]

In Calvin's "refutation of the false accusations" of the Roman Church against the Reformation doctrine of justification in the *Institutes*, he emphasizes the inseparability of the two aspects of the *duplex gratia*. Here he says:

> Why, then, are we justified by faith? Because by faith we grasp Christ's righteousness, by which alone we are reconciled to God. Yet you could not grasp this without at the same time grasping sanctification also.... Therefore Christ justifies no one whom he does not at the same time sanctify. These benefits are joined together by an everlasting and indissoluble bond.... Although we may distinguish them, Christ contains both of them inseparably in himself.... Thus it is clear how true it is that we are justified not without works yet not through works, since in our sharing in Christ, which justifies us sanctification is just as much included as righteousness.[204]

Such an insistence upon the inseparability of sanctification and justification could have been enough for the defense of the Reformation doctrine of justification by faith *alone*. Yet Calvin uses another method to defend this doctrine still further: the organization of the material of the *Institutes*. In fact, we find this intention stated at the beginning of his discussion of justification.[205] After Calvin had stated that we receive a twofold grace (justification and sanctification) by partaking of Christ, he goes on to say:

> Of regeneration, indeed, the second of these gifts, I have said what seemed sufficient. The theme of justification was therefore more lightly touched upon because it was more to the point to under-

---

203. *Com. Rom* 8:13 (C. O. XLIX, 147).

204. *Inst.*, III, xvi, 1 (O. S. IV, 249, 3–22).

205. Niesel, *Theology of Calvin*, 131; Van Buren, *Christ in Our Place*, 107ff.; Wendel, *Sources et é volution*, 175.

stand first how little devoid of good works is the faith, through which alone we obtain free righteousness by the mercy of God; and what is the nature of the good works of the saints.[206]

In this way, the *duplex gratia* enables us to understand the *duplex cognitio* more clearly. Now we can see that although Calvin distinguishes between knowledge of the Creator and knowledge of the Redeemer, he never separates the two. We have stated this fact before,[207] yet we can see it now more fully.[208]

Furthermore, we can now understand why Calvin presented the knowledge of the Creator before the knowledge of the Redeemer. We do not need to say with Dowey that "the redemptive revelation is actually the presupposition of the knowledge of the Creator which in Calvin precedes it,"[209] nor do we need to state with Butin that "a careful study of apparently 'dialectical' passages in Calvin's writings confirms the hypothesis that these typically pertain to the relationship of God to sinful human beings, apart from the redemption God offers in Christ to the elect."[210]

Calvin follows the same procedure in his presentation of the offices of Christ.[211] He speaks of knowledge of the Creator before discussing knowledge of the Redeemer and speaks of sanctification before justification. Thus he discusses Christ's kingly office of ruling through his Spirit in the lives of believers *before* he describes Christ's priestly office as the Mediator who reconciles us to God by his sacrifice and freely confers on us his righteousness. We have seen how Calvin transforms Luther's *simul iustus et peccator* principle with its emphasis on justification, placing more emphasis upon sanctification.[212] For Calvin pres-

---

206. *Inst.*, III, xi, 1 (O. S. IV, 249, 23–25).

207. Cf. page 00 above.

208. With this in mind we shall not need to subdivide the *Institutes* in the manner Dowey does in *Knowledge of God* (1994), 41. Nor shall we need to say with him about *Inst.*, II, vi, 1, "From this transitional point Calvin's doctrine has a whole new orientation. All that he says subsequently lies within the vast background he has given of the Trinitarian God, his creation of the universe and of man in a state of perfection and his providential care of that creation." Ibid., 45ff.

209. Ibid., 46.

210. Butin, *Revelation, Redemption and Response*, 23ff.

211. *Inst.*, II, xv, 306 (O. S. III, 474, 19–481, 18).

212. We should not forget that Calvin observes that sanctification is given prior consideration not to shift the emphasis from justification to this doctrine but rather to point out more clearly the fact that justification is by faith alone and grace alone, *sola*

ents the knowledge of ourselves as restored even as we are yet sinners in order to point out that sanctification must accompany justification, although justification is by faith alone. Edgar suggests two reasons why Calvin treated sanctification before justification.[213] First, to head off possible objections from the Roman Catholics who would accurse him of antinomianism (*libertinage*). Thus he forestalls any objection against justification by faith alone that undermines the importance or even the necessity of good works and makes for a careless life.[214] Second, Calvin's arrangement of the material drives home the point that justification and sanctification are inseparable. Moreover, Calvin stresses that it is only those who are being sanctified who realize how sinful they are and how little they can depend on works to stand justified in the sight of God. Thus the experience of the grace of sanctification enables believers to fully realize that their justification is by faith alone. It is as they know God as their Creator and try to respond to him in trust and reverence that they come to realize their lack of responsiveness, and thus come to see their own sinfulness. It is this experience that enables them to know God as their Redeemer who justifies them freely. Thus we do not need to agree with George, who followed Dowey's reasoning when he said:

> However, when Calvin spoke of the twofold knowledge of God *duplex cognitio domini* he was not talking about the ever present duality of the divine-human encounter. Rather he referred to the knowledge of God as Creator, manifested in the fashioning of the universe, and the knowledge of God as Redeemer, seen only in the face of Christ.[215]

We have now arrived at the full meaning and significance of the twofold knowledge of God and of ourselves as we find it in the first two books of the *Institutes*. In light of this whole discussion we can appreciate Geoffrey W. Bromiley's remark:

> The Reformers in general can hardly be said to have presented a comprehensive view of Christian salvation and the Christian life in a way which brings out the full relationship of justification and sanctification. This was to be the great achievement of Calvin.[216]

---

gratia. Cf. *Inst.*, III, iii, 1; III, xi, 1 (O. S. IV, 55, 12–15; 182, 8–14).

213.. Edgar, "Ethics," 320–46.

214. Niesel, *Theology of Calvin*, 130ff.

215. George, *Theology of the Reformers*, 190.

216. Bromiley, *Historical Theology*, 237.

Conclusion

We have finally arrived at the key to understanding the root meaning and significance of the *duplex cognitio Domini*, the twofold knowledge of God (and ourselves) as used by Calvin for the first time in 1559. We know that Calvin emphasized the relationship between knowledge of God and of ourselves in the opening words of the *editio princeps* of the *Institutes* in 1536. He expressed the same idea with an enlarged scope in 1539. He continued to use the same wording in all subsequent editions including the definitive edition of 1559. Yet throughout all editions of the *Institutes* prior to 1559, Calvin separated knowledge of God, which we have seen to be twofold as Creator and Redeemer, and knowledge of humankind, which is also twofold as created and as sinner, in the first two chapters.

We noted that Calvin pointed out in the *Institutes* of 1539 and in all subsequent editions that believers receive a twofold grace (*duplex gratia Dei*), the grace of justification and of regeneration (sanctification). We have also pointed out that Calvin repeatedly taught the twofold grace in his commentaries, sermons, and various other writings. Furthermore, we noted that the *duplex gratia Dei* is distinctive to Calvin, who more than any other reformer used it to express the full relationship between justification and sanctification.

In light of the studies and comparisons we have presented, the present writer contends that Calvin's continued use of the *duplex gratia Dei* inspired him to rearrange the materials of the two chapters he continued to use from 1539 onwards on knowledge of God (Creator and Redeemer) and knowledge of humankind (as originally created and as sinner), to express in 1559 the correlation between the knowledge of God and ourselves, which he continued to emphasize in the opening words of all editions of the *Institutes*. Thus Book I became the knowledge of God the Creator *and ourselves* as originally created, and Book II the knowledge of God the Redeemer *and ourselves* as sinners. Calvin also used for the first time in 1559 the term *duplex cognitio Domini*, and added the words "joined by many bonds" (I, i, 1). In this way, Calvin indicated the new arrangement of the material that had been separated in previous editions. Meanwhile, he used the phrase *duplex cognitio Domini* to express the *duplex gratia* as applied in the life of believers as it relates to the twofold knowledge of God and of ourselves.

We have also pointed out that the *duplex cognitio Domini* is another way to express the *duplex gratia Dei*: justification and regeneration (sanctification). The first expresses what God has done to enable the believer to know God as his or her Redeemer and one's self as sinner, while the second speaks of the believer's experience of knowing God as his or her Creator and one's self as being restored to what he or she was when first created (before the fall). The first is the basis while the second pertains to a continuous process. Thus justification and sanctification are inseparable and simultaneous. They can be distinguished but not divided. Thus, we can use the christological formula of Chalcedon to say about justification and sanctification what we previously said about knowledge of God the Creator and Redeemer: that they are "without confusion, without change, without division, without separation."[217]

With the above understanding most of the problems some have found in Calvin's theology can be resolved. We do not need to claim with Venema that the knowledge of God and of ourselves comprise the whole subject matter of Calvin's theology.[218] Nor do we need to agree that Calvin's arrangement of the material of the *Institutes* is partly dependent upon rhetorical considerations.[219] We also do not need to say with Dowey and others that Calvin "must be judged to have two not entirely reconcilable theological explanations of the faithful man's knowledge of God's special revelation,"[220] or claim that "the doctrines of Scripture and faith are separated throughout Calvin's thought."[221]

We have seen that studies of Calvin have dealt with his theology and its structure almost exclusively from the perspective of his teaching on the knowledge of God.[222] In so doing, scholars have encountered several problems that they sought to resolve by suggesting as Armstrong and others have done that Calvin's theology is based on "a broad, general philosophical dialectic between the ideal and the real"[223] or by speaking of a hypothetical or conditional structure of the *Institutes*.[224] It is this

---

217. See page 46 above; Garcia, *Life in Christ*, 222.
218. Venema, *Accepted and Renewed in Christ*, 34.
219. Ibid., 63.
220. Dowey, *Knowledge of God*, 161.
221. Ibid., 6ff.
222. Gamble, ed., *Articles on Calvin and Calvinism*, 180.
223. McKee and Armstrong, *Probing the Reformed Tradition*, 138.
224. Ibid., 142ff.

writer's contention that the twofold knowledge of God and ourselves (*duplex cognitio Domini*) should be understood in light of the twofold grace (*duplex gratia Dei*), not vice versa, as such writers as Venema propose when they state that the *duplex gratia Dei* must be understood from within the framework of the understanding of knowledge of God and ourselves.[225] Likewise, we do not need to reconcile the contents of the knowledge of God the Creator with the knowledge of God the Redeemer through suggesting a dialectical relationship, as Dowey and others suppose.[226] Thus, the understanding we are presenting resolves the problems many claim to encounter in the study of Calvin's theology. Further study will provide a better understanding of the structure of the *Institutes* of 1559 and Calvin's theology. With this outline in mind, the following chapters will address Calvin's doctrine of the authority of Scripture and the teaching ministry of the church.

---

225. Venema, *Accepted and Renewed in Christ*, 34.
226. Dowey, *Knowledge of God*, 256.

PART TWO

Word and Spirit

3

Word and Spirit: Illumination of the Mind

CALVIN CONSIDERS THE HUMAN soul to consist of two faculties, understanding and will, or mind and heart.[1] Explaining the function of each, he says,

> Let the office . . . of understanding be to distinguish between objects, as each seems worthy of approval or disapproval; while that of the will, to choose and follow what the understanding pronounces good, but to reject and flee what it disapproves.[2]

Later Calvin explains that these two faculties of the soul are "situated in the mind and the heart."[3] Both faculties are now affected by the fall. Calvin found that Paul teaches that "corruption subsists not in one part only, but that none of the soul remains pure or untouched by that mortal disease."[4] Thus "the mind is given over to blindness and the heart to depravity."[5]

It is against this background that we can understand Calvin's definition of faith as "a firm and certain knowledge of God's benevolence toward us, founded upon the truth of the freely given promise in Christ, both *revealed to our minds and sealed upon our hearts* through the Holy Spirit."[6] Here we see the dual function of faith, which is also a dual operation of the Holy Spirit. Therefore, immediately before defining faith

---

1. *Inst.*, I, xv, 7–8 (O. S. III, 184, 26–186, 11).
2. Ibid. I, xv, 7 (O. S. III, 185, 2–6).
3. *Inst.*, II, ii, 2.
4. *Inst.*, II, i, 9 (O. S. III, 239, 2–4).
5. Ibid. (239, 6ff.).
6. *Inst.*, III, ii, 7 (O. S. IV, 16, 31–35); italics added.

in this manner Calvin says, "Our mind must be . . . illumined and our heart strengthened."[7]

Calvin consistently emphasizes these two steps of faith, which correspond to what he considered the two operations of the Holy Spirit. He says, "It will not be enough for the mind to be illumined by the Spirit of God unless the heart is also strengthened and supported by his power."[8] Referring to these two operations he goes on to say, "In both ways, therefore, faith is a singular gift of God, both in that the mind of man is purged so as to be able to taste the truth of God and in that the heart is established therein."[9] Emphasizing this dual operation of the Holy Spirit still further, Calvin says:

> But if it is true that the mind's real understanding is illumination by the Spirit of God, then in such confirmation of the heart his power is much more clearly manifested, to the extent that the heart's distrust is greater than the mind's blindness. It is harder for the heart to be furnished with assurance than for the mind to be endowed with thought.[10]

Again in the *Geneva Catechism*, which Calvin prepared, after pointing out that faith is the "singular gift of the Holy Spirit," he wrote the following response to Question 113:

> Our mind is too weak to comprehend the spiritual wisdom of God which is revealed to us by faith, and our hearts are too prone either to defiance or to a perverse confidence in ourselves or creaturely things. But the Holy Spirit enlightens us to make us capable of understanding what would otherwise be incomprehensible to us, and fortifies us in certitude, sealing and imprinting the promises of salvation on our hearts.[11]

The same thought finds clear expression in Calvin's comments on the words "in whom also, after that ye believed" (Eph 1:13). Here he says:

> There are two operations of the Spirit in faith, corresponding to the two parts of which faith consists, as it enlightens, and as it

---

7. Ibid. (16, 29ff.).
8. *Inst.*, III, ii, 33 (O. S. IV, 44, 11ff).
9. Ibid. (44, 15–17).
10. *Inst.*, III, ii, 36 (O. S. IV, 46, 37–47, 3).
11. Torrance, *School of Faith*, 23 (C. O. VI, 45).

establishes the mind. (*Nam et mentes illuminat, et animos confirmat.*) The commencement of faith is knowledge: the completion of it is a firm and steady conviction, which admits of no opposing doubt. Both, I have said, are the work of the Spirit.[12]

Again, in his comments on the words "And ye also bear witness (John 15:27)," Calvin says, "There is no faith until God's Spirit enlightens our minds and seals our hearts."[13] Many more references could be produced to demonstrate that Calvin clearly taught two operations of the Holy Spirit.[14] He consistently calls the first *illumination* and the second *sealing*. He sometimes, however, uses the first term for the heart as well as the mind;[15] and at one place he uses the second term for the mind.[16] These variations are not essential because Calvin found the word *heart* to be used in the Scriptures as a synonym for understanding.[17] It is in this sense that he uses the term *illumination* in connection with the heart.

For clarity, we shall use *illumination* in connection with the mind and *sealing* in connection with the heart. This pattern is, of course, in line with Calvin's common usage and distinction as we have just seen. Meanwhile, it would be helpful for us to remember that Calvin's main interest in his insistence on the two operations of the Holy Spirit is to show that faith has to do with the whole being of a person whose soul he defines as consisting of mind and heart.

We have seen how Calvin insisted that "faith is the principal work of the Holy Spirit,"[18] and that "there is a permanent relationship between faith and the Word."[19] Therefore we can see both operations of the Spirit in faith under the correlation of word and Spirit, which is one of Calvin's favorite phrases.[20] Within this correlation we can also consider Calvin's doctrine of inspiration. In this and the following chapter we shall study

12. *Com.* Eph 1:13 (C. O. LI, 153).
13. *Com.* John 15:27 (C. O. XLVII, 354).
14. Krusche, *Das Wirken*, 255ff., especially 259, n. 727.
15. *Inst.*, III, ii, 8 (O. S. IV, 17, 4ff.); *Com.* Rom 1:16 (C. O. XLIX, 19).
16. *Inst.*, I, ix, 1 (O. S. III, 83, 7).
17. Commenting on the words, "And I will give them a heart to know me," Calvin says: "The word *heart* is to be taken here for the mind or understanding, as it means often in Hebrew." *Com.* Jer 24:7 (C. O. XXXVIII, 462).
18. *Inst.*, III, i, 4 (O. S. IV, 5, 14).
19. *Inst.*, III, ii, 6 (O. S. IV, 14, 8).
20. *Inst.*, I, vii–ix, III, ii, especially 34; IV, viii, 13.

the two operations of the Spirit in faith, leaving the discussion of inspiration for consideration in the last chapter. As we survey Calvin's doctrine of faith with its two parts under the correlation of word and Spirit, we come to an interesting aspect of Calvin's theology that defines the context within which Calvin considered the Holy Spirit to work through the word. It is here that we come to his doctrine of the church. This is a large topic; however, we shall limit ourselves to the material relevant to our subject.

FAITH AND THE TEACHING MINISTRY OF THE CHURCH

In Calvin's discussion of the Roman Catholic doctrine of implicit faith, he observes that "it would be the height of absurdity to label ignorance tempered by humility 'faith!' For faith consists in the knowledge of God and Christ (John 17:3), not in reverence for the church."[21] At first glance this statement might lead one to expect that Calvin would now place the word over against the church and thus teach submission to Scripture. Yet this is exactly what he does not do, for Calvin never considered church and word to be antithetical. Rather, his criticism of implicit faith is based on the belief that this doctrine made people submissive to the Roman Church and their submission resulted in complacent ignorance. It is this latter development that disturbed Calvin. Immediately after dismissing the Roman doctrine, he enunciates a new doctrine of implicit faith, in which he commends reverent attention to the word. This new form of *fides implicita* can be called teachableness with the desire to learn, which Calvin considers to be "far different from sheer ignorance in which those sluggishly rest who are content with the sort of 'implicit faith' the papists invent."[22] It is against this background that we can fully appreciate Calvin's doctrine of the teaching ministry of the church.

As we investigate this subject, it is worthwhile to remember that Calvin considered Scripture a special gift from God to the church. He says:

> Scripture, gathering up the otherwise confused knowledge of God in our minds, having dispersed our dullness, clearly shows us the true God. This, therefore, is a special gift, where God, to instruct the church . . . opens his own most hallowed lips . . . . He has from the beginning maintained this plan for his Church.[23]

---

21. *Inst.*, III, ii, 3 (O. S. IV, 11, 8–11).
22. *Inst.*, III, ii, 5 (O. S. IV, 13, 9–11).
23. *Inst.*, I, vi, 1 (O. S. III, 60, 29-61, 6).

We can now partially understand why Calvin says that "the authority of the Church is an introduction through which we are prepared for faith in the gospel."[24] Yet what is essential for us to notice here is that Calvin considers the word to be in the church in order that it may be preached and heard. This teaching is clearly expressed in the *Geneva Catechism*. We find the following questions and answers in reference to the Scriptures:

> Minister: How are we to use it [the Word] in order to profit by it?
>
> Child: By receiving it with the full consent of our conscience, as truth come down from heaven, submitting ourselves to it in right obedience, loving it with a true affection by having it imprinted in our hearts, we may follow it entirely and conform ourselves to it.
>
> Minister: Is all this within our own power?
>
> Child: None of it; but God works them in us in this way by His Holy Spirit.
>
> Minister: But are we not to take trouble and be diligent, and zealously strive by hearing and reading its teaching, as it is declared to us?
>
> Child: Yes, indeed: first each one of us in particular ought to study it; and above all, we are frequently to attend the sermons in which this Word is expounded in the Assembly of the Christians.
>
> Minister: Do you mean that it is not enough for people to read it privately at home, without altogether hearing its teaching in common?
>
> Child: That is just what I mean, while God provides the way for it.
>
> Minister: Why do you say that?
>
> Child: Because Jesus Christ has established this order in His Church (Eph 4:11), and He had declared this to be the only means of edifying and preserving it. Thus we must keep ourselves to it and not be wiser than our Master.[25]

Here we can observe Calvin's emphasis on the teaching ministry of the church. This same emphasis also finds clear expression in the *Institutes*. In the opening sentences of Book IV Calvin says:

---

24. *Inst.*, I, vii, 3 (O. S. III, 68, 9ff.).
25. Torrance, *School of Faith*, 52ff. (C. O. VI, 109, Q. 302–306).

> I shall start, then, with the church, into whose bosom God is pleased to gather his sons, not only that they may be nourished by her help and ministry as long as they are infants and children, but also that they may be guided by her motherly care until they mature and at last reach the goal of faith . . . so that, for those to whom he is Father the Church may also be Mother.[26]

This emphasis on the role of the Church provides the context within which we can address the issue of authority in Calvin's theology, since the church is the setting of the efficacy of the word:

> For there is no other way to enter into life unless this mother conceive us in her womb, give us birth, nourish us at her breast, and lastly, unless she keep us under her care and guidance until, putting off mortal flesh, we become like the angels (Matt. 22:30).[27]

This context then gives insight into Calvin's emphasis on preaching. "God, who could in a moment perfect his own, nevertheless desires them to grow up into manhood solely under the education of the church."[28] Moreover, "Our weakness does not allow us to be dismissed from her school until we have been pupils all our lives."[29] The same teaching is found in Calvin's remarks on "But Jerusalem, which is above (Gal. 4:26)." He says:

> The heavenly Jerusalem, which derives its origin from heaven, and dwells above by faith, is the mother of believers. To the Church, under God, we owe it that we are 'born again, not of corruptible seed, but of incorruptible,' (1 Pet 1:23) and from her we obtain the milk and the food by which we are afterward nourished.
>
> Such are the reasons why the Church is called the mother of believers. And certainly he who refuses to be a son of the Church in vain desires to have God as his Father; for it is only through the instrumentality of the Church that we are 'born of God,' (1 John 3:9) and brought up through the various stages of childhood and youth, till we arrive at manhood. This designation, 'the mother of us all,' reflects the highest credit and the highest honor on the Church.[30]

---

26. *Inst.*, IV, I, 1 (O. S. V, 1, 29–32, 2).
27. *Inst.*, IV, i, 4 (O. S. V, 7, 7–10).
28. *Inst.*, IV, i, 5 (O. S. V, 8, 6–8).
29. *Inst.*, IV, i, 4 (O. S. V, 7, 11ff.).
30. *Com.* Gal 4: 26 (C. O. L, 239ff).

We see then that Calvin gives a high place to the preaching ministry of the church and therefore accords great authority to those who hold this office. "As He did not entrust the ancient folk to angels but raised up teachers from the earth truly to perform the angelic office, so also today it is his will to teach us through human means."[31] These human means, according to Calvin, are doubly useful for us:

> On the one hand, He proves our obedience by a very good test when we hear his ministers speaking just as if he himself spoke. On the other, he also provides for our weakness in that he prefers to address us in human fashion through interpreters in order to draw us to himself.[32]

Attributing so great an authority to preaching, Calvin understands that his readers might think that this would diminish the authority of the word. Therefore, he goes on to say:

> Those who think the authority of the Word is dragged down by the baseness of the men called to teach it disclose their own ungratefulness. For, among the many excellent gifts with which God has adorned the human race, it is a singular privilege that he designs to consecrate to himself the mouths and tongues of men in order that his voice may resound in them. Let us accordingly not in turn dislike embracing obediently the doctrine of salvation put forth by his command and by his own mouth.[33]

Again, in his comments on Paul's words "As an angel of God (Gal 4:14)," Calvin says:

> In this light every true minister of Christ ought to be regarded.... Godly teachers are divinely raised up to administer to us the most excellent of all blessings, the doctrine of eternal salvation....
>
> But the apostle rises still higher, and adds, *even as Christ Jesus*; for the Lord himself commands that his ministers shall be viewed in the same light as himself. 'He that heareth you heareth me.' (Luke 10:16).... Such is the highly commendatory language which reveals to us at once the majesty of the gospel, and the honorable character of its ministry. If it be the command of Christ that his ministers shall be thus honored, it is certain that contempt of them

---

31. *Inst.*, IV, i, 5 (O. S. V, 8, 36–39). Cf. MacGregor, *Corpus Christi*, 52.
32. Ibid. (9, 2–7).
33. *Com.* Gal 4:14 (C. O. l, 232ff.).

proceeds from the instigation of the devil; and indeed they never can be despised so long as the word of God is esteemed.[34]

It should be remembered, however, that this power and authority that Calvin assigned to the ministers does not belong to these persons in themselves. "For Christ has not given this power properly to men but to his word, of which he has made these men ministers."[35] Meanwhile, Calvin states that if we do not submit to the yoke of being taught by human words and ministry, such insubordination would be "like blotting out the face of God which shines upon us in teaching."[36]

In his doctrine of preaching Calvin thus steers a middle course between Lutheran and Zwinglian doctrines of the word and Spirit. This middle course, as Parker indicates, is:

> between those who exaggerate the dignity of the ministry beyond measure (Lutheran), and those who contend 'that it is a criminal transfer to mortal man of what properly belongs to the Holy Spirit, to suppose that ministers and teachers penetrate the heart and mind' (Zwinglian).[37]

Calvin says, "God breathes faith into us only by the instrument of his gospel. . . . Likewise, the power to save rests with God (Rom 1:16); but . . . He displays and unfolds it in the preaching of the gospel."[38]

This doctrine of the church and its teaching ministry must be kept clearly in mind in order to reach a proper understanding of Calvin's doctrine of biblical authority; the authority of the church and its ministry is the context and the perspective from which we must view Calvin's correlation of word and Spirit. This is the basis on which he rejects the Roman doctrine of authority as well as the teaching of the Anabaptist fanatics. Against Rome, Calvin says, "Our opponents locate the authority of the Church outside God's Word; but we insist that it be attached to the Word, and do not allow it to be separated from it."[39]

---

34. Ibid. (9, 9–15); cf. Wallace, *Calvin's Doctrine of Word and Sacrament*.
35. Fuhrmann, *Instruction in Faith*, 73. (O. S. I, 414). Also *Inst.*, IV, ii, 1 (O. S. V, 197, 17–32); cf. Jansen, *Calvin's Doctrine of the Work of Christ*, 46ff.
36. *Inst.*, IV, i, 5 (O. S. V, 9, 32ff.).
37. Parker, *Oracles of God*, 50.
38. *Inst.*, IV, i, 5 (O. S. V, 8, 17–21).
39. *Inst.*, IV, viii, 13 (O. S. V, 146, 29–31).

> For seeing how dangerous it would be to boast of the Spirit without the Word, he declared that the Church is indeed governed by the Holy Spirit, but in order that that government might not be vague and unstable, he annexed it to the Word.[40]

On the other hand, against the so-called fanatics, Calvin points out that "we are to expect nothing more from his Spirit than that he will illumine our minds to perceive the truth of his teaching."[41] Again he says, "Let us not believe anything that is thrust in under the title of the Spirit apart from the Gospel."[42]

Moreover, it is from the perspective of the teaching ministry of the church that Calvin establishes the permanent relationship between faith and the word. It is within this context that he says, "This . . . is the true knowledge of Christ, if we receive him as he is offered by the Father: namely, clothed with his gospel."[43] Thus we can see that Calvin conceives of the word within the context of the church and of Christ as being offered in the word. The reader must keep this pattern in mind when considering Calvin's doctrine of authority.

Now we shall turn to the doctrine of illumination by the Holy Spirit, which is the first part of faith and the first operation of the Spirit within it. We shall also view this doctrine from the perspective of the twofold knowledge. It is obvious that we must start with knowledge of God as Redeemer before we consider knowledge of God as Creator because we must discuss humankind's fallen condition before we can see it restored; that is, as human beings were originally created.

KNOWLEDGE OF GOD THE REDEEMER

Illumination by the Holy Spirit can best be understood against the background of the darkness of mind that makes this illumination necessary. Calvin's systematic discussion of this subject, as we have already observed, can be found in the first five chapters of Book II of the *Institutes*. Calvin presents his doctrine of sin against the background of his doctrine of creation. He says,

---

40. Calvin, "Reply to Sadoleto," *Tracts and Treatises*, I, 35 (O. S. I, 465).
41. Ibid. (147, 16–18).
42. Ibid. (147, 22ff.).
43. *Inst.*, III, ii, 6 (O. S. IV, 13, 15ff.).

> Now away with those persons who dare write God's name upon their faults, because we declare that men are vicious by nature! They perversely search out God's handiwork in their own pollution, when they ought rather to have sought it in that unimpaired and uncorrupted nature of Adam. Our destruction therefore comes from the guilt of our flesh not from God, inasmuch as we have perished solely because we have degenerated from our original condition.[44]

Likewise, as previously shown, Calvin discusses the fall and knowledge of ourselves as sinners in correspondence to knowledge of God the Redeemer, and he teaches that we arrive at both sides of this knowledge when we receive the grace of justification. Believers know their sinfulness at its darkest only against the bright light of their redemption in Christ, while redemption is not seen in its full meaning except against human depravity.

Thus we can see that Calvin presents his doctrine of humanity from beginning to end within the context of grace. For this reason he points out that:

> When he [man] had been advanced to the highest degree of honor, Scripture attributed nothing else to him than that he had been created in the image of God (Gen 1:27), thus suggesting that man was blessed, not because of his own good actions, but by participation in God. What, therefore, now remains for man, bare and destitute of all glory, but to recognize God for whose beneficence he could not be grateful when he abounded with the riches of his grace; and at least, by confessing his own poverty, to glorify him in whom he did not previously glory in recognition of his own blessings?
>
> Also, it is no less to our advantage than pertinent to God's glory that we be deprived of all credit for our wisdom and virtue.[45]

As Torrance has stated, "By starting from the fact of grace, Calvin forms his doctrine of man's present depravity only as a corollary of grace."[46] Or again,

> It is because faith must speak of salvation and forgiveness in total terms that it must also speak of sin and depravity in total terms. It is only within this context of grace, and only on the ground of

---

44. *Inst.*, II, i, 10 (O. S. III, 239, 26–33); cf. I, xv, I (O. S. III, 173, 37ff.).
45. *Inst.*, II, ii, 1 (O. S. III, 241, 32–242, 9).
46. Torrance, *Calvin's Doctrine of Man*, 85.

this grace, that we have any right to make such a total judgment upon man as he is, but on this ground, that is, of a new creation, we must set aside the old man and all that pertains to him as having come under the total judgment of God manifested on the Cross.[47]

A detailed discussion of Calvin's doctrine of humanness would take us beyond the purpose of this study. Therefore we shall satisfy ourselves here by surveying the role that Calvin assigned to the Scriptures in illumining our minds within the sphere of knowledge of God as Redeemer. Keeping in mind his emphasis on grace and with an eye on the sinfulness of humankind which, as we have seen, was taken lightly by the Schoolmen,[48] we can now understand why Calvin insisted that "faith properly begins with the promise, rests in it, and ends in it."[49] Explaining the reason for such teaching, he says:

> For in God faith seeks life: a life that is not found in commandments or declarations of penalties, but in the promise of mercy, and only in a freely given promise. For a conditional promise that sends us back to our own works does not promise life unless we discern its presence in ourselves. Therefore, if we would not have our faith tremble and waver, we must buttress it with the promise of salvation, which is willingly and freely offered to us by the Lord in consideration of our misery rather than our deserts. . . . There is nothing that can establish faith except that generous embassy by which God reconciles the world to himself.[50]

As we have seen in the last chapter, Calvin differentiates between the "freely given promise" and the "whole of Scripture." The elements that are excluded here, as Dowey has said, are "various oracles of condemnation, the precepts, promises, and threats, or altogether, the conditional salvation of the law."[51] This differentiation is what we now need to examine more closely.

---

47. Ibid.
48. Cf. page 54 above.
49. *Inst.*, III, ii, 29 (O. S. IV, 39, 5ff).
50. Ibid. (39, 6–25).
51. Dowey, *Knowledge of God* (1994), 157.

THE CONDEMNATORY FUNCTION OF THE LAW

We have established Calvin's position that it is impossible for us to attain the knowledge of God the Creator, the true God, and the knowledge of ourselves as restored except on the basis of knowledge of the Redeemer and of ourselves as sinners. It is because of this concept that he gives a fuller definition of faith, singling out the freely given promise in Christ while emphasizing the knowledge of ourselves as sinners. The function of the law from this point of view is only negative.

> Let us survey briefly the function and use of what is called the 'moral law.' Now, so far as I understand it, it consists of three parts. The first part is this: while it shows God's righteousness, that is, the righteousness alone acceptable to God, it warns, informs, convicts, and lastly condemns, every man of his own unrighteousness. For man, blinded and drunk with self-love, must be compelled to know and to confess his own feebleness and impurity.[52]

The law here does not produce faith but rather convicts and condemns. But, Calvin would tell us,

> We ask only what faith finds in the Word of the Lord upon which to lean and rest. Where our conscience sees only indignation and vengeance, how can it fail to tremble and be afraid? Or to shun the God whom it dreads? Yet faith ought to seek God, not to shun him .... Accordingly, we need the promise of grace, which can testify to us that the Father is merciful; since we can approach him in no other way, and upon grace alone the heart of man can rest.[53]

Thus, for the believer *as a sinner*, the relationship between the law and the freely given promise can be understood in this manner:

> By our wickedness and depravity we are prevented from enjoying the blessed life set openly before us by the law. Thereby the grace of God, which nourishes us without the support of the law, becomes sweeter, and his mercy which bestows that grace upon us, becomes more lovely. From this we learn that he never tires in repeatedly benefiting us and in heaping new gifts upon us.[54]

---

52. *Inst.*, II, vii, 6 (O. S. III, 332, 3–10).
53. *Inst.*, III, ii, 7 (O. S. IV, 15, 19–16, 4).
54. *Inst.*, II, vii, 7 (O. S. III, 333, 32–334, 4).

Word and Spirit: Illumination of the Mind   105

This is the thought Calvin wanted to emphasize. It is for this reason, after he had contrasted the Roman doctrine of merits with the Evangelical teaching, that he closes his chapter on faith saying, "But for our part . . . *we as sinners* . . . let us so willingly presume upon his truth that, relying upon his mercy alone, abandoning reliance upon works, we dare to have good hope."[55]

Within this context of the knowledge of the Redeemer and of ourselves as sinners, faith looks to the freely given promise in Christ as its object. As for the law, it cannot at this point serve more than its negative first function. Anything other than this role would obscure God's grace. Interestingly, this is the thought which Calvin expresses in the last lecture that he ever delivered:

> Moreover, since God wishes his glory to shine prominently in his free mercy, we must conclude that those who obscure his compassion or minimize it, or attempt to reduce its greatness to nothing, are the most hardened and open enemies of his glory.
>
> And we know that the teaching of the papacy aims in that direction, for in it, God's free kindness lies buried, or is hidden in a fog, or has wholly vanished. For they set forth *merits* of various sorts which they oppose to God's grace.[56]

Thus we can see the role of Scripture in bringing us to knowledge of God the Redeemer. The law judges and convicts; in order to bring us to God it reveals to us our wickedness. "Yet this is not done to cause us to fall down in despair or, completely discouraged, to rush headlong over the brink."[57] "For God does not despoil us with the view of leaving us bare."[58]

It is true that through the first use of the law "the wicked are terrified." Yet Calvin shows that this is "because of their obstinacy of heart."[59] Thus "for the Children of God the knowledge of the law should have another purpose."[60]

> 'For God has shut up all men in unbelief,' not that he may destroy all or suffer all to perish, but 'that he may have mercy upon all' (Rom 11:32). This means that, dismissing the stupid opinion of

55. *Inst.*, III, ii, 43 (O. S. IV, 54, 28–31); italics added.
56. *Com.* Ezek 20:44; Haroutunian, *Calvin: Commentaries*, 128 (C. O. XL, 514).
57. *Inst.*, II, vii, 8 (O. S. III, 334, 6–8).
58. *Com.* 1 Cor 1:31 (C. O. XLIX, 332).
59. *Inst.*, II, vii, 8 (O. S. III, 334, 8ff.).
60. Ibid. (334, 9ff.).

their own strength, they come to realize that they stand and are upheld by God's hand alone . . . . In the precepts of the law, God is but the rewarder of perfect righteousness, which all of us lack, and conversely, the severe judge of evil deeds. But in Christ his face shines, full of grace and gentleness, even upon us poor and unworthy sinners.[61]

Once again Calvin has posited a connection between the knowledge of the Redeemer and justification by faith alone; and therein the freely given promise in Christ is offered to us in the specific or proper teaching of Scripture.

KNOWLEDGE OF GOD THE CREATOR

In humankind's predicament of a darkened, blinded mind, revelation from creation cannot be of any help. "For the natural man refuses to be led to recognize the disease of his lusts. The light of nature is extinguished before he even enters upon this abyss."[62] The only remedy that Calvin can find for the eyes of the human mind is the illumination of the Holy Spirit. Thus having referred to some of the prayers of David and Paul, he says:

> Augustine so recognizes this inability of the reason to understand the things of God that he deems the grace of illumination no less necessary for our minds than the light of the sun for our eyes. Not content with this, he adds the correction that we ourselves open our eyes to behold the light, but the eyes of the mind, unless the Lord opens them, remain closed.[63]

At this point we must consider the effects that Calvin ascribes to illumination of the mind by the Holy Spirit. Calvin does not consider illumination by the Holy Spirit to be something that takes place once for all but rather as an ongoing experience of the believer. He says:

> Nor does Scripture teach that our minds are illumined only on one day and that they may thereafter see of themselves. For what I have just quoted from Paul has reference to continuing progress and increase.[64]

---

61. Ibid. (334, 13–25); cf. *Instruction in Faith*, 34ff. (O. S. I, 382).
62. *Inst.*, II, ii, 24 (O. S. III, 267, 13–16).
63. *Inst.*, II, ii, 25 (O. S. III, 268, 21–26).
64. Ibid. (268, 27–30).

The illumination of the Holy Spirit is not an operation by which the eyes of the mind regain the full clearness of vision they had before the fall. Rather,

> David has aptly expressed it in these words: 'With my whole heart I have sought thee, let me not wander from thy commandments!' (Ps. 119:10). Although he had been reborn and had advanced to no mean extent in true godliness, he still confesses that he needs continual direction at every moment, lest he decline from the knowledge with which he has been endowed.[65]

Calvin thus depicts a life of inner spiritual tension. On the one hand, believers are illumined, while on the other, they are in need of further illumination. Believers are both sinners and restored at the same time.

We are now ready to understand Calvin's discussion of knowledge of God the Creator in Book I of the *Institutes*, although we must confine ourselves to considering the role that Calvin assigns to Scripture in this book. For Calvin, knowledge of God the Creator is only possible because of Christ[66] and depends on the illumination of the Holy Spirit.[67] Calvin says, "As much in the fashioning of the universe as in the general teaching of Scripture, the Lord shows himself to be the Creator."[68] Now, as we consider knowledge from creation as it is expressed in Chapter v, we notice that Calvin summarizes the whole subject by referring to a passage from the Epistle to the Hebrews:

> The apostle, in that very passage where he calls the world the image of things invisible, adds that through faith we understand that they have been fashioned by God's word (Heb 11:3). He means by this that the invisible divinity is made manifest in such spectacles, but that we have not the eyes to see this unless they be illumined by the inner revelation of God through faith.[69]

Thus it becomes obvious that Calvin has been speaking throughout the chapter as a person whose eyes are being illumined through faith.

---

65. Ibid. (268, 30–35).
66. *Inst.*, I, ii, 1 (O. S. III, 34, 15–17).
67. *Inst.*, I, v, 1 (O. S. III, 59, 7ff.).
68. *Inst.*, I, ii, 1 (O. S. 34, 22ff.).
69. *Inst.*, I, v, 14 (O. S. III, 59, 3–8).

As we gain knowledge of God the Creator from Scripture, Calvin assigns to the Scriptures the role of a better help.[70] "The knowledge of God, otherwise quite clearly set forth in the system of the universe and in all creatures, is nonetheless more intimately and also more vividly revealed in his Word."[71] One should remember that Calvin is speaking here about believers; he has just said that God had "added the light of his Word by which to become known unto salvation; and he regarded as worthy of this privilege those whom he pleased to gather more closely and intimately to himself."[72] It is within this role that Calvin's simile of spectacles should be understood.

> Just as old or bleary-eyed men and those with weak vision, if you thrust before them a most beautiful volume, even if they recognize it to be some sort of writing, yet can scarcely construe two words, but with the aid of spectacles will begin to read distinctly; so Scripture, gathering up the otherwise confused knowledge of God in our minds, having dispersed our dullness, clearly shows us the true God.[73]

We know that Calvin is speaking here of the experience of believers, for he says of Scripture: "since otherwise even those who seem to stand firm before all others would soon melt away."[74] We have shown that believers know themselves to be sinners and blind in spiritual matters.[75] Their sight is restored in Christ, but this restoration cannot be complete as long as they are in the flesh. Therefore, they are always dependent on the spectacles of Scripture for accurate vision.

We now find ourselves bordering on the issue of natural theology in Calvin's thought. To engage in the debate would take us beyond our purpose,[76] so we shall merely try to present a positive and constructive

---

70. *Inst.*, I, vi, 1 (O. S. III, 60, 15).
71. *Inst.*, I, x, 1 (O. S. III, 85, 7–9).
72. *Inst.*, I, vi, 1 (O. S. III, 60, 17–19).
73. Ibid. (60, 25–30).
74. Ibid. (60, 23ff.).
75. *Inst.*, II, ii, 19 (O. S. III, 261, 27–29).

76. The two sides of the debate can be found in Brunner's *Nature and Grace* and Barth's reply, *No!* On the basis of our analysis of the twofold knowledge, we can say that both Barth and his school on one hand and Brunner and his school on the other present Calvin correctly, depending on which aspect we are considering. Concerning knowledge of God the Creator, which corresponds to knowledge of ourselves as restored in Christ, Brunner would certainly be correct when he speaks of believers as

Word and Spirit: Illumination of the Mind   109

statement, showing the exact relationship that Calvin considers to exist between knowledge of God the Creator within creation and knowledge gained from the general teaching of Scripture. We are dealing here with a knowledge offered "as much in the fashioning of the universe as in the general teaching of Scripture."[77] Calvin does not consider the general teaching of Scripture to offer any knowledge content over and above what creation supplies.[78] Instead, the spectacles metaphor allows us to see that Calvin considers the function of Scripture to be clarification. Referring again to a previous quotation, we see that "the knowledge of God, otherwise quite clearly set forth in the system of the universe . . . is nonetheless more intimately and also more vividly revealed in his Word."[79]

The content of knowledge of the Creator from creation is found, as we have seen, in Chapter v of the book under discussion, while knowledge of the Creator as found in the general teaching of Scripture is discussed in Chapters xi through xviii. A comparison of these two portions of the book reveals what Calvin had in mind. Chapter v teaches that even the person of faith who has been illumined cannot see more than that there is *a* creator or that there is *a* God from creation alone. Then, holding the spectacles of Scripture before their eyes, they come to

---

"those whose eyes have been opened by Christ" (26ff.) (*"dem durch Christus der Star gestochen ist . . ." Nature und Gnade*, 14). It should be remembered that Peter Barth opposed Brunner on this point since he thought that Brunner had changed Calvin's metaphor of the spectacles into one of his own, namely Christ piercing our cataracts. On this basis Barth charged Brunner with teaching that the believer by faith becomes a "clear-sighted person" rather than a "dim-sighted man" as Calvin presents him. (*Das Problem der natürlichen Theologie bei Calvin*, 9–10). Peter Barth is also true to Calvin on this point, for he speaks within the context of ourselves as (blind) sinners. From this point of view there is no knowledge of the true God that can be derived from creation. Moreover, within this context Karl Barth can say that this is true "also of those 'whose eyes have been opened by Christ!'" (126). The present writer thinks that both sides can find sufficient support in Calvin's writings for the battle to continue! Meanwhile, I suggest that in reality, both views are complementary to each other. Believers know God as their Creator and Redeemer, and as long as they are in the flesh they are restored while still being sinners. Schreiner takes up this matter and points out that "The main problem for a 'Christian natural theology' is not the disputed 'point of contact' debated by Barth and Brunner. Calvin clearly stated that the work of the Spirit and of Scripture corrects the noetic effect of sin in so far as one remains within the bounds of Scripture." Schreiner, *Theater of His Glory*, 122.

77. *Inst.* I, ii,1 (O.S. III,34, 21); author's translation.
78. Cf. pages 24–26 above
79 *Inst.*, I, x, 1 (O. S. III, 85, 7–9).

know the Creator, who is the true God. It is for this reason that Calvin emphasizes so emphatically the necessity of Scripture. He says:

> Now, in order that true religion may shine upon us, we ought to hold that it must take its beginning from heavenly doctrine and that no one can get even the slightest taste of right and sound doctrine unless he be a pupil of Scripture.[80]

Even believers whose eyes have been opened cannot do without Scripture:

> We must come, I say, to the Word, where God is truly and vividly described to us from his works, while these very works are appraised not by our depraved judgment but by the rule of eternal truth. If we turn aside from the Word ... though we may strive with strenuous haste, yet, since we have got off the track, we shall never reach the goal.[81]

Calvin closed Chapter vi with the same thought which he later added at the end of Chapter x as an introduction to the following chapters. In Chapter vi Calvin quoted references from the Psalms about knowledge, first from creation and then from the Scriptures. Here Calvin says: "Since God in vain calls all peoples to himself by the contemplation of heaven and earth, this [Scripture] is the very school of God's children."[82] This same thought is repeated again at the end of Chapter x when Calvin points out that "Whatever ... [the heathen] had naturally sensed concerning the sole God had no value beyond making them inexcusable."[83] Then he goes on to say: "Habakkuk, when he condemned all idols, bade men seek God 'in his temple' (Hab 2:20) lest believers admit someone other than him who revealed himself by his Word."[84] The function of Scripture then is to clarify that knowledge which believers understand from Creation, thus leading them to the true God.

This point is a recurring refrain in Book I of the *Institutes*, and it is an important clue to understanding the full content of the book. When Calvin first introduces Scripture he says:

---

80. *Inst.*, I, vi, 2 (O. S. III, 63, 5–9).
81. *Inst.*, I, vi, 3 (O. S. III, 63, 25–31).
82. *Inst.*, I, vi, 4 (O. S. III, 64, 19–21).
83. *Inst.*, I, vi, 4 (O. S. III, 88, 1ff.
84. Ibid. (88, 10–13).

> So Scripture, gathering up the otherwise confused knowledge of God in our minds, having dispersed our dullness, clearly shows us *the true God*.... He also put forth his Word, which is a more direct and more certain mark whereby he is to be recognized.[85]

In explaining the purpose of Book I he says, "Here I shall discuss only how we should learn from Scripture that God, the Creator of the universe, can by sure marks be distinguished from all the throng of feigned gods."[86] His concern therefore is the knowledge of the true God. Again in introducing the subject matter of Chapters xi through xviii, Calvin says:

> But here I propose to summarize the general doctrine. And first, indeed, let readers observe that Scriptures, to direct us to *the true God*, distinctly excludes and rejects all the gods of the heathen.[87]

Given the importance of the idea, Calvin makes it the title for his entire tenth chapter. Moreover, from Chapter xi onward we find a clear emphasis on the concept of the true God, which is so obvious even in the chapter titles that it does not need to be spelled out here. Thus it is obvious that the true God is the organizing principle that enables us to interpret the following chapters; it is not misleading, as Dowey claims.[88]

Now it becomes clear why we previously stated that Calvin had found the twofold knowledge in John 17:3.[89] The whole of Book I can be seen as a commentary on the words, "This is eternal life, that they know thee the only true God." The reference to this verse at the beginning of Chapter v cannot be just incidental. As we consider Calvin's doctrines of creation and providence we again notice the same relationship between knowledge from creation and that derived from the general teaching of Scripture. In Chapter v we see how creation presents these doctrines to persons of faith, and in Chapters xiv through xviii we see how Scripture clarifies them. Therefore, referring to the notion that the Creator reveals his lordship over creation, Calvin says in Chapter v:

> Belonging to this theme are the praises of God's power from the testimonies of nature which one meets here and there especially

---

85. *Inst.*, I, vi, 1; italics added (O. S. III, 60, 29ff).
86. Ibid. (61, 25–28).
87. *Inst.*, I, x, 3 (O. S. III, 87, 20-24); italics added.
88. Dowey, *Knowledge of God*, 87.
89. Cf. pages 37f above.

indeed in the Book of Job and in Isaiah. These I now intentionally pass over, for they will find a more appropriate place where I shall discuss *from the Scriptures* the creation of the universe.[90]

This he does in Chapters xiv through xviii.[91] Referring to the revelation of God as Creator, however, Calvin says in Chapter xiv:

> Nothing is to be gained by further discussing what direction the contemplation of God's works should take and to what goal such contemplation ought to be applied, in as much as the greater part of this topic has been disposed of in another place.[92]

It is evident that he is referring here to the discussion in Chapter v.[93]

Therefore, as far as Calvin is concerned, there is no additional content to be found in Scripture concerning creation. For, "as much in the fashioning of the universe as in the general teaching of Scripture, the Lord shows himself to be the Creator."[94] Thus the believer is sent by Scripture to discover God in the creation and is *helped* by Scripture to see him clearly. Scripture is "the very school of God's children,"[95] "lest believers admit someone other than him who revealed himself by his Word."[96] This clarification is essential "since otherwise [without Scripture] even those who seem to stand firm before all others would soon melt away."[97]

We should not forget, however, that when Calvin maintains that the knowledge of God from creation is identical with knowledge obtained from Scripture, he is speaking only within the context of knowledge of God *as Creator*. Therefore it would be incorrect to say with Stuermann that "nature displays God as Creator *and Redeemer*."[98] Calvin never conceived of knowledge of the Redeemer except in Christ.

---

90. *Inst.*, I, v, 6 (O. S. III, 51, 13–18); italics added.

91. The doctrines of creation and providence are inseparable for Calvin. He treats them together in Book I, Chapter v, while providence is introduced in I, xvi, 1 in this manner: "Unless we pass on to his providence . . . we do not yet properly grasp what it means to say: 'God is Creator'" (O. S. III, 187, 19–21).

92. *Inst.*, I, xiv, 21 (O. S. III, 171, 18–22).

93. *Inst.*, I, v, 1–4, *passim*.

94. *Inst.*, I, ii, 1 (O. S. III, 34, 22ff.).

95. *Inst.*, I, vi, 4 (O. S. III, 64, 21ff.).

96. *Inst.*, I, x, 3 (O. S. III, 88, 12ff.).

97. *Inst.*, I, vi, 1 (60, 23ff.).

98. Stuermann, *Critical Study*, 129; italics added.

As we consider the content of knowledge of God the Creator, we come to understand more fully the role that Calvin assigns to Scripture in this context. At several places in Book I, Calvin observes that knowledge of God involves trust and reverence. Closely associated with reverence we find the element of worship.[99] Here we see that Calvin makes the whole of Scripture (the general teaching of Scripture), the common object of faith.

THE PEDAGOGICAL FUNCTION OF THE LAW

We noted in our discussion of faith that Calvin distinguishes between the freely given promise and Scripture as a whole. We have seen that within the context of knowledge of God the Redeemer, faith does not embrace all of the Scriptures; rather, it "properly begins with the promise, rests in it, and ends in it."[100] The law here performs its first function, which is negative—conviction and condemnation. In the context of knowledge of God the Creator, however, when the believer relates to God as a restored human being, the role of Scripture is different. Now the believer can embrace the whole of Scripture, including the law. It is at this stage that the law performs its pedagogical function, which Calvin calls its third use. "The third . . . use . . . finds its place among believers in whose hearts the Spirit of God already lives and reigns."[101] Here believers "profit by the law in two ways: . . . to learn more thoroughly each day the nature of the Lord's will, [and] . . . by frequent meditation upon it to be aroused to obedience."[102] It is obvious that Calvin is speaking here of the believer's experience of the grace of sanctification and knowledge of the Creator. He goes on to say:

> Certain ignorant persons, not understanding this distinction [between the different uses of the law], rashly cast out the whole of Moses, and bid farewell to the two Tables of the Law. For they think it obviously alien to Christians to hold to a doctrine that contains the 'dispensation of death' (Cf. 2 Cor 3:7). Banish this wicked thought from your minds! For Moses has admirably taught that the law, which among sinners can engender nothing

---

99. *Inst.*, I, ii, 2; I, v, 10; I, x, 2; I, xiv, 21, 22 (O. S. III, 37, 10; 54, 1; 87, 16–19; 171, 34–173, 23).

100. *Inst.*, III, ii, 29 (O. S. IV, 39, 5ff.).

101. *Inst.*, II, vii, 12 (O. S. III, 337, 23–25).

102. *Inst.* II, vii, 12 (O. S. III, 337, 27–29); and III, vi, 2.

but death, ought among the saints to have a better and more excellent use.... The life of a righteous man is a continual meditation upon the law.[103]

Here we can see why Calvin says that "when we say that faith must rest upon a freely given promise, we do not deny that believers embrace and grasp the Word of God in every respect."[104]

According to Calvin, the law first convicts and condemns; and third,[105] it is used to both instruct and inspire the believer in obedience. In its first use the law relates to the knowledge of God as Redeemer and his freely given promise, while its latter function relates to knowledge of God as Creator and the word of God in general. Understanding this dual relationship, which likewise relates to justification and sanctification, is important for rightly interpreting Calvin's theology.

We have seen already that Calvin rejected the Schoolmen's claim to knowledge of God the Creator or faith in God's truth (the whole of Scripture) because he thought that they had, "as it were, drawn a veil over Christ to hide him."[106] Accordingly he insisted that knowledge of God as Creator must be founded on the knowledge of him as Redeemer; and that the word cannot obtain full faith until we have arrived at the freely given promise in Christ.[107] When faith is defined as "knowledge of God's benevolence toward us, founded upon the truth of the freely given promise in Christ,"[108] the law appears in its first use. But Calvin considered the law's pedagogical function as "the third and principal use, which pertains more closely to the proper purpose of the law."[109] It is in this context that Calvin emphasizes faith as the "knowledge of God's

---

103. *Inst.*, II, vii, 13 (O. S. III, 338, 29–339, 13).

104. *Inst.*, III, ii, 29 (O. S. IV, 39, 25–27). This statement should be contrasted with another by Dowey in which, after pointing out Calvin's distinction between the law and the freely given promise, he goes on to say about the law, "But faith never did embrace the whole of this." Dowey, *Knowledge of God* (1994), 157.

105. The second use of the law, which is known as the civil use, is intentionally left out of discussion here since its consideration would take us beyond our purpose. For the second use, which Calvin identifies as "To restrain malefactors and those who are not yet believers" and a "deterrent to those not yet regenerate", the reader is referred to *Inst.* II, vii, 10 and 11 *passim*.

106. *Inst.*, III, ii, 2 (O. S. IV, 10, 2).

107. *Inst.*, III, ii, 7 (O. S. IV, 16, 22–35).

108. Ibid. (16, 32–34).

109. *Inst.*, II, vii, 12 (O. S. III, 337, 23ff.).

will toward us, perceived from his Word,"[110] which results in a life that responds to God in trust and reverence—a life that is not realized except through the grace of sanctification. Here we see in broad and general terms the difference between Luther and Calvin. For Luther, the proper and main function of the law is condemnation (Com. Gal 3:19), while for Calvin, as we have just seen, the pedagogical function whereby the law guides believers in the knowledge of God's will is primary.[111]

THE TWOFOLD KNOWLEDGE

We have previously seen that by faith we have a twofold knowledge of God corresponding to a twofold knowledge of ourselves. Illumined by the Holy Spirit, we receive a twofold grace that results in a twofold relationship with God. Consequently, we know God as our Creator and Redeemer, and we know ourselves as being restored to what we were before the fall, while still remaining sinners. As far as Calvin is concerned, faith could not achieve one of these without the other, because there cannot be knowledge of the Creator nor an acceptance of all of the Scriptures leading to a life of trust and reverence unless it were founded on the knowledge of the Redeemer and the freely given promise in Christ. Rather, when we come to the knowledge of the Redeemer and when we lean and rest upon the freely given promise in Christ, then we also know the Creator, and the word does obtain full faith among us. This concept is crucial for understanding biblical authority in Calvin's theology, and we will continue to examine it in the following chapter.

As we consider the twofoldness of the knowledge of faith, we should remember that for Calvin, salvation or eternal life does not consist of one side of the twofold knowledge without the other. They are inseparable, as seen in Calvin's explication of John 17:3: "This is eternal life, that they know thee the only true God, and Jesus Christ whom thou hast sent."

---

110. *Inst.*, III, ii, 6; II, vii, 12; I, ii, 2 (O. S. IV, 15, 10f.; III, 337, 29-338, 1; III, 35, 11–37, 13).

111. Garcia, *Life in Christ*, 74ff. Furthermore, it should be noted that Luther's "liberty" in handling the Scriptures owes much to his views on the law as a tool of condemnation. Calvin, however, did not exercise such "liberty" because he considered the condemning function to be "accidental." (*Com.* Rom 7:10ff., 2 Cor. 3:7; C. O. XLIX, 126; L, 41). Therefore, faith regards the whole of Scripture, for the law finds its principal and proper purpose among believers.

Otherwise we would be tearing Christ to pieces.[112] Parker says toward the end of his discussion of knowledge of the Creator:

> It remains to see of what religious value this revelation is to man. It does not, despite a sentence to the contrary in *Institutio* I, vi, 1, lead us to salvation. That is to say, it does not bring us the forgiveness of our sins and eternal life. We know God as Creator, not as Redeemer. We learn the very first lesson of religion—to be religious. And the nature of pure religion is this: 'It consists in faith.' ... *Fides* here comprises both belief and trust; belief that God is, that He has revealed Himself to us in His works, and in His Word, that He is our Creator and Preserver, our loving Father ... and trust that is assured that it may in all circumstances rely upon His help, that He will supply all needs and that under the shadow of His wing there is safety.... One wonders: is all of this just the 'very first lesson of religion?' And if we could learn to relate ourselves to God in this manner before we know him as Redeemer, would there have ever been a need for Redemption?[113]

The difficulty in Parker's position arises when he considers it possible for a person to have faith, to relate to God in reverence and trust, and to worship him properly without knowing him as Redeemer. Because of this interpretation, Parker had to set what he calls Calvin's "strange statement" against other statements and is finally left "wondering why ever Calvin used them."[114] In response to Parker's argument, Calvin would say that "God is comprehended in Christ alone.... 'He that does not have the Son does not have the Father.'"[115] For, as we have pointed out before, there can never be knowledge of God as the Creator in isolation from knowledge of him as the Redeemer, while knowing him as Redeemer carries with it knowledge of him as Creator.

The full meaning of Book I becomes clear when we remember that for Calvin, we receive in faith a twofold grace and that eternal life means knowledge of God and of Christ. Knowledge of God the Redeemer is only one side of the life of faith. It is basic, essential, central, and fundamental because believers, as long as they are burdened with the flesh, know that they are still sinners. Nevertheless, they also know what they were like before the fall and know that their Father has restored them in

---

112. Cf. pages 77, 83 above.
113. Parker, *Calvin's Doctrine of the Knowledge of God*, 55.
114. Ibid. n. 1.
115. *Inst.*, II, vi, 4 (O. S. III, 326, 6–8).

Christ, and that this restoration goes beyond themselves to include the whole creation.[116] For "we well know why Christ was promised from the beginning: to restore the fallen world and to succor lost men."[117]

This then is the basic assumption and foundation for interpreting the work of Christ as presented in Book II of the *Institutes*. Moreover, it is essential for us to remember that Calvin considers knowledge of the Redeemer to correspond to knowledge of ourselves as fallen.[118] When this correlation is kept in mind, Calvin will not be blamed for a "failure to integrate Christology with Soteriology," as Hendry claims:[119]

> In all of this Calvin appears to be laying an objective foundation for the vicariousness of the work of Christ. When we turn to the third book of the *Institutes*, however, we note with surprise that not a trace of it remains. The Christ who, we learned earlier, came and joined himself to us and took our nature and put on the person of Adam in order that he might act for us, has now got separated from us and is outside us.[120]

It is important to note that all that Calvin says about the Redeemer in Book II does not correspond to ourselves as *joined to* him, as Hendry supposes, but rather as fallen sinners, in anticipation of what Book III offers: "The Way in Which We Receive the Grace of Christ."[121]

When discussing restoration as presented in Book I, Calvin views knowledge of God the Creator in the following manner:

> Whenever we call God the Creator of heaven and earth, let us at the same time bear in mind that the dispensation of all those things which he has made is in his own hand and power and that we are indeed his children, whom he has received into his faithful protection to nourish and educate. We are therefore to await the fullness of all good things from him alone and to trust completely that he will never leave us destitute of what we need for salvation, and to hang our hopes on none but him! We are therefore, also, to petition him for whatever we desire; and we are to recognize as a blessing from him, and thankfully to acknowledge, every benefit

---

116. Cf. *Com. Rom* 8:19ff.; Luke 17:20 (C.O. XLIX, 151–53; XLV, 425); Schreiner, *Theater of His Glory*, 99ff.

117. *Inst.*, II, xii, 4 (O. S. III, 440, 28–31).

118. Cf. *Com. Rom* 5:17 (C. O. XLIX, 99ff.).

119. Hendry, *Gospel of the Incarnation*, 68–71.

120. Ibid., 69.

121. Book III, title.

that falls to our share. So, invited by the great sweetness of his beneficence and goodness, let us study to love and serve him with all our heart.[122]

Reading such a statement and mindful of Calvin's emphasis on the third use of the law, one can see why Calvin believed Christ to be the transformer of culture.[123] This understanding also explains the interest of Calvin and the whole Reformed tradition in human society, science, politics, ethics, and economics.[124] It is this side of Calvin's theology that can easily be lost whenever there is an overemphasis on the christocentric nature of his doctrine of faith. Instead, Calvin wanted to hold together in one movement the various themes of creation and redemption, of incarnation and atonement. It is probably in light of this that Butin explains: "Approaches focusing on Christology or 'union with Christ' provide significant help in appreciating the coherence of Calvin's thought. Nevertheless, when advanced as inclusive explanations, they are insufficiently comprehensive."[125] An analysis of these aspects would take us beyond our purpose. Yet we have now advanced far enough to see that Calvin is consistent in his statements regarding the freely given promise and Scripture as a whole. Hence we can understand his remark:

> When we say that faith must rest upon a freely given promise, we do not deny that believers embrace and grasp the Word of God in every respect: but we point out the promise of mercy as the proper goal of faith.[126]

Believers are sinners who are justified by faith alone on the basis of the freely given promise. But they are also sanctified and thus being restored, knowing themselves to be part of a creation for whose restoration Christ has died. From this viewpoint the believer "embraces and grasps the Word of God *in every respect*." It is this word that makes us know the will of our Creator.

---

122. *Inst.*, I, xiv, 22 (O. S. III, 173, 11–23).

123. Niebuhr, *Christ and Culture*, 190 ff.

124. André Biéler, *La penséte économique*, 184ff., 223ff., and *passim*; Dillenberger, *Protestant Thought and Natural Science*; Dowey, *Knowledge of God* (1994); 138ff.; Harkness, *John Calvin*, 158.

125. Butin, *Revelation, Redemption and Response*, 127.

126. *Inst.*, IIII, ii, 29 (O. S. IV, 39, 25–28).

4

Word and Spirit: Sealing of the Heart

INTRODUCTORY REMARKS

We have seen that Calvin considers faith to consist of two aspects that correspond to the two operations of the Holy Spirit: illumination of the mind and sealing of the heart. Both are expressed in his fuller definition of faith.[1] We have also seen that Calvin's whole discussion of faith was affected by his attack on the Schoolmen and their teaching on the subject. We have pointed out that he did not object to the content, or rather claimed content, of faith as they saw it. He could subscribe "to the common saying that God is the object of faith,"[2] and he could say, "I admit . . . that God's truth is, as they call it, the common object of faith"[3]

Calvin did, however, reject the scholastic doctrine of implicit faith, believing that it kept ordinary church members in ignorance. He said, "Is this what believing means—to understand nothing, provided only that you submit your feeling obediently to the church? Faith rests not on ignorance, but on knowledge."[4] Moreover, he also thought that the scholastic doctrine of assent resulted in empty speculation or a quasi-knowledge that just flits vainly in the brain, leading souls astray rather than directing them to a definite goal.[5] Over against the scholastic approach, Calvin claimed to direct his readers to firm and certain knowledge.

---

1. *Inst.*, III, ii, 7 (O. S. IV, 16, 31–35).
2. *Inst.*, II, vi, 4 (O. S. III, 325, 22ff.).
3. *Inst.*, III, ii, 30 (O. S. IV, 39, 37ff.).
4. *Inst.*, III, ii, 2 (O. S. IV, 10, 11ff.).
5. *Inst.*, III, ii, 1; 36; I, v, 9 (O. S. IV, 7, 18–21; 46, 33–37; III, 53, 10–14).

Calvin's emphasis on firm and certain knowledge and his attack upon the idle speculations of the Schoolmen were not only elucidations of a doctrine but also functioned as a counterattack or defense of evangelical teaching against the charges of the Roman Church. This purpose is what we now need to examine.

The Roman Case against the Evangelicals

In Calvin's prefatory address to King Francis I of France, he summarized the different charges that the Roman Church had against the Evangelicals:

> They do not cease to assail our doctrine and to reproach and defame it with names that render it hated or suspect. They call it new and *of recent birth*. They reproach it as *doubtful and uncertain*. They ask what miracles have confirmed it. They inquire whether it is right for it to prevail against the agreement of so many holy fathers and against most ancient customs. They urge us to acknowledge that it is schismatic . . . . Finally, they say that . . . one can judge by its fruits what it is, seeing that it has engendered such a heap of sects, so many seditious tumults, such great licentiousness.[6]

Calvin then took the charges, one after the other, examined them and gave his defense of evangelical doctrine. In reading this defense, one should not fail to notice his repeated emphasis on the concept of certainty. We shall consider here only the first two charges against the evangelicals—novelty and ambiguity—since they are important for understanding of Calvin's doctrine of Biblical authority. Regarding the first he says:

> By calling it *new* they do great wrong to God, whose Sacred Word does not deserve to be accused of novelty. Indeed, I do not at all doubt that it is new to them, since to them both Christ himself and his gospel are new. But he who knows that this preaching of Paul is ancient, that 'Jesus Christ died for our sins and rose again for our justification' (Rom 4:25), will find nothing new among us.[7]

We see here that Calvin equates Scripture and the doctrine of the Evangelicals. He considers his teaching to be nothing but Scripture put

---

6. *Inst.*, 14ff. (O. S. III, 14, 26–15, 4).
7. *Inst.*, 15ff. (O. S. III, 15, 9–15).

in a systematic form,[8] or as Peter Barth puts it, "The *Institutio* is as it were Calvin's forefinger, pointing to the Scriptures."[9] Coming to the charge of uncertainty, Calvin says:

> The same ignorance leads them to regard it as doubtful and uncertain. This is precisely what the Lord complains of through his prophet . . . . But however they may jest about its uncertainty, if they had to seal their doctrine with their own blood, and at the expense of their own life, one could see how much it would mean to them. Quite the opposite is our assurance, which fears neither the terrors of death nor even God's judgment seat.[10]

It is important to understand Calvin's defense of this point. The Roman Catholic charge was against the doctrine of the Evangelicals. Because Calvin regards this doctrine to be nothing but Scripture, he considers it ignorance on the Roman part to call it doubtful. He goes on to say that the Evangelicals are so sure of their doctrine that they have been willing to die for it. It will be very important for us as we progress in our study of Calvin's doctrine of biblical authority to remember that the concept of certainty for him does not concern the *objective* authority of Scripture but rather its *subjective* dimension in the life and faith of believers.

As we look back at Calvin's definition of faith and also note his emphasis on certainty, it becomes evident that several purposes are served by this approach. On the one hand he is directing his readers to a sure goal while on the other he is exposing the uncertainty engendered by the Roman doctrine. Thus he is able to defend the certainty of the evangelical faith and even reverse the Roman charge, thereby putting the Roman controversialists on the defensive. We should keep in mind, however, that it was the certainty of the evangelical doctrine that was at stake at this time. It would be doing Calvin less than justice to think that he moved away from the concept of *fiducia* toward an intellectualized faith. This pattern becomes clearer when we study his theology as a whole, especially his concepts of knowledge and certainty.[11]

---

8. *Inst.*, 4 (O. S. III, 6, 19–25).
9. Cited in Parker, *Calvin's Doctrine of the Knowledge of God*, 45.
10. *Inst.*, 16 (O. S. III, 15, 13–26).
11. Cf. Dowey, *Knowledge of God* (1994), 184ff; Krusche, *Das Wirken*, 261.

Illumination and Sealing

In the previous chapter we studied Calvin's concept of illumination, in which the blind, sin-darkened mind of the believer is given new vision as a new creation in Christ. Now as we examine the phrase *sealing of the heart*, we see that it is not about adding to knowledge. Instead, the sealing work of the Holy Spirit is meant to confirm and give certainty rather than an increase in knowledge. With the scholastic doctrine in mind, Calvin says that "the Word of God is not received by faith if it flits about in the top of the brain, but when it takes root in the depth of the heart."[12] Then he adds,

> But if it is true that the mind's real understanding is illumination by the Spirit of God, then in such confirmation of the heart his power is much more clearly manifested, to the extent that the heart's distrust is greater than the mind's blindness. It is harder for the heart to be furnished with assurance than for the mind to be endowed with thought. The Spirit accordingly serves as a seal, to seal up in our hearts those very promises the certainty of which it has previously impressed upon our minds; and takes the place of a guarantee to confirm and establish them. . . . Do you see how Paul . . . calls him the *Spirit of promise* (Eph 1:13), because he makes firm the gospel among us?[13]

Here we see how receiving the word by faith and making the gospel firm are based on the sealing of the heart by the Holy Spirit.[14] We have now finally arrived at the basis of the authority of Scripture in Calvin's theology. Before exploring this subject further, however, it would be worthwhile to reconsider some of the points that we have discussed before—but from a different point of view.[15]

Sealing, Certainty, and Authority

In his discussion of faith, Calvin is trying to lead the Schoolmen and those who are under their sway to see Christ and the freely given promise found in him. He starts with the Schoolmen's point of view, mov-

---

12. *Inst.*, III, ii, 36 (O. S. IV, 46, 34ff.).

13. Ibid. (46, 37–47, 10).

14. It should also be remembered that for Calvin, "One important function of the sacraments is to confirm and seal the Word." Wallace, *Calvin's Doctrine of the Word and Sacrament*, 137ff.

15. Cf. Wallace, *Calvin's Doctrine*, 54ff.

Word and Spirit: Sealing of the Heart

ing step by step toward his objective. This is what we shall now briefly explore. First, one should remember that the Schoolmen called God the object of faith.[16] Calvin accepts this definition; his first step is to state it in the following manner:

> In understanding faith it is not merely a question of knowing that God exists, but also—and this especially—of knowing what is his will toward us. For it is not so much our concern to know who he is in himself, as what he wills to be toward us.[17]

With this step, Calvin introduces his first definition of faith by saying: "Therefore, we hold faith to be knowledge of God's will toward us perceived from his Word."[18] So far, he is still close enough to the Schoolmen in that they also say regarding the Word, that "God's truth is . . . the common object of faith, whether he threaten or hold out hope of grace."[19]

At this point Calvin raises the question of certainty, which he associates with the problem of authority. After defining faith in the manner which we have just seen, he goes on to say: "But the foundation of this is a preconceived conviction of God's truth. As for its certainty, as long as your mind is at war with itself, the Word will be of doubtful and weak authority, or rather of none."[20] This statement is very important for understanding the issue of biblical authority in Calvin's theology. For it is here that we can see him relating his discussion of the authority of Scripture in Book I[21] to his doctrine of faith, and particularly to the second aspect of faith, which pertains to certainty or the sealing of the heart.

Calvin has already pointed out that it is the knowledge of God's will toward humans that causes them to respond to God in trust and reverence and thus produces good works in them.[22] This subject greatly interested the Roman Church, which mounted a formidable attack against the Reformation regarding the place of good works. It was to forestall these attacks that Calvin emphasized the importance of good works in

16. *Inst.*, II, vi, 4; III, ii, 1 (O. S. III, 325, 22ff.; IV, 7, 18ff.).

17. *Inst.*, III, ii, 6 (O. S. IV, 15, 6–10). Cf. I, ii, 2; I, x, 2 (O. S. III, 35, 11–14; 86, 17ff.).

18. *Inst.*, III, ii, 6 (O. S. IV, 15, 10ff.).

19. *Inst.*, III, ii, 30 (O. S. IV, 39, 37–39).

20. *Inst.*, III, ii, 6 (O. S. IV, 15, 12–15).

21. *Inst.*, I, vii–ix, *passim*.

22. *Inst.*, I, ii, 2 (O. S. III, 35, 17–37, 14).

the life of faith. But now he wants readers to understand that this knowledge of God's will requires the word of God to have full authority as its foundation, meaning that it should have full certainty. Here Calvin tries to make his readers recognize that a difficulty stands between human beings as sinners and the certainty of the word. For, "this bare and external proof of the Word of God should have been amply sufficient to engender faith, did not our blindness and perversity prevent it."[23] Therefore, after pointing to the necessity of the certainty and authority of the word for faith as he has first defined it, Calvin goes on to say, "But since man's heart is not aroused to faith at every word of God, we must find out at this point what, strictly speaking, faith looks to in the Word."[24]

It is at this place in his argument that Calvin points to the freely given promise as the way to illumine the minds of human beings and to seal their hearts. It is only as these two operations of the Holy Spirit take place in the life and experience of a person that the word obtains full faith and its authority becomes certain. Leading into his fuller definition of faith Calvin says:

> Far indeed is the mind of man, blind and darkened as it is, from penetrating and attaining even to perception of the will of God! And the heart, too, wavering as it is in perpetual hesitation, is far from resting secure in that conviction! Therefore *our mind must be otherwise illumined and our heart strengthened, that the Word of God may obtain full faith among us.*[25]

This is the key to a proper understanding of Calvin's discussion of the authority of Scripture in Book I.[26] In this book his doctrine of the *testimonium internum Spiritus Sancti* is presented within a wider discussion of the Holy Spirit's work of sealing of the believer's heart resulting in certainty and full faith. Therefore he says:

> They who strive to build up firm faith in Scripture through disputation are doing things backwards . . . . Even if anyone clears God's Sacred Word from man's evil speaking, he will not at once imprint upon their hearts that certainty which piety requires. Since for unbelieving men religion seems to stand by opinion alone, they, in order not to believe anything foolishly or lightly,

---

23. *Inst.*, III, ii, 33 (O. S. IV, 44, 4–6).
24. *Inst.*, III, 7 (O. S. IV, 15, 19–21).
25. Ibid. (16, 26–31); italics added.
26. *Inst.*, I, vii–ix, *passim*.

> both wish and demand rational proof that Moses and the prophets spoke divinely. But I reply: the testimony of the Spirit is more excellent than all reason. For as God alone is a fit witness of himself in his Word, so also the Word will not find acceptance in men's hearts before it is sealed by the inward testimony of the Spirit.[27]

Now we can see that the question of biblical authority and certainty for Calvin is linked up with piety, which he considers the believer's active relationship to God in trust and reverence, and which is also the experience of sanctification. Consequently, the question of the authority of Scripture is neither to be raised nor answered in the area of knowledge of ourselves as sinners who have fears and doubts. Calvin tells us:

> As for its certainty, as long as your mind is at war with itself, the Word will be of doubtful and weak authority, or rather of none. And it is not even enough to believe that God is trustworthy (cf. Rom 3:3), who can neither deceive nor lie (cf. Titus 1:2), unless you hold to be beyond doubt that whatever proceeds from him is sacred and inviolable truth.[28]

Thus Scripture becomes fully authoritative only as we know ourselves as restored in Christ, when "we hold faith to be a knowledge of God's will toward us, perceived from his Word,"[29] which is the knowledge of God as our Creator.

We can now see why Calvin places his doctrine of the authority of Scripture in Book I of the *Institutes*.[30] The authority of Scripture is tied to the work of the Holy Spirit in the heart and the obedient life of the believer. With this in mind we are now ready to examine Chapters vii through ix of Book I, which we had previously left out of consideration.[31] In these three chapters, Calvin presents his doctrine of Biblical authority

---

27. *Inst.*, I, vii, 4, *passim*. The last sentence in the original is: *Nam sicuti Deus solus de se idoneus est testis in suo sermone: ita etiam non ante fidem reperiet sermo in hominum cordibus quam interiore spiritus testimonio obsignetur.* The word *fidem*, translated "acceptance" by Battles, obscures the meaning. Henry Beveridge's "full credit" is closer to Calvin's meaning.

28. *Inst.*, III, ii, 6 (O. S. IV, 15, 13–18).

29. *Inst.*, III, ii, 6 (O. S. IV, 15, 10ff.).

30. There is no need to say with Wallace, "It is possible that Calvin himself . . . might, if he had lived to-day, have placed his chapter on Scripture a little further back in his *Institutes*." Wallace, *Calvin's Doctrine*, 114.

31. See pages 13f above.

with the Roman Catholics, the humanists, and those whom he calls the fanatics in mind. We shall study each of these groups separately.

BIBLICAL AUTHORITY AND THE ROMAN CHURCH

Roman theologians charged that the Evangelicals' doctrine was "doubtful and uncertain."[32] This charge carried both theological and psychological significance, and one can see in it Rome's attempts to keep ordinary believers away from evangelical doctrine. Yet we have shown that in his discussion of faith, Calvin reversed this charge by pointing out the uncertainty of the Roman Catholic position. We will see this same reversal as we study his doctrine of Scripture and its authority. Calvin titled Chapter vii, "Scripture Must Be Confirmed by the Witness of the Spirit. Thus May Its Authority Be Established as Certain; and It is a Wicked Falsehood that Its Credibility Depends on the Judgment of the Church." It is obvious that Calvin is here discussing the question of authority in opposition to the teaching of the Roman Catholic Church. He discusses the issue in two steps. First he deals with the authority of Scripture in its objective aspect. This aspect is found in the first three sections of the chapter. Then he addresses the subjective side of the problem in the fourth and fifth sections.[33]

To use Calvin's terminology, the objective aspect concerns the issue of credibility, while the subjective aspect speaks to the problem of certainty. The concept of certainty for Calvin is always an experience of faith that stems from the sealing of the heart by the Holy Spirit. It has an objective foundation yet it is a subjective experience. Faith does not regard something that is "out there"; rather it involves the whole being of the individual, for it is an existential certainty. Speaking of Scripture in its objective reality, Calvin addresses the Roman Church in this manner: "When that which is set forth is acknowledged to be the Word of God, there is no one so deplorably insolent—unless devoid also both of common sense and of humanity itself—as to dare impugn the credibility of Him who speaks."[34]

---

32. See pages 120f above.

33. A similar view is expressed by Krusche, *Das Wirken*, 204ff. The present writer has arrived at his conclusions independently and develops them differently. Cf. also Murray, *Calvin on Scripture and Divine Sovereignty*, 44ff.

34. *Inst.*, I, vii, 1 (O. S. III, 65, 8–11).

Calvin begins with a belief which he and the Roman Church share and have in common. He then argues against their position, showing its inconsistency and absurdity. For if they say that Scripture in itself is the word of God, then they should not make its objective authority depend on the decrees of the church, although this is precisely what they wanted to do. Calvin says:

> But a most pernicious error widely prevails that Scripture has only so much weight as is conceded to it by the consent of the Church. As if the eternal and inviolable truth of God depended upon the decision of men! For they mock the Holy Spirit when they ask: who can convince us that these writings came from God? Who can assure us that Scripture has come down whole and intact even to our very day? . . . What reverence is due Scripture and what books ought to be reckoned within its canon depend, they say, upon the determination of the Church. Thus these sacrilegious men, wishing to impose an unbridled tyranny under the cover of the Church, do not care with what absurdities they ensnare themselves and others, provided they can force this one idea upon the simple-minded that the church has authority in all things.[35]

It should be clear that Calvin is dealing here with the problem of authority in its objective aspect. He is considering Scripture in itself, in its credibility. This objective dimension is very important, for it provides the foundation for the subjective aspect of the problem. Accordingly, he goes on to say: "To what mockeries of the impious is our faith subjected, into what suspicion has it fallen among all men, if we believe that it has a precarious authority dependent solely upon the good pleasure of men."[36]

Here Calvin tries to show that the church cannot be the firm objective foundation for the authority of Scripture. If this were the case then humanity would not subjectively experience the certainty that can be established on none other than God. "The foundation of faith would be frail and unsteady, if it rested on human wisdom."[37] Having stated his position, he then turns to the arguments that Rome had used against the Evangelicals. Rome had claimed that the church's authority is above Scripture and appealed to Augustine to support their views. Answering

---

35. Ibid. (65, 19–66, 8).
36. Ibid. (66, 12–15).
37. *Com*. Eph 1:13 (C. O. LI, 153).

their challenge Calvin contends that the church itself is grounded on Scripture.

> Such wranglers are neatly refuted by just one word of the apostle. He testifies that the church is "built upon the foundation of the prophets and apostles" (Eph 2:20). If the teaching of the prophets and apostles is the foundation, this must have had authority before the church began to exist.[38]

As for the canon, he goes on to say:

> Groundless, too, is their subtle objection that ... the writings to be attributed to the prophets and apostles ... remain in doubt until decided by the Church. For if the Christian church was from the beginning founded upon the writings of the prophets and the preaching of the apostles, wherever this doctrine is found, the acceptance of it—without which the church itself would never have existed—must certainly have preceded the church.[39]

Having made his case, Calvin comes to the conclusion that

> It is utterly vain, then, to pretend that the power of judging Scripture so lies with the church that its certainty depends upon churchly assent. Thus, while the church receives and gives its seal of approval to the Scriptures, it does not thereby render authentic what is otherwise doubtful or controversial. But because the church recognizes Scripture to be the truth of its own God, as a pious duty it unhesitatingly venerates Scripture.[40]

The same thought is found in Calvin's remarks on *The True Method of Giving Peace to Christendom and Reforming the Church* when he says:

> That it is the proper office of the Church to distinguish genuine from spurious Scripture, I deny not, and for this reason, that the Church obediently embraces whatever is of God. The sheep hear the voice of the shepherd, and will not listen to the voice of strangers. But to submit the sound oracles of God to the Church, that they may obtain a kind of precarious authority among men, is blasphemous impiety. The Church is, as Paul declares, founded on the doctrine of Apostles and Prophets; but these men

---

38. *Inst.*, I, vii, 2 (O. S. III, 66, 16–20).
39. Ibid. (66, 21–27).
40. Ibid. (66, 27–67, 2).

speak as if they imagined that the mother owed her birth to the daughter.[41]

This is the role which Calvin assigned to the church in connection with the canon. Thus he continues his answer to the Roman challenge saying:

> As to their question—How can we be assured that this has sprung from God unless we have recourse to the decree of the church?—it is as if someone asked: Whence will we learn to distinguish light from darkness, white from black, sweet from bitter? Indeed, Scripture exhibits fully as clear evidence of its own truth as white and black things do of their color, or sweet and bitter things do of their taste.[42]

Calvin has made no mention up to this point of the inner testimony of the Holy Spirit, which relates to the subjective side of the question that he has not yet considered. We should remember that in his discussion of the objective authority of the Scripture and its relationship to the authority of the church, Calvin is not trying to make the inner witness of the Holy Spirit take the place of the church.[43] These are different aspects of the discussion that should not be confused.

Calvin's remarks in the *Institutes* regarding the biblical canon are in harmony with his teaching in the *Commentaries*. In the *Arguments* for the different books of the Bible on which he commented, nowhere does Calvin appeal to the inner testimony of the Holy Spirit as the ground for establishing the canonicity of any book.[44] Rather, criticisms and objections are always met on the merits of the individual book.[45] Thus in the first three sections of Chapter vii Calvin is saying that the word does not derive its authority from the church but rather Scripture has authority over the church. Calvin expressed this same thought in Book IV of the *Institutes*: "Our opponents locate the authority of the church outside God's Word; but we insist that it be attached to the Word, and do not al-

---

41. Calvin, *Tracts and Treatises*, III, 267.
42. *Inst.*, I, vii, 2 (O. S. III, 67, 2–7).
43. Krusche, *Das Wirken*, 206.
44. See page 132 below.
45. Dowey, *Knowledge of God* (1994), 120. Cf. Hodge, *Witness of the Holy Spirit*, 71; Warfield, *Calvin and Calvinism*, 90ff.

low it to be separated from it."⁴⁶ Calvin believed that the church should be subject to the word:

> What wonder if Christ's bride and pupil be subject to her Spouse and Teacher, so that she pays constant and careful attention to his words! For this is the arrangement of a well-governed house, that the wife obey the husband's authority. This is the plan of a well-ordered school, that there the teaching of the schoolmaster alone be heard. For this reason, the church should not be wise of itself, should not devise anything of itself but should set the limit of its own wisdom where Christ has made an end of speaking.⁴⁷

This then is the relationship that exists between Scripture and the church as Calvin sees it. Accordingly, he says to Cardinal Sadoleto, "The Spirit goes before the Church, to enlighten her in understanding the Word, while the Word itself is like the Lydian Stone, by which she tests all doctrines."⁴⁸

The Roman *Church appealed to Augustine to support their teaching* in response to Calvin's argument. *To this Calvin replies, "Indeed, I know that statement of Augustine is commonly referred to, that he would not believe the gospel if the authority of the church did not move him to do so."*⁴⁹ *After discussing Augustine's words in context Calvin concludes that*

> The holy man's intention was not to make the faith that we hold in Scripture dependent upon the assent or judgment of the church.... He avers, the authority of the church is an introduction through which we are prepared for faith in the gospel.... It never occurs to him to teach that the authority which we ascribe to Scripture depends upon the definition or decree of men.⁵⁰

To summarize: we can see that the Roman Catholics planned to strike at the very foundations of the Reformation. For this reason they charged the evangelical doctrine with being uncertain and doubtful. They even contended that Scripture, on which the Evangelicals so confidently established themselves, would be doubtful and uncertain unless it were rendered authoritative by the church. Thus Rome attached the question of certainty to the objective aspect of authority.

46. *Inst.*, IV, viii, 13 (O. S. V, 146, 29–31).
47. Ibid. (146, 31–147, 6).
48. Calvin, *Tracts and Treatises*, I, 37 (O. S. I, 465ff.).
49. *Inst.*, I, vii, 3 (O. S. III, 67, 8–10).
50. Ibid. (68, 4–6; 18ff.).

In answering this charge, Calvin asserted that the objective question of the nature of Scripture itself should not be considered a question of certainty but rather of credibility. Further, he stated that because the Roman church acknowledged Scripture as the word of God its theologians should then admit that it does not need authentication. For God alone is fit witness of himself in his word. Scripture is self-authenticating. Continuing to deal with the issue on the objective level, Calvin points out that in its zeal to establish the certainty of the Scriptures, the Roman church placed the certainty of believers on shaky grounds. Instead of deriving the credibility of Scripture "from the fact that God in person speaks in it,"[51] Roman theologians derive it from the church, which is a human institution. Therefore, says Calvin, "If this is so, what will happen to miserable consciences seeking firm assurance of eternal life if all promises of it consist in and depend solely upon the judgment of men?"[52]

Having established this point, Calvin stated that the question of certainty posed by Rome should be seen as subjective. Thus, instead of making God's truth doubtful until authenticated by the church, as Rome claimed, Calvin believed that it is the believer's faith that can be either doubtful and unsure *or firm and certain. Now we can understand why Calvin contrasts what he calls the "fleeting speculations" of the Schoolmen with the firm and certain faith at which he is aiming.*

This concept provides insight into Calvin's doctrine of the ordained ministry as well as his doctrine of the church. Calvin does not offer any grounds for the objective authority of Scripture other than the fact that it is God's word. He expects the ministers of the church to preach it as such without trying to support it with any proofs. For, as long as the word is "out there," it has no certainty in the hearts of people. Therefore, preachers and teachers should claim the authority of God in their use of Scripture and expect him to generate certainty in the hearts of believers.

> Thus, the highest proof of Scripture derives in general from the fact that God in person speaks in it. The prophets and apostles do not boast either of their keenness or of anything that obtains credit for them as they speak, nor do they dwell upon rational

---

51. *Inst.*, I, vii, 4 (O. S. III, 68, 30ff.).
52. *Inst.*, I, vii, 1 (O. S. III, 66, 8–11).

proofs. Rather they bring forward God's holy name, that by it the whole world may be brought into obedience to him.[53]

Thus we can see that Calvin does not suggest that the inner witness of the Holy Spirit is given as an objective ground by which a nonbeliever comes to certainty about Scripture. Instead, an unbeliever must first be illumined by the Holy Spirit before arriving at this certainty. Moreover, it is not the inner witness of the Spirit but rather the authority of the church that serves as an introduction to faith. Calvin is therefore in agreement with Augustine:

> *Those* who have not yet been illumined by the Spirit of God are rendered teachable by reverence for the church, so that they may persevere in learning faith in Christ from the gospel. Thus . . . the authority of the church is an introduction through which we are prepared for faith in the gospel.[54]

Here we find ourselves moving from the objective side of the authority of Scripture to the subjective aspect; from the area of credibility to that of certainty. Mindful of the fact that these two sides of the problem should not be confused,[55] we shall now consider their relationship. The following passage is helpful in this connection.

> For as God alone is a fit witness of himself in his Word, so also the Word will not find acceptance [*fidem*[56]] in men's hearts before it is sealed by the inward testimony of the Spirit. The same Spirit, therefore, who has spoken through the mouths of the prophets, must penetrate into our hearts to persuade us that they faithfully proclaimed what had been divinely commanded. Isaiah very aptly expresses this connection in these words: 'My Spirit which is in you, and the words that I have put in your mouth, and the mouths of your offspring, shall never fail' (Isa 59:21).[57]

We have begun to see that between objective credibility and subjective certainty lies the authority of the church, which introduces people

---

53. *Inst.*, I, vii, 4 (O. S. III, 68, 30–69, 4).

54. *Inst.*, I, vii, 3 (O. S. III, 68, 7–10).

55. Regarding this point Krusche says, "*Beachtet man diese Distinktion nicht, so kommt man mit der Interpretation Calvin's in Teufels Küche!*" Krusche, *Das Wirken*, 207, n. 428.

56. The Latin term is supplied by the present writer as a reminder that the English translation "acceptance" obscures Calvin's intention. Cf. page 000, n 27 above.

57. *Inst.*, I, vii, 4 (O. S. III, 70, 2–11).

Word and Spirit: Sealing of the Heart 133

to faith through its preaching ministry. This point becomes clear as we supplement this passage with another:

> We see how God, who could in a moment perfect his own, nevertheless desires them to grow up into manhood solely under the education of the church. We see the way set for it: the preaching of the heavenly doctrine has been enjoined upon the pastors. We see that all are brought under the same regulation, that with a gentle and teachable spirit they may allow themselves to be governed by teachers appointed to this function. Isaiah had long before distinguished Christ's Kingdom by this mark: 'My Spirit which is upon you, and my words which I have put in your mouth, shall never depart out of your mouth, or out of the mouth of your children . . . ' (Isa 59:21). From this it follows that all those who spurn the spiritual food, divinely extended to them through the hand of the church, deserve to perish in famine and hunger. God breathes faith into us only by the instrument of his gospel . . . . Likewise, the power to save rests with God (Rom 1:16); but . . . he displays and unfolds it in the preaching of the gospel.[58]

We should also remember, however, that the authority of the church and teachableness on the part of human beings cannot guarantee that Scripture is experienced as certain. For the illumination of the Holy Spirit must take place before the heart can be sealed and Scripture obtain full faith. Calvin says:

> Some good folk are annoyed that a clear proof is not ready at hand when the impious, unpunished, murmur against God's Word. As if the Spirit were not called both seal and guarantee (2 Cor 1:22) for confirming the faith of the godly; because until he illumines their minds, they ever waver among many doubts.[59]

Now we can see more clearly the relationship between the authority of Scripture and the two aspects of faith that correspond to the two operations of the Holy Spirit: the illumination of the mind and the sealing of the heart. Unless these take place, Scripture would not be certain, and "the Word will be of doubtful and weak authority, or rather of none."[60] "Therefore," Calvin tells us, "our mind must be otherwise illumined

---

58. *Inst.*, IV, i, 5 (O. S. v, 8, 6–21).

59. *Inst.*, I, vii, 4(O. S. III, 70, 11–15). Also 3: "Those who have not yet been illumined by the Spirit of God are rendered teachable by reverence for the church. . . ." (O. S. III, 68, 7ff.).

60. *Inst.*, III, ii, 6 (O. S. IV, 15, 14ff.).

and our heart strengthened, that the Word of God may obtain full faith among us."[61]

Thus Calvin never conceived of a certainty of Scripture that would precede faith. Nor did he teach a certainty of Scripture that is separate from a certainty of salvation.[62] For this reason his language in Book I, Chapters vii–ix, is identical with that in III, ii.[63] Regarding the certainty of Scripture he says:

> Illumined by his power, we believe neither by our own nor by anyone else's judgment that Scripture is from God; but above human judgment we affirm with utter certainty ... that it has flowed to us from the very mouth of God by the ministry of men ....
>
> Such, then, is a conviction that requires no reasons; such, a knowledge with which the best reason agrees—in which the mind truly reposes more securely and constantly than in any reasons; such, finally, a feeling that can be born only of heavenly revelation. I speak of nothing other than what each believer experience within himself—though my words fall far beneath a just explanation of the matter.[64]

In discussing the certainty of faith he says:

> When we call faith 'knowledge' we do not mean comprehension of the sort that is commonly concerned with those things which fall under human sense perception. For faith is so far above sense that man's mind has to go beyond and rise above itself in order to attain it. Even where the mind has attained, it does not comprehend what it feels. But while it is persuaded of what it does not grasp, by the very certainty of its persuasion it understands more than if it perceived anything human by its own capacity .... This kind of knowledge is far loftier than all understanding.[65]

Again, concerning the certainty of Scripture he says: "We seek no proofs.... This we do, not as persons accustomed to seize upon some unknown thing, which, under closer scrutiny, displeases them, but fully

---

61. *Inst.*, III, ii, 7 (O. S. IV, 16, 29–31).

62. Krusche, *Das Wirken*, 217. Cf. Runia, *Karl Barth's Doctrine of Holy Scripture*, 148ff.; Dorner, *History of Protestant Theology*, I, 389ff.

63. Cf. Dowey, *Knowledge of God* (1994), 183ff.; and Warfield, *Calvin and Calvinism*, 71ff.

64. *Inst.*, I, vii, 5 (O. S. III, 70, 22–27; 71, 8–14).

65. *Inst.*, III, ii, 14 (O. S. IV, 24, 34–25, 5).

conscious that we hold the unassailable truth!"[66] Once more we find the same language expressing the certainty of salvation:

> We add the words 'sure and firm' in order to express a more solid constancy of persuasion. For, as faith is not content with a doubtful and changeable opinion, so is it not content with an obscure and confused conception; but requires full and fixed certainty, such as men are wont to have from things experienced and proved.[67]

Concluding his discussion of the certainty of Scripture, Calvin clearly demonstrates that he considers this subject to be part of the whole certainty of faith when he says: "I now refrain from saying more, since I shall have opportunity to discuss this matter elsewhere. Let us, then, know that the only true faith is that which the Spirit of God seals in our hearts."[68] Or again, when Calvin comments on the words, "In whom also, after that ye believed" (Eph 1:13), says:

> Having maintained that the gospel is certain, he now comes to the proof. And what higher surety can be found than the Holy Spirit? 'Having denominated the gospel *the word of truth*, I will not prove it by the authority of men; for you have the testimony of the Spirit of God himself, who seals the truth of it in your hearts.' This elegant comparison is taken from Seals, which among men have the effect of removing doubt. Seals give validity . . . . A seal distinguishes what is true and certain, from what is false and spurious. This office the apostle ascribes to the Holy Spirit . . . . Our minds never become so firmly established in the truth of God . . . until we have been confirmed in it by the Holy Spirit. The true conviction which believers have of the word of God, of their own salvation, and of religion in general, does not spring from the judgment of the flesh, or from human and philosophical arguments, but from the sealing of the Spirit, who imparts to their consciences such certainty as to remove all doubt.[69]

Calvin has set forth a relationship between the inner testimony of the Holy Spirit and the sealing of the hearts of the believers, which gives them certainty about the word of God, their own salvation, and religion

---

66. *Inst.*, I, vii, 5 (O. S. III, 70, 27, 33).
67. *Inst.*, III, ii, 15 (O. S. IV, 25, 24, 28).
68. *Inst.*, I, vii, 5 (O. S. III, 71, 14–17).
69. *Com.* Eph 1:13.

in general. This understanding of Calvin can be contrasted with the opinion of Hendry, who says:

> The position [of Calvin] is not that men, finding the *message* of Scripture confirmed in their hearts by the testimony of the Holy Spirit, are led to a conviction of its divine origin and authority; but first they receive by the Spirit certification of the authority of Scripture, and then they experience the power of its message.[70]

As we have shown, however, Calvin does not speak of a prior certification of Scripture by the inner witness of the Holy Spirit before experiencing the power of its message. Rather, in order for the word to obtain full faith, full authority and certainty, "our mind must be otherwise illumined and our heart strengthened"[71] Thus Calvin would not consider it possible for the word to be firm and have authority in a sin-darkened mind unless that mind is first illumined by the Holy Spirit. This is the point that he wished to make to his contemporaries when they raised the issue of certainty.

> Accordingly, we need not wonder if there are many who doubt as to the Author of the Scripture; for, although the majesty of God is displayed in it, yet none but those who have been enlightened by the Holy Spirit have eyes to perceive what ought, indeed, to have been visible to all, and yet is visible to the elect alone.[72]

George correctly expresses Calvin's mind in this way:

---

70. Hendry, *Holy Spirit in Christian Theology*, 76. A similar view is expressed by Warfield when he points out that from the logical point of view "Calvin would certainly have said that our faith in Christ presupposes faith in the Scriptures, rather than that we believe in the Scriptures for Christ's sake." Warfield, *Calvin and Calvinism*, 106ff. He goes on to say, however, "But if our minds are set on chronological sequence, the response to the question which is raised is more doubtful." Ibid.

Hodge points out that the "inner witness of the Holy Spirit" gives assurance and certainty to the believers, yet distinguishes rather sharply between assurance of salvation and assurance about the Bible. He says, "The testimony of the Holy Spirit to the Bible . . . is not to be identified with the gift to the believer of assurance of faith." Hodge, *Witness of the Holy Spirit*, 71. In this connection Preiss says, "On the part of Calvin the inner testimony of the Holy Spirit occurred at two points: it made the believer know, on the one hand, the authority of Scripture, and on the other hand the certainty of his own personal salvation. Calvin still bound these two points together, although with a bond sometimes a little loose." Preiss, "Inner Witness of the Holy Spirit," 263.

71. *Inst.*, III, ii, 7 (O. S. IV, 16, 29–31).

72. *Com.* 2 Tim 3: 16 (C. O. III, 383).

How do we know that the Bible is the Word of God? For Calvin there was no independent epistemological platform on which believers could stand and objectively decide for or against the Bible. How could one know that the Bible was the Word of God? Such assurance could only come if the same Spirit who inspired the prophets and apostles was present to *illuminate* one's mind and *confirm* within one the truth which had been revealed.[73]

For this reason Calvin taught that Scripture in its totality cannot be accepted nor can it be certain for us unless we first arrive at the freely given promise.

We have now progressed far enough to see that Calvin does not separate what were later called the material and formal principles of the Reformation nor does he introduce any discrepancy between the two, as Dowey claims.[74] Rather, Calvin speaks in the same breath of the certainty of the word and of our salvation because he cannot conceive of a distinction between faith in the word and faith in Christ.[75] Thus in emphasizing that "there is a permanent relationship between faith and the Word,"[76] he says, "This . . . is the true knowledge of Christ, if we receive him as he is offered by the Father: namely, clothed with his gospel."[77] Explaining this assertion he says, "Yet I do not so restrict faith to the gospel without confessing that what sufficed for building it up had been handed down by Moses and the Prophets."[78] Then he goes on to say, "The same Word is the basis whereby faith is supported and sustained; if it turns away from the Word, it falls. Therefore, take away the Word and no faith will remain."[79] This principle of "Christ clothed with his gospel"[80] is very important because it shows how the two principles of the Reformation are joined together: *sola Scriptura* and *sola fide*. Even in Calvin's time, however, this unity of Christ clothed with his gospel was fiercely debated. In exploring this debate it is necessary to briefly restate

---

73. George, *Theology of the Reformers*, 196; italics added.
74. Dowey, *Knowledge of God*, 161.
75. Krusche, *Das Wirken*, 217ff.
76. *Inst.*, III, ii, 6 (O. S. IV, 14, 7–9).
77. Ibid. (13, 15ff.).
78. Ibid. (13, 22–25).
79. Ibid. (14, 26–28).
80. Cf. Torrance, *School of Faith*, lxxxiii.

the role that Calvin intended for the doctrine of the *testimonium Spiritus Sancti internum* as well as the ways in which others used his concepts.

To recapitulate: Calvin considered faith to consist of both illumination and sealing, with the inner testimony of the Holy Spirit always operating in connection with the latter. This distinction must be kept in mind.[81] Furthermore, we have noted that Calvin distinguished between the objective and subjective aspects of the authority of Scripture. The objective aspect is the basis and the foundation. Scripture is authoritative in itself as the word of God and thus is self-authenticated. Accordingly, the objective authority of Scripture is not dependent on the subjective faith and certainty of the believer[82] nor is it founded on the inner testimony of the Holy Spirit. Subjectively, however, the authority of Scripture cannot be established as certain without this testimony. Between the objective credibility and the subjective certainty of Scripture lie both the teaching ministry of the church and the illumination and sealing of the Holy Spirit.

If we contrast Calvin's approach with that of the Roman Catholic Church we again notice that there is both an objective and a subjective aspect of Scripture's authority. Rome makes the objective authority of Scripture dependent on the church;[83] subjectively speaking, Scripture becomes authoritative through the believer's assent. The reader should remember that in Calvin's dispute with the Roman Church, he is not trying to prove that Scripture is authoritative or that it is the word of God. This doctrine was accepted without question by both parties. The question that Roman theologians raised concerned the objective ground

---

81. This is to be compared with Dowey's view when he says, "'Illumination' seems to be a more basic and comprehensive category of the Spirit's work than the 'testimony.' The latter . . . is the 'smaller' term. When seen in the context of Calvin's more general doctrine, the 'internal testimony' appears to be used as a technical term which is particularly concerned with the accrediting of Scripture. 'Illumination' occurs a few times in the doctrine of Scripture, but is greatly outnumbered and outweighed by the other . . . . No great importance can be attached to the terms themselves, since the function signified is largely the same, the use is not entirely consistent, and Calvin does not give any description of the relation . . . that would indicate that he conceived them differently. Dowey, *Knowledge of God* (1994), 173ff. Émile Doumergue expresses a similar view: «La doctrine sur le témoignage du Saint-Esprit n'est pas pour Calvin une doctrine spéciale, se rapportant exclusivement a l'autorité des Écritures. Loin de là!» Doumergue, *Jean Calvin*, IV, 68.

82. Krusche, *Das Wirken*, 213.

83. *Inst.*, I, vii, 1-3, *passim*.

of the authority of Scripture.[84] We have seen that Calvin notes the absurdity of the Roman position, affirming that "God alone is a fit witness of himself in his Word."[85] Calvin's entire concern here is to show that the authority which we ascribe to Scripture does not depend on human definitions or decrees.[86] The certainty of the godly should rest on a far different foundation.[87] The "credibility of doctrine is not established until we are persuaded beyond doubt that God is its Author. Thus, the highest proof of Scripture derives in general from the fact that God in person speaks in it."[88] All these quotes concern the objective aspect of authority and show that Scripture does not require the judgment of human beings or church authority to authenticate it. Bloesch expresses this idea very aptly as follows:

> Against their Catholic opponents the Reformers contended that scripture authenticates itself and interprets itself. It gains its credence neither from the church nor from reason but from the One to whom it testifies and who is himself its living center, Jesus Christ.[89]

When we come to the subjective side of the issue, we notice another agreement between the Roman theologians and Calvin. As we have seen before, both sides agreed that Scripture in its totality is the "common object of faith."[90] Yet the question that arises here is concerning the way in which the credibility of Scripture comes to be certainty. In other words the question is: How does Scripture become a living, authoritative reality in the life of the believer? Rome gave a clear answer to this question: assent to the church. Against this position Calvin taught that mere assent as presented by the Schoolmen cannot give believers a firm and certain faith, nor can it establish the certainty of the authority of Scripture in their lives. The reason for this position is that assent defined in that manner does not take the sinfulness of human beings seriously.

---

84. Reid, *Authority of Scripture*, 32.
85. *Inst.*, I, vii, 4 (O. S. III, 70, 2ff.).
86. *Inst.*, I, vii, 3 (O. S. III, 68, 18ff.).
87. Ibid. (68, 10–12).
88. *Inst.*, I, vii, 4 (O. S. III, 68, 28–69, 1).
89. Bloesch, *Essentials of Evangelical Theology*, I, 59.
90. *Inst.*, III, ii, 30 (O. S. IV, 39, 37ff.).

If we keep in mind that Calvin used the terms "word of God," "God's truth," and "Scripture in its totality" interchangeably,[91] we shall be able to grasp his point in the following passage:

> This bare and external proof of the Word of God should have been amply sufficient to engender faith, did not our blindness and perversity prevent it. But our mind has such an inclination to vanity that it can never cleave fast to the truth of God; and it has such a dullness that it is always blind to the light of God's truth. Accordingly, without the illumination of the Holy Spirit, the Word can do nothing . . . . And it will not be enough for the mind to be illumined by the Spirit of God unless the heart is also strengthened and supported by his power. In this matter the Schoolmen go completely astray, who in considering faith identify it with a bare and simple assent arising out of knowledge, and leave out confidence and assurance of heart. In both ways, therefore, faith is a singular gift of God, both in that the mind of man is purged so as to be able to taste the truth of God and in that his heart is established therein.[92]

Thus Calvin rejects assent, not because of the *content* of the knowledge it offers, but rather because it leads to idle speculations and to insubstantial knowledge of God and his word. Over against this approach he maintains that a firm and certain knowledge of God must be established on knowledge of Christ; and that the word of God in its totality will not be certain nor have its full authority until one arrives at the freely given promise in Christ. We have found the same argument in his discussion of the twofold knowledge.

Now when our minds are illumined and our hearts are sealed, we receive the Spirit of adoption who gives us confidence and assurance and thus makes the Word as well as our salvation certain.[93] It is at this stage that the *testimonium Spiritus Sancti internum* is experienced and it is only then that the authority of Scripture is "established as certain"[94]

---

91. *Inst.*, I, vii, 1; III, ii, 6; 7; 8; 30 *passim*; *Com.* John 3:33 (C. O. XLVII, 73ff.). In this connection Taylor says, "God, asserted Calvin confidently, imprinted his image in Scripture, where he intends that we meet him face to face. And because God himself is in his Word, the preaching of it becomes the truth. In saying this without so much as pausing to explain, Calvin indicates the extent to which he considers Word, Scripture and truth interchangeable." Taylor, "John Calvin the Teacher," 69.

92. *Inst.*, III, ii, 33 (O. S. IV, 44, 5–17).

93. *Inst.*, III, ii, 7 (O. S. IV, 16, 29–31); *Com.* Eph 1: 13 (C. O. LI, 153).

94. *Inst.*, I, vii, chapter title.

in the life of the believer. Calvin considers this understanding of assent to be the scriptural view, as over against the Scholastic view, which he found to be nothing but vain speculation. He says:

> If we possessed only this one reason, it would have been sufficient to end the dispute: that very assent itself . . . is more of the heart than of the brain, and more of the disposition than of the understanding. For this reason, it is called 'obedience of faith' (Rom. 1:5), and the Lord prefers no other obedience to it—and justly, since nothing is more precious to him than his truth. To this truth believers set their seal. . . . Since there is no doubt about the matter, we establish in one word that they are speaking foolishly when they say that faith is *formed* when pious inclination is added to assent. For even assent rests upon such pious inclination—at least such assent as is revealed in the Scriptures.[95]

It is essential to remember that Calvin never considers the inner testimony of the Holy Spirit the ground of the objective authority of Scripture. Scripture is authoritative objectively speaking because "God is its Author."[96] Thus it is not the inner testimony of the Holy Spirit that lends credibility to the word, for this would mean that the word in itself is doubtful. As far as Calvin is concerned, this assertion would be as absurd as the Roman position, which makes the church authenticate, as it were, "what is otherwise doubtful or controversial."[97] Thus the inner testimony of the Holy Spirit does not serve the purpose of authenticating Scripture in order that people might accept it; rather, it gives believers who have already accepted the word of God in their hearts certainty and assurance, so that their faith might not waver. "The faithful are doubtless often shaken but are never utterly cast down. In short . . . the godly soul ought to rely on the inward testimony of the Holy Spirit."[98]

It is also important to keep in mind what we have said previously, that between the objective and the subjective sides of the authority of Scripture there is the introductory authority of the church, the preaching ministry, the inward teaching of the Holy Spirit, and the illumination of the mind. These guides can be seen in the following passage:

---

95. *Inst.*, III, ii, 8 (O. S. IV, 17, 23–18, 8).
96. *Inst.*, I, vii, 4 (O. S. III, 8, 29ff.).
97. *Inst.*, I, vii, 2 (O. S. III, 66, 31).
98. *Com.* Rom 8: 31 (C. O. XLIX, 162).

> Those whom the Holy Spirit has inwardly taught truly rest upon Scripture, and . . . Scripture indeed is self-authenticated; hence, it is not right to subject it to proof and reasoning. And the certainty it deserves with us, it attains by the testimony of the Spirit. For even if it wins reverence for itself by its own majesty, it seriously affects us only when it is sealed upon our hearts through the Spirit. Therefore, illumined by his power, we believe neither by our own nor by anyone else's judgment that Scripture is from God; but above human judgment we affirm with utter certainty . . . that it has flowed to us from the very mouth of God by the ministry of men.[99]

Indeed, "when God has effectually called us to faith in Christ it should have as much force with us as if He confirmed His decree concerning our salvation with an engraven seal. For the testimony of the Spirit is nothing but the sealing of our adoption."[100]

Both the Roman theologians and Calvin agreed that Scripture is to be communicated to the faithful through the church. But the difference comes when each tries to answer the question: On whose authority is Scripture to be presented to people so that they might believe? For the Roman teachers, people must accept Scripture on the authority of the church. For Calvin, if the church confesses that Scripture is the word of God, then it would be absurd for it to offer this word on its own authority rather than God's.

> Thus, the highest proof of Scripture derives in general from the fact that God in person speaks in it. The prophets and apostles do not boast either of their keenness or of anything that obtains credit for them as they speak; nor do they dwell upon rational proofs. Rather, they bring forward God's holy name, that by it the whole world may be brought into obedience to him.[101]

This is what Calvin has in mind when he says, "Our opponents locate the authority of the church outside God's Word; but we insist that it be attached to the Word, and do not allow it to be separated from it."[102]

On the subjective level, as we have pointed out repeatedly, Calvin saw faith as taught by the Roman Church to be mere assent. He consid-

---

99. *Inst.*, I, vii, 5 (O. S. III, 70, 16–27).

100. *Com.* John 6: 40 (C. O. XLVII, 147).

101. *Inst.*, I, vii, 4 (O. S. III, 68, 30–69, 4).

102. *Inst.*, IV, viii, 13 (O. S. V, 146, 29–31). Cf. Reply to Sadoleto, *Tracts and Treatises*, I, 37 (O. S. I, 465ff).

ered this definition to be no more than fleeting speculations. He emphasized instead that faith involves illumination of the mind and sealing of the heart. These two parts of faith or two operations of the Holy Spirit must be considered in the order in which Calvin presented them. He never conceived of a heart that can be sealed—that is to say, a heart to which the Holy Spirit gives assurance and confidence unless the mind had already been illumined. Thus as the inner witness of the Holy Spirit seals our hearts, the word of God "obtains full faith among us."[103] For "Scripture must be confirmed by the witness of the Spirit. Thus may its authority be established as certain."[104]

As believers, however, move from the subjective experience of the authority of Scripture to discuss the ground of this authority, Calvin would never allow them to authenticate Scripture nor establish the canon on the basis of their own certainty. Thus Calvin would not base the credibility of Scripture on the inner testimony of the Holy Spirit. Otherwise, the objective truth of God would depend on the subjective experience of the believer. To this misunderstanding Calvin would repeat what he said to the church of Rome: "If this is so, what will happen to miserable consciences seeking firm assurance of eternal life if all promises of it consist in and depend solely upon the judgment of men?"[105]

Calvin does not consider the judgment of the church here to be wrong. All that is being affirmed at this point is the fact that Scripture is the word of God. Thus Calvin does not deny for a moment the role of the church in the formation of the biblical canon. His disagreement with Rome concerns the nature and significance of this role. The Roman Church saw in the formation of the canon an indication that the church has authority over Scripture. Accordingly, they considered its credibility—that is to say, the foundation or ground of its objective authority—to be the church. Thus Scripture must be presented to Christians on the authority of the church in order that they might believe. Calvin strongly opposed this view. In addressing his Roman opponents he said, "To what mockeries of the impious is our faith subjected, into what suspicion has it fallen among men, if we believe that it has a precarious authority dependent solely upon the good pleasure of men!"[106] As far as the credibility of Scripture is con-

---

103. *Inst.*, III, ii, 7 (O. S. IV, 16, 31).
104. *Inst.*, I, vii, chapter title.
105. *Inst.*, I, vii, 1 (O. S. III, 66, 8–11).
106. Ibid. (66, 12–15).

cerned, he stated that the Word of God demands obedience on its own authority rather than on the authority of the church.

We have pointed out that Calvin does not deny the role of the church in the formation of the canon. He interprets this role, however, in terms of acknowledgment rather than accreditation. Consequently he accepts the biblical canon as he finds it and does not think that this acceptance weakens his position at all. To cite one example, in discussing the questionable passage of John 8: 1–11, he says:[107]

> It is quite clear that this story was unknown to the ancient Greek Churches. Hence some conjecture that it was inserted from another place. But it has always been received by the Latin Churches and is found in many Greek manuscripts, and contains nothing unworthy of an apostolic Spirit; so there is no reason why we should refuse to make use of it.[108]

Thus as far as the canon goes, Calvin would expect believers to study it. But he would never allow them as a church or as individuals to claim that the word of God receives objective authority (credibility) on the basis of their judgment. Their entire role is that of acknowledgment rather than authentication. When they present this word, they should proclaim it on the authority of God.

We have also seen, however, that Calvin considered that the church has an important role in the proclamation of the word, with an authority that serves as "an introduction through which we are prepared for faith in the gospel."[109] Moreover, he strongly emphasized the need for docility and teachableness among the laity, whereby they should humbly and obediently listen to the preaching of the word in the church.[110]

> For, among the many excellent gifts with which God has adorned the human race it is a singular privilege that he deigns to consecrate to himself the mouths and tongues of men in order that his voice may resound in them. Let us accordingly not in turn dislike to embrace obediently the doctrine of salvation put forth by his command and by his own mouth.[111]

---

107. Many more examples can be added, such as *Com.* Hebrews, Argument; *Com.* 2 Peter, Argument.
108. *Com.* John 8: 3 (C. O. XLVII, 188).
109. *Inst.*, I, vii, 3 (O. S. II, 68, 9ff,).
110. Cf. Forstman, *Word and Spirit*, 132ff.; MacGregor, *Corpus Christi*, 52.
111. *Inst.*, IV, i, 5 (O. S. V, 9, 11–15).

Calvin then, wants the church to preach the word of God authoritatively. Such authoritativeness, however, does not mean that the church has authority over the word or authenticates it, because it derives its authority from the word. Now, within the context of the church and through the secret and inner work of the Holy Spirit, human beings are brought into a teachable condition,[112] their minds are illumined and their hearts sealed. It is at this stage that the authority of Scripture is established in their hearts as certain by the inner witness of the Holy Spirit and they are also assured of their own salvation.

BIBLICAL AUTHORITY AND HUMANISM

The doctrine of the *testimonium Spiritus Sancti internum* can be seen from a different perspective in the eighth chapter of Book I of the *Institutes*, where Calvin is addressing himself to the challenges of several humanists. Here he is discussing the objective authority of Scripture and its credibility rather than its certainty. Calvin therefore titles this chapter "So Far as Human Reason Goes, Sufficiently Firm Proofs Are at Hand to Establish the Credibility of Scripture." It is obvious that the whole chapter is written from the perspective of human reason. As we read this chapter we notice that Calvin intended it to serve two purposes. On the one hand he is trying to point out to critical humanists that the certainty of faith stemming from the inner witness of the Holy Spirit is different from taking refuge in ignorance.[113] In other words one can be a Christian and at the same time intelligent and well educated. On the other hand he is suggesting that these arguments and proofs can also be helpful to believers as secondary aids to their feebleness.[114] This is the controlling thought of the chapter.

We have mentioned earlier that Calvin makes no separation between the so-called formal and material principles of the Reformation. Now we can see how Calvin is indebted to Hilary of Poitiers, using the

112. Calvin writes regarding his own experience in the preface of his commentary on the Psalms: "First, since I was too obstinately devoted to the superstition of Popery to be easily extricated from so profound an abyss of mire, God by a sudden conversion subdued and brought my mind to a teachable frame, which was more hardened in such matters than might have been expected from one at my early period of life. Having thus received some taste and knowledge of true godliness, I was immediately inflamed with so intense a desire to make progress therein." (C. O. XXXI, 22). ET, xi ff.

113. Krusche, *Das Wirken*, 210.

114. *Inst.*, I, viii, 13 (O. S. III, 81, 27).

fourth-century bishop's principle on the material as well as the formal level. For if God alone is fit witness of himself in his word, this fact explains two features of the *Institutes* that cannot be separated. First, we can understand why the *Institutes* does not contain proofs of the existence of God, since human proofs are not fit witnesses. Second, we can see why Calvin repeatedly teaches that one cannot prove that Scripture is the word of God through disputation.[115] As far as Calvin is concerned, it is only through the inner witness of the Holy Spirit that we can be certain of both our knowledge of God as well as our faith in Scripture. Knowledge of God and Scripture are one and the same for Calvin.

This point becomes clearer when we remember that the doctrine of the *testimonium Spiritus Sancti internum* as related to the authority of Scripture was introduced by Calvin to the theological world in the *Institutes* of 1539, in the same year in which he published his *Commentary on the Epistle to the Romans*. His struggle with the Roman Church on the question of certainty was probably the immediate reason that enabled him to discover this doctrine in the Epistle to the Romans and to express through it the firm faith of the Evangelicals.[116] At the same time, this doctrine was specifically related to the question of biblical authority in the *Institutes*. Preiss has said that in the New Testament the testimony of the Holy Spirit "always testifies in some manner of Jesus Christ and of his work of salvation. Furthermore, if we look for a text which directly sets forth the doctrine on the basis of a formal authority, we shall never find any."[117] Thus we should not expect that Calvin, the biblical theologian par excellence, would conceive of a separate operation of the inner witness of the Holy Spirit to authenticate Scripture. Otherwise he would be establishing the certainty of believers on a twisted interpretation of Scripture.

In the chapter that we are now considering, Calvin deals with the humanists' attack upon Scripture and uses the approach of a humanist scholar who is searching the Scripture as far as human reason goes. We do not need to consider the different proofs that Calvin adduces here, though they might have been impressive in the sixteenth century. Rather, we need to understand the relationship which Calvin perceives between

---

115. *Inst.*, I, vii, 4&5; I, viii, 1 and 13 (O. S. III, 69, 24ff.; 70, 18ff.; 71, 39–72, 1; 81, 17–22).

116. Cf. *Com.* Rom 8:16 (C. O. XLIX, 150).

117. Preiss, "Inner Witness of the Holy Spirit," 264.

Word and Spirit: Sealing of the Heart 147

these proofs and the inner testimony of the Holy Spirit. Doumergue considers the latter to be *la grande prevue*, while the former are *preuves subsidiaires*.[118] Warfield goes still further than Doumergue. Calling these proofs *indicia*, he says:[119]

> It . . . remains . . . to inquire precisely how Calvin conceived the Spirit to operate in bringing the soul to a hearty faith in the Word . . . . Are we to understand him as teaching that the Holy Spirit by His almighty power creates, in the souls of those whom God has set upon to bring to a knowledge of Him an entirely ungrounded faith in the divinity of the Scriptures and the truth of their contents, so that the soul embraces them and their contents with firm confidence as a revelation from God wholly apart from and in the absence of all *indicia* of their divinity or of the truth of their contents?[120]

The difficulty here is in the formulation of the question. Warfield wants the reader to choose between two extremes. A few pages later he correctly points out that for Calvin "the *indicia* are ineffective for the production of a 'sound faith' apart from the . . . testimony of the Spirit."[121] With this thought he goes on to say:

> But what about the *indicia* in connection with the testimony of the Spirit? It would seem to be evident that, on Calvin's ground, they would have their full part to play here, and that we must say that, when the soul is renewed by the Holy Spirit to a sense for the divinity of Scripture, it is through the *indicia* of that divinity that it is brought into its proper confidence in the divinity of Scripture.[122]

We see then that Warfield realizes that he cannot find enough support in Calvin's writings for his thesis. Accordingly he says, "In treating of the *indicia*, Calvin does not, however, declare this in so many words. . . . Of their part in forming faith under the operation of the testimony of the Spirit he does not appear explicitly to speak."[123] Yet this does not stop Warfield from concluding:

118. Doumergue, *Jean Calvin*, 60–62.
119. Warfield, *Calvin and Calvinism*, 84ff.
120. Ibid., 84.
121. Ibid., 87.
122. Ibid.
123. Ibid., 87ff.

> Nevertheless, there are not lacking convincing hints that there was lying in his mind all the time the implicit understanding that it is through these *indicia* of the divinity of Scripture that the soul, under the operation of the testimony of the Spirit, reaches its sound faith in Scripture, and that he has been withheld from more explicitly stating this only by the warmth of his zeal for the necessity of the testimony of the Spirit.[124]

Thus Warfield ends up formulating for Calvin a doctrine that is contrary to Calvin's own.[125]

There is no doubt that Calvin considered the inner witness of the Holy Spirit to be the only source for the confidence and assurance of believers. For all these proofs in Chapter viii are governed by the criterion "so far as human reason goes." As for the inner witness of the Holy Spirit, Calvin says, "We ought to seek our conviction in a higher place than human reasons, judgments, or conjectures, that is, in the secret testimony of the Spirit."[126] Or again, "the testimony of the Spirit is more excellent than all reason."[127] "Such, then, is a conviction that requires no reasons; such a knowledge with which the best reason agrees—in which the mind truly reposes more securely and constantly than in any reasons."[128] Calvin closes his chapter on the proofs saying:

> There are other reasons, neither few nor weak . . . yet of themselves these are not strong enough to provide a firm faith, until our Heavenly Father, revealing his majesty there, lifts reverence for Scripture beyond the realm of controversy. Therefore Scripture will ultimately suffice for a saving knowledge of God only when its certainty is founded upon the inward persuasion of the Holy Spirit . . . . But those who wish to prove to unbelievers that Scripture is the word of God are acting foolishly, for only by faith can this be known.[129]

The same thought, and indeed Calvin's whole doctrine of the inner witness of the Holy Spirit, is clearly stated in his comments on the words, "But when the Comforter is come (John 15:26)." Here he says:

---

124. Ibid., 89.
125. Dowey, *Knowledge of God* (1994), 115.
126. *Inst.*, I, vii, 4 (O. S. III, 69, 9–11).
127. Ibid. (70, 1ff.).
128. *Inst.*, I, vii, 5 (O. S. III, 71, 8–10).
129. *Inst.*, I, viii, 13 (O. S. III, 81, 17–29).

When Christ has shown the apostles that they must not think less of the Gospel because it has many adversaries, even within the Church itself, He now opposes the testimony of the Spirit to the ungodly fury of those men. And if this supports their consciences, they will never give away. As if he had said, 'The world will indeed rage against you. Some will mock and others will curse your teaching. But none of their attacks will be so violent as to break the firmness of your faith when the Holy Spirit has been given to you to establish you by His testimony.' Indeed, when the world rages on all sides, our one protection is that God's truth, sealed by the Holy Spirit in our hearts, despises all that is in the world. For if it were subject to men's judgment, our faith would be overwhelmed a hundred times a day.

We must therefore carefully note where we should stand among so many turmoils. It is because we have received, not the Spirit of the world, but the Spirit which is of God, that we might know the things which are given to us by God (1 Cor 2:12). This one testimony is powerful to drive away, scatter and overturn whatever the world sets up to obscure or destroy the truth of God. Whoever is endowed with this Spirit is so far from the danger of despairing over the hatred or contempt of the world that he will be victorious over the whole world. Yet we must beware of depending on the good opinion of men; for so long as faith wanders like this, or rather, as soon as it has left God's sanctuary, it must waver miserably. It must therefore be recalled to the inward and secret testimony of the Spirit, which believers know has been given to them from heaven. Apart from this witness men are carried about in all sorts of ways and have no firm resting place anywhere; but wherever He speaks, He frees men's minds from all doubt and fear of deception.[130]

BIBLICAL AUTHORITY AND THE FANATICS

We outlined Calvin's response to Rome's teaching about the authority of Scripture in our discussion of the seventh chapter. We noticed that he considered Scripture, objectively speaking, to be self-authorizing; and that subjectively, believers by faith are given confidence and assurance through the inner witness of the Holy Spirit. In this way, they come to be certain that Scripture is the word of God.

Yet many Evangelicals felt themselves to be at a disadvantage. They wanted decisive arguments to prove to skeptics that Scripture is the word

---

130. *Com.* John 15:26 (C. O. XLVII, 353ff.). Cf. Also *Com.* John 3:33 (C. O. XLVII, 122).

of God. The inner testimony of the Holy Spirit, in spite of all the certainty that it gives to the believers themselves, is by its nature subjective and lacks the tangibility that makes it useful as an argument. Consequently, the Evangelicals were more exposed to challenges from humanists than the Roman Catholics. It is in this connection that Calvin says, "Some good folk are annoyed that a clear proof is not ready at hand when the impious, unpunished, murmur against God's Word."[131] The eighth chapter was intended by Calvin to offer the believers some "secondary aids" to their "feebleness."[132] Yet he reminds them repeatedly that "godliness and peace of mind ought to come first if a man is to understand anything of such great matters."[133]

Now as we turn to the ninth chapter we find Calvin addressing himself to a problem raised by the so-called fanatics. The question is no longer the certainty of the word but rather the certainty of the Spirit. The problem arose because the radical Anabaptists so exalted the teaching ministry of the Spirit that they despised the Scriptures.[134] Arguing against them, Calvin poses the following challenge:

> I should like to know from them what this spirit is by whose inspiration they are borne up so high that they dare despise the Scriptural doctrine as childish and mean. For if they answer that it is the Spirit of Christ, such assurance is utterly ridiculous. Indeed, they will, I think, agree that the apostles of Christ and other believers of the primitive church were illumined by no other Spirit. Yet no one of them thence learned contempt for God's Word; rather, each was imbued with greater reverence as their writings most splendidly attest.[135]

This is the essence of Calvin's case against the fanatics. Then, referring to Isa 50:21, he demonstrates the unity of word and Spirit. "Under the reign of Christ the new church will have this true and complete happiness: to be ruled no less by the voice of God than by the Spirit."[136] The

---

131. *Inst.*, I, vii, 4 (O. S. III, 70, 11–13).
132. *Inst.*, I, viii, 13 (O. S. III, 81, 27).
133. Ibid. (81, 30–32).
134. *Inst.*, I, ix, 1, *passim*.
135. *Inst.*, I, ix, 1 (O. S. III, 82, 4–12).
136. Ibid. (82 , 17–19).

fanatics are therefore "tearing apart those things which . . . (are) joined together with an inviolable bond."[137]

Moreover, Calvin points out that the Spirit whom the Lord promised to his disciples "has not the task of inventing new and unheard-of revelations, or of forging a new kind of doctrine."[138] He is "One that would speak not from himself but would suggest to and instill into their minds what he had handed on through the Word."[139] Thus he teaches that the certainty of the Spirit must be examined by the word. This precaution is the more necessary since even Satan disguises himself as an angel of light (2 Cor 11:14).[140] This caveat, however, should not be considered a derogation of the Holy Spirit for he is to be recognized "in his own image, which he has stamped upon the Scriptures."[141]

> He is the Author of the Scriptures: he cannot vary and differ from himself. Hence he must ever remain just as he once revealed himself there. This is no affront to him, unless perchance we consider it honorable for him to decline or degenerate from himself.[142]

Thus "the Scripture has primacy not only over the Church but also over religious experience."[143]

The fanatics, however, used Scripture to support their views, citing Paul's words that "the letter kills" (2 Cor 3:6). To this argument Calvin answered:

> It is clear enough that Paul . . . contends against the false apostles, who indeed, in commending the law apart from Christ, were calling the people away from the benefits of the New Testament. . . . The letter . . . is dead, and the law of the Lord slays its readers where it both cut off from Christ's grace (2 Cor 3:6) and, leaving the heart untouched, pounds in the ears alone. But if through the Spirit it is really branded upon hearts, if it shows forth Christ, it is the word of life.[144]

---

137. Ibid. (82, 20ff.).
138. Ibid. (83, 3–5).
139. Ibid. (83, 1–3). Cf. I, vii, 1 (O. S. III, 65, 11–14).
140. *Inst.*, I, ix, 2 (O. S. III, 83, 15–18).
141. Ibid. (83, 32ff.).
142. Ibid. (83, 33–36).
143. Bloesch, *Essentials of Evangelical Theology*, 61.
144. *Inst.*, I, ix, 3 (O. S. III, 83–84, 7).

Calvin then argued that there is no illumination except through the word. For "the written word is the instrument by which the Lord dispenses the illumination of his Spirit to believers."[145]

Calvin considered the separation between word and Spirit to be a problem with both Roman Catholic and Anabaptist theology. Answering Cardinal Sadoleto's letter he says:

> We are assailed by two sects, which seem to differ most widely from each other. For what similitude is there in appearance between the Pope and the Anabaptists? And yet, that you may see that Satan never transforms himself so cunningly, as not in some measure to betray himself, the principal weapon with which they both assail us is the same. For when they boast extravagantly of the Spirit, the tendency certainly is to sink and bury the Word of God.... And you, Sadolet, by stumbling on the very threshold, have paid the penalty of that affront which you offered to the Holy Spirit, when you separated him from the Word. It is no less unreasonable to boast of the Spirit without the Word, than it would be absurd to bring forward the Word itself without the Spirit.[146]

Again in his remarks on the words "He shall glorify me," Calvin remarks that the Roman Catholic Church maintains a similar attitude towards Scripture to that of the Anabaptists.

> Having said goodbye to Christ's law, as if His reign were ended, and He is now nothing at all, they substitute the Spirit in His place.... As soon as the Spirit is severed from Christ's Word the door is open to all sorts of craziness and impostures. Many fanatics have tried a similar method of deception in our own age....
>
> What then is the purpose of the Spirit's teaching? Not to lead us away from the school of Christ, but rather to ratify that voice in which we are commanded to listen to Him; otherwise He would detract from Christ's glory.[147]

We see then that Calvin binds together the certainty of the word with the certainty of the Spirit. In his teaching on Biblical authority, his

---

145. Ibid. (84, 37ff.).
146. Calvin, *Tracts and Treatises*, I, 36ff. (O. S. I, 465ff.).
147. *Com.* John 16:14 (C. O. XLVII, 363); Cf. *Inst.*, IV, viii, 13 *passim*.

doctrine of word and Spirit strikes a balance between subjectivism and objectivism.

> For by a kind of mutual bond the Lord has joined together the certainty of his Word and of his Spirit so that the perfect religion of the word may abide in our minds when the Spirit who causes us to contemplate God's face, shines; and that we in turn may embrace the Spirit with no fear of being deceived when we recognize him in his own image, namely, in the Word.[148]

Yet Calvin was not naïve. He saw the difficulties that this presented. Therefore he says in his remarks on "Prove the spirits" (1 John 4:1):

> But it might be asked where we get this discernment from. Those who reply that God's Word is the rule by which everything that men put forward should be tried, say something but not everything. I grant that doctrines should be tested by God's Word. But unless the Spirit of wisdom is present, there is little or no profit in having God's Word in our hands, for its meaning will not be certain for us. . . . But the Spirit will only guide us to a true discrimination if we subject all our thoughts to the Word.[149]

Calvin insists on the unity of word and Spirit, but he knows that this unity cannot guarantee the certainty of Christian teaching and doctrine. He suggests the following solution:

> There is a twofold trial of doctrine, private and public. The private is that by which each one settles his own faith and safely rests in that doctrine which he knows has come from God. For conscience will never find a safe and quiet harbor elsewhere than in God. The public trial relates to the common consent πολιτεία of the Church. For since there is the danger of fanatical men arising and presumptuously claiming that they are endued with the Spirit of God, it is a necessary remedy that believers shall meet together and seek a way of godly and pure agreement. But the old proverb is true. So many heads, so many viewpoints; and therefore it is a remarkable work of God when he tames our obstinacy and makes us think alike and agree in a pure unity of faith.[150]

---

148. *Inst.*, I, ix, 3 (O. S. III, 84, 14 –20).
149. *Com.* I John 4:1 (C. O. LV, 347ff.).
150. Ibid. (C. O. LV, 348).

5

Word and Spirit: A Corollary

The Doctrine of Inspiration

It should be stated at the outset that Calvin never gives a systematic account of his doctrine of inspiration. Yet there are many scattered references in his writings from which Calvin scholars have constructed differing theories and doctrines. Before discussing any of these, it is worthwhile to consider the reasons that one cannot find a doctrine of inspiration in Calvin; it does not seem to be a "curious omission" on the part of Calvin, as some writers often suppose.[1]

Calvin was chiefly concerned with the controversial questions of his day. He probably spent as much time and energy in combating the Anabaptists as in his battles with Rome.[2] Yet he did not discuss the doctrine of inspiration on either front because he did not disagree with either group of opponents in this regard. Rather this doctrine was commonly assumed by all parties. Thus Calvin's remarks on inspiration are actually nothing but a corollary to his doctrine of word and Spirit, as we have seen in the previous two chapters. Moreover, as we have already shown, Calvin's teaching on the authority of Scripture is not based on a doctrine of inspiration. The authority of Scripture is not established as certain except through the inner testimony of the Holy Spirit.[3] Calvin moves from the authority of Scripture to its inspiration rather than leading from a theory of inspiration to the authority of Scripture. Therefore, the doctrine of inspiration in Calvin's theology acts as a statement of

---

1. Cf. Forstman, *Word and Spirit*, 49.
2. Preiss, "Inner Witness of the Holy Spirit," 260.
3. *Inst.*, I, vii, *passim*.

faith that the believer could be certain of only through the *testimonium Spiritus Sancti internum*. It is now evident why we have left this doctrine of inspiration until the end of our discussion of biblical authority.

THE CASE FOR VERBAL INERRANCY

Calvin's doctrine of inspiration is in some sense a doctrine of *dictation*. Many statements can be produced to support such a contention. Commenting on the words, "All Scripture is given by the inspiration of God," (2 Tim 3:16) Calvin says:

> Our religion is distinguished from all others in that the prophets have spoken not of themselves, but as instruments of the Holy Spirit; and what they have brought to us, they received by heavenly commission . . . . The teaching of the law and the prophets came to us not by the will of man, but as dictated by the Holy Spirit (*Spiritu sancto dictatam*).[4]

The same thought is also found in the *Institutes*, where Calvin says:

> But where it pleased God to raise up a more visible form of the church, he willed to have his Word set down and sealed in writing . . . . This means that they should teach nothing strange or foreign to that doctrine which God included in the law. . . .
>
> There then followed the prophets, through whom God published new oracles which were added to the law—but not so new that they did not flow from the law and hark back to it. . . . But because the Lord was pleased to reveal a clearer and fuller doctrine in order better to satisfy weak consciences, he commanded that the prophecies also be committed to writing and be accounted part of his Word. At the same time, histories were added to these, also the labor of the prophets, but composed under the Holy Spirit's dictation (*dictante Spiritu Sancto*). I include the psalms with the prophecies.[5]

This passage gives us Calvin's fullest statement regarding the formation of the Old Testament, after which he spoke of God's self-revelation in Christ. He then says of Scripture as a whole:

---

4. Haroutunian and Smith, *Calvin: Commentaries*, 84; *Com.* 2 Tim 3:16 (C.O. LII, 383); Latin supplied

5. *Inst.*, IV, viii, 6 (O. S. V, 137, 24–138, 14); Latin supplied.

> Let this be a firm principle: No other word is to be held as the Word of God, and given place as such in the church, than what is contained first in the Law and the Prophets, then in the writings of the apostles; and the only authorized way of teaching in the church is by the prescription and standard of his Word.
>
> From this also we infer that the only thing granted to the apostles was that which the prophets had had of old. They were to expound the ancient Scripture.... Yet they were not to do this except from the Lord, that is, with Christ's Spirit as precursor in a certain measure dictating the words (*verba quodammodo dictante Christi Spiritu*).[6]

Again in a sermon on Deuteronomy Calvin says:

> Let us note that this word Scripture implies that Moses was not at all the author of the Law or Psalms; but that he was only a scribe or secretary under the mouth of God. Thus, just as a secretary will write what is given him, so it is precisely declared here that Moses wrote what he received from God, and not what he fabricated in his own head.[7]

All these are not mere casual references. Calvin is quite explicit in expressing his dictation doctrine of inspiration. Referring to the apostles he says, "This ... is the difference between the apostles and their successors: the former were sure and genuine scribes of the Holy Spirit (*certi et authentici Spiritus Sancti amanuenses*), and their writings are therefore to be considered oracles of God."[8] In all this Calvin is insisting that everything in Scripture must be taken seriously. This insistence is clearly demonstrated in his discussion of the doctrines of providence and predestination. In connection with the first he says, "Our wisdom ought to be nothing else than to embrace with humble teachableness, and at least without finding fault, whatever is taught in Sacred Scripture."[9] Again in his discussion of predestination he remarks:

> Scripture is the school of the Holy Spirit, in which, as nothing is omitted that is both necessary and useful to know, so nothing is taught but what is expedient to know. Therefore, we must guard against depriving believers of anything disclosed about predestina-

---

6. *Inst.*, IV, viii, 8 (O. S. V, 139, 29–140, 6); Latin supplied.
7. Quoted in Reid, *Authority of Scripture*, 34.
8. *Inst.*, IV, viii, 9 (O. S. V, 141, 11–13); Latin supplied
9. *Inst.*, I, xviii, 4 (O. S. III, 227, 27–30).

tion in Scripture, lest we seem either wickedly to defraud them of the blessing of their God or to accuse and scoff at the Holy Spirit for having published what it is in any way profitable to suppress.[10]

The question now is precisely what did Calvin mean by dictation? One could easily surmise that he believes that God dictates the specific words of Scripture. Consider the following: "The words which God dictated to his servant were called the words of Jeremiah; yet, properly speaking, they were not the words of man, for they did not proceed from a mortal man but from the only God."[11] Indeed Dowey says about Calvin: "He incontrovertibly did mean literal dictation in his description of Jeremiah's inspiration." Likewise, "The utter seriousness with which he [Calvin] takes every word of the text is an indication that he believes the revelation to have been given word for word by the spirit."[12] After extensive references to Calvin's writings in support of the dictation theory, Dowey goes on to say:

> To Calvin the theologian an error in Scripture is unthinkable . . . but Calvin the critical scholar recognizes mistakes with a disarming ingeniousness . . . I know of no instance in which Calvin draws any theological conclusions from the existence of error in the text.[13]

In light of all of the above, many scholars have come to the conclusion that Calvin held a verbal inerrancy theory of inspiration.[14]

Other scholars have held variations of this theory. Warfield, for example, suggested that the mode of inspiration is not necessarily dictation, but the result of inspiration is as if it were by dictation.[15] Still others claim a duality in Calvin's thought: infallible verbal inspiration side by side with a christocentric emphasis.[16] This claim is based on the sup-

---

10. *Inst.*, III, 21, 3 (O. S. IV, 372, 1–7).

11. *Com.* Jer 36: 8 (C. O. XXXIX, 121).

12. Dowey, *Knowledge of God* (1994), 99.

13. Ibid., 104.

14. Bauke, *Die Probleme der Theologie Calvins*, 47ff.; Davies, *Problem of Authority in the Continental Reformation*, 114ff.; Hunter, *Teaching of Calvin*, 67ff.; Kantzer, "Calvin and the Holy Scriptures," 137ff.; Moore, "Calvin's Doctrine of Holy Scripture," 49ff.; Murray, *Calvin on Scripture*, 11ff.; Runia, *Karl Barth's Doctrine of Holy Scripture*, 39ff.; Seeberg, *Lehrbuch der Dogmengeschichte* IV, part 2, 566ff.

15. Warfield, *Calvin and Calvinism*, 63.

16. Forstman, *Word and Spirit*, 64f; Gerrish, "Biblical Authority and the Continental

position that Calvin operated with what Forstman called "two distinct epistemologies."[17] We have noted, however, that Calvin's thought is more coherent than has been presented by these writers. The case for verbal inerrancy becomes more plausible in light of his many remarks regarding several of the writers of Scripture. Ezekiel, for example, "put off, as it were, his human infirmities when God intrusted to him the office of instructor."[18] Likewise Daniel's writings are "free . . . from any human delusion or invention."[19] And Calvin says concerning the Apostle Paul, "Now it is the duty of an apostle to make known publicly only what he has received from the Lord, so that he is, directly (as it were, from hand to hand *de manu (quod aiunt) in manum*) responsible for giving out the pure Word to the Church."[20] Again, commenting on the words "As the Holy Spirit says," Calvin remarks "It is useful for us to familiarize ourselves with such expressions, so that we may remember that the words adduced from the books of the prophets are those of God and not of men."[21]

In light of all of these remarks, some scholars have concluded that Calvin taught that "the Holy Spirit was, not simply in a purposeful but in a quite direct and instrumental fashion, the 'author' of the Bible."[22] And that "the expression 'the Holy Spirit says' is synonymous in Calvin for 'the Scripture says.'"[23] More recently Raymond defended the inerrancy of Scripture very strongly.[24] Before we draw any conclusions, however, other aspects must be taken into consideration.

THE CASE AGAINST VERBAL INERRANCY

Doumergue reminds us that many of the terms which Calvin uses, such as *scribe*, *secretary*, and *mouth of God* are figurative.[25] They are similar

Reformation," 349ff.
17. Forstman, *Word and Spirit*, 38.
18. *Com.* Ezek. 1:1 (C.O. XL, 27).
19. *Com.* Dan 10:21 (C. O. XLII, 215).
20. *Com.* 1 Cor 15:3 (C. O. XLIX, 538).
21. *Com.* Heb 3:7 (C. O. LV, 39).
22. Johnson, *Authority in Protestant Theology*, 50.
23. Parker, *Calvin's Doctrine of the Knowledge of God*, 42.
24. Raymond, *Calvin's Doctrine of Holy Scripture*, 57ff.
25. Doumergue, *Jean Calvin*, IV, 73.

to calling Scripture a mirror.[26] Moreover, he points out that the decisive and most characteristic words favoring verbal inspiration disappeared from the French translation of 1560.[27] Doumergue thus concludes that the expressions which Calvin uses "say that the Bible comes not from men, but from God; they do not say *how*."[28] Doumergue also suggests that for Calvin, "the important thing is not the words but the *doctrine*, the *spiritual doctrine*, the *substance*."[29] Pannier, probably influenced by his professor Sabatier, under whom he wrote his dissertation, expresses a view that is similar to Doumergue's. Pannier differentiates between what he calls the contents and the container. One is the message of grace while the other is Scripture.[30] "The container is perhaps of clay, it is the content that is divine."[31] Thus Pannier concludes that there is nothing in Calvin that supports a doctrine of literal inspiration.[32] Fuhrmann agrees with Pannier on this point.[33] Both see Scripture in Calvin to be better defined as *Dei verbum* rather than *Dei verba*.[34] "The diversity of the writers disappears before the unity of the Spirit."[35] Heppe comes to a similar conclusion regarding Calvin's views of Scripture:

> There is no word of a peculiar inspiration of the record. The authority of Scripture then rests not upon the form of its recording, but upon its content, i.e. upon the reality of the revealed facts attested in the writing. Hence God is described not so much as the 'author' of Scripture, as rather the author of the doctrine attested in it, which He Himself has announced to men.[36]

The same opinion was later voiced by Clavier,[37] and a strong case for it has also been made by Reid and McNeill. Reid says:

26. Cf. *Inst.*, III, ii, 6 (O. S. IV, 14, 31ff.).
27. Doumergue, *Jean Calvin*, IV, 73.
28. Ibid., 74.
29. Ibid., 78.
30. Pannier, *Témoignage du Saint-Esprit*, 198; Cf. Sabatier, *Religions of Authority and the Religion of the Spirit*, 155ff.
31. Ibid., 199.
32. Ibid., 200.
33. Fuhrmann, *God-Centered Religion*, 85.
34. Ibid.
35. Pannier, "L'autorité de l'Écriture Sainte," 203.
36. Heppe, *Reformed Dogmatics*, 16.
37. Clavier, *Études sur le Calvinisme*, 27.

> Calvin's emphasis and interest is placed, not on the record as such, but on the content of the record. Nowhere is it affirmed that the record itself is inspired … God is the author, not of Holy Scripture, but of the 'doctrine' contained and transmitted by the Holy Spirit.[38]

Mindful of the many references in Calvin that can give an impression that contradicts his thesis, Reid concludes that "the kind of interest that Calvin manifests in the content of Scripture is not compatible with verbal inspiration."[39]

In his article "The Significance of the Word of God for Calvin," McNeill starts by pointing out that for Calvin it is not that Scripture is God's Word, but rather that God's Word is contained in the Scripture.[40] He then makes a detailed and careful study of passages from the *Institutes* as well as the *Commentaries*, showing that the contexts refer to doctrine and not words. For example, referring to Calvin's comments on 2 Tim 3:16 from which we have quoted earlier, McNeill says:

> It is not said that the Scripture is verbally dictated; the point is simply that its teaching (doctrine) is not of men but of God. And when he adds that we should hold it in that reverence that we owe to God since it has proceeded from Him alone and has nothing belonging to man mingled with it, it is still the doctrine, the content and spiritual message, rather than the mere words of which he is speaking.[41]

It is also worthy of notice that whenever a reference to dictation occurs in the *Institutes*, Ford Battles supplies in his translation of the *Institutes*, "the adverb (dictating) is, however, a deliberate qualification, discounting any doctrine of exact verbal inspiration. The context has reference to teaching, not words merely, showing that Calvin's point is not verbal inerrancy, but the authoritative message of Scripture."[42]

In addition to these arguments it is helpful to remember that Calvin admits the presence of inaccuracies in the Scripture texts and yet these do not seem to present a problem for him. He considers that many textual irregularities resulted from God's accommodation to our capaci-

---

38. Reid, *Authority of Scripture*, 43.
39. Ibid., 44.
40. McNeill, "Significance of the Word of God for Calvin," 133.
41. Ibid., 141ff.
42. *Inst.*, IV, viii, 8, n. 7; also *Inst* IV, viii, 9, n. 9

ties. Mistakes are also attributed to copyists.[43] Indeed Calvin does not betray an interest in the *words* of Scripture as such. For example, noticing a discrepancy between Luke and "Moses," he says: "We ought rather to weigh the miracle which the Spirit commends to us in this place than to stand long about one letter whereby the number is altered."[44] Again, in substituting the name of Abraham for that of Jacob, Calvin says: "This verse must be corrected accordingly."[45]

Likewise, the fact that New Testament writers change the meaning of Old Testament words does not seem to disturb Calvin. At one place he remarks, "To serve the purpose of his argument, Paul has departed not a little from the true meaning of this quotation."[46] Because no value is attached to the words in themselves, Calvin says: "We indeed know that the Apostles in quoting Scripture often used a freer language than the original; for they counted it enough to quote what was suitable to their subject: hence they made no great account of words."[47] From these examples we can see that Calvin's references to copyists' mistakes are not necessarily an indication of his concern for a flawless original text.[48] In a sense, he was doing what any humanist scholar of his time would have done with an ancient text.

That for Calvin the original text does not serve the role which Warfield and others assign to it can also be seen when we compare some of his sermons with what he says in the *Commentaries* about the same passages. Taylor has shown that in his sermons, Calvin uses the text that the people had in their hands (Jerome's Vulgate) and shows no concern for copyists' mistakes or even errors in translation.[49] Moreover, in spite of all the references to dictation that we noted earlier, Calvin did not believe in a so-called mechanical theory of inspiration. Commenting on 2 Pet 1:20, he says:

---

43. Dowey, *Knowledge of God* (1994), 99ff.; Gerrish, "Biblical Authority and Continental Reformation," 354ff.

44. *Com.* Acts 7:14 (C. O. XLVIII, 137); cf. Wallace, *Calvin's Doctrine of the Word and Sacrament*, 111.

45. George, *Theology of the Reformers*, 196.

46. *Com.* Eph 4:8 (C. O. LI, 193).

47. *Com.* Rom. 3;4 (C. O. XLIX, 49); cf. 10:9 (C. O. XLIX, 201); Wallace, *Calvin's Doctrine of the Word and Sacrament*, 112.

48. Cf. Dowey, *Knowledge of God* (1994), 100, 103; Warfield, *Calvin and Calvinism*, 65.

49. Taylor, "John Calvin the Teacher," 149ff.

> The holy men spoke as they were moved by the Spirit of God; that is, they did not babble out fables.... Peter says they were *moved*, not because they were bereft of their own minds (as the Gentiles imagined their prophets to have been during their 'enthusiasm'), but because they did not dare to say anything of their own.[50]

Again, referring to John 11:49 Calvin remarks, "When the Evangelist says that Caiaphas *said not this of himself*, he does not mean that Caiaphas, like a madman or a fanatic, uttered what he did not understand, for he voiced his own opinion."[51]

More recently, in an extended lecture that Neuser gave at the International Congress on Calvin Research concerning "Calvin's Understanding of the Holy Scriptures,"[52] Neuser claims that "It is not the form and structure of doctrine that is given prominence in his [Calvin's] thought, but rather its relation to the salvation of his fellow men."[53] He goes on to claim that "since Calvin holds firm to the idea that doctrine must be related to preaching and limited to that which is 'wholesome' (salvific), so he cannot be counted amongst the representatives of later Orthodoxy."[54] Referring to Calvin's comments on 2 Tim 3:16, Neuser says:

> Whoever seeks to find the teaching of Reformed Orthodoxy in Calvin's doctrine of inspiration will not find it. The Reformers were concerned about the exegesis and proclamation of Scripture, its 'utility' for the recipient of the Biblical message. They understand the inspiration of Scriptures as both functional and personal.[55]

Neuser's most important contribution was his categorization of the forty places where the word *dictation* occurs in Calvin's writings.[56] Using Battles's research, Neuser grouped and discussed these loci, proving that the forty references for *dictare* are used figuratively rather than in the literal sense of dictation.[57]

More recently still, Bloesch in an extended chapter titled "The Primacy of Scripture" writes that "while it is important to underscore

---

50. Haroutunian, *Calvin: Commentaries*, 89; *Com.* 2 Pet 1:20 (C. O. LV, 458).
51. *Com.* John 11:49 (C. O. XLVII, 274).
52. Neuser, ed., *Calvinus Sacrae Scripturae Professor*, 41–71.
53. Ibid., 55.
54. Ibid.
55. Ibid., 58.
56. Neuser, *Calvinus Sacrae Scripturae Professor*, 67–71.
57. Ibid., 60.

the inseparability of the Biblical text and divine revelation, one must not make the mistake of equating them."[58] He expresses his understanding of Calvin as follows:

> Calvin, too, upheld biblical infallibility and inerrancy without falling into the delusion that this means that everything that the Bible says must be taken at face value. He felt remarkably free to exercise critical judgment when dealing with textual problems . . . . While referring to the Bible as 'the certain and unerring rule,' he clearly meant by this the rule of faith. He contended that the biblical writers when referring to matters of science might well be speaking 'in mere accommodation to mistaken, though generally received opinion,' . . . Calvin was committed to a high view of the Scriptures, even regarding them as the oracles of God, but this did not prevent him from examining the text critically.[59]

He goes on to say:

> With the Reformers we wish to maintain that the heavenly doctrine of scripture is infallible but that this doctrine can only be discerned by the eyes of faith . . . . The Bible contains a fallible element in the sense that it reflects the cultural limitations of the writers. But it is not mistaken in what it purports to teach, namely, God's will and purpose for the world. There are no errors or contradictions in its substance and heart. It bears the imprint of human frailty, but it also carries the truth and power of divine infallibility. It is entirely trustworthy in every area in which it claims to be trustworthy.[60]

TOWARD AN ANSWER

As we look back at all the references in Calvin related to inspiration we can see why scholars are so divided in their analysis. On the one hand, Calvin reminds us of the humanness of Scripture. For "we must allow that there is a degree of impropriety in the language when what is borrowed from created things is transferred to the hidden majesty of God."[61] Yet he also insists that Scripture is free from errors and human

---

58. Bloesch, *Essentials of Evangelical Theology*, I, 52
59. Ibid., 66.
60. Ibid., 68ff.
61. *Com.* Heb 1:3 (C. O. I.V, 11ff.).

infirmities. After careful study of the matter, Hamilton wrote, "To exact absolute consistency of thought throughout his [Calvin's] voluminous writings is to forget that Calvin, though a great theologian, was also a fallible one!"[62] We shall see, however, that we do not need to leave matters where Hamilton left them. By contrast, Parker remarks:

> Calvin's concept of Scripture as the word of God presents probably the most difficult problem in all his theology, one on which much has been written and about which there is considerable disagreement. It is a question of relating the numerous passages where he speaks of the Holy Spirit 'dictating' the Scriptures to the prophets and apostles, his 'amanuenses,' and the no less frequent places where he treats the text as a human production and, as such, sometimes incorrect on matters of fact. Some scholars emphasize the one side, some the other.... Both views are quite right and can be supported easily by quotations from Calvin's writings. For this reason the problem is insoluble so long as the discussion is confined to this single point. If, however, it is treated as part of a larger doctrine, in fact in reference to Calvin's general concept of God's dealings with men, the urgency of the tension is removed but the tension itself is seen to be, not merely incapable of removal, but necessary to his doctrine of revelation.[63]

Then he goes on to say: "It is more true to Calvin's thought to say that God reveals himself in Scripture than that God is revealed in Scripture."[64]

I would suggest, however, that it was easy for Calvin to make the above seemingly dissonant remarks in connection with inspiration without being contradictory because of the fact that he lived in the sixteenth century. Dowey expresses this opinion though in the context of Calvin's struggle against Rome and the Anabaptists as follows: "Calvin did not face or did not realize that he was facing serious historical criticism of the Bible, which has driven theology since the nineteenth century to discard the doctrine of verbal inspiration."[65] It is essential to remember that the debates carried on during the latter part of the nineteenth, twentieth, and even the twenty-first centuries regarding Calvin's doctrine of inspiration were in response to the radical effects and challenges of Biblical

---

62. Hamilton, *Calvin's Doctrine of Scripture*, 18.
63. Parker, *Calvin's New Testament Commentaries*, 56, 57.
64. Ibid., 57.
65. Dowey, *Knowledge of God*, 162.

criticism. Calvin lived prior to this revolution and is not to be interpreted in terms of it either for or against the theory of verbal inerrancy. As Gamble points out clearly, "Calvin is a sixteenth-century thinker, and we must not abstract him from the sixteenth century."[66]

Inspiration was not a problem for Calvin. Of more importance was the question of interpretation. It should be remembered that the allegorical method was predominant in the Middle Ages. The Reformers thought that this method of interpretation opened the door to idle speculations. Especially in his sermons Calvin emphasized the literal or historical meaning of Scripture.[67] Commenting on Paul's use of allegory Calvin says:

> But as the apostle declares that these things are allegorized, Origen, and many others along with him, have seized the occasion of torturing Scripture, in every possible manner, away from the true sense. They concluded that the literal sense is too mean and poor, and that, under the outer bark of the letter, there lurk deeper mysteries, which cannot be extracted but by beating out allegories. And this they had no difficulty in accomplishing; for speculations which appear to be ingenious have always been preferred, and always will be preferred, by the world to solid doctrine.
>
> With such approbation the licentious system gradually attained such a height, that he who handled Scripture for his own amusement not only was suffered to pass unpunished, but even obtained the highest applause. For many centuries no man was considered to be ingenious, who had not the skill and daring necessary for changing into a variety of curious shapes the sacred word of God.[68]

Then Calvin concludes:

> Let us know, then, that the true meaning of Scripture is the natural and obvious meaning; and let us embrace and abide by it resolutely. Let us not only neglect as doubtful, but set aside as deadly corruptions, those pretended expositions, which lead us away from the natural meaning.[69]

---

66. Gamble, ed., *Articles on Calvin and Calvinism*, 194.
67. Schreiner, *Where Shall Wisdom Be Found*, 25; also 91.
68. *Com.* Gal 4:22 (C. O. L, 236).
69. Ibid. (C. O. L, 237).

It is against the background of this problem rather than within the context of a doctrine of inspiration that much of Calvin's emphasis upon the words of Scripture should be seen. It is the method of interpretation rather than the doctrine of inspiration that was the problem of his day. Moreover, to understand Calvin's doctrine of inspiration, it would be helpful to remember that he did not need to be as precise in his vocabulary as we like to be in the twenty-first century. This change can probably best be illustrated by his use of the verb *dictate* (*dictare* in Latin). Dowey has called Calvin's expression, "*dictante Spiritu Sancto*,"[70] the most extreme of these expressions for the divine origin and complete objective validity of Scripture.[71] Yet it is interesting that only a few lines before the same reference Calvin says:

> Among the patriarchs God used secret revelations, but at the same time to confirm these he added such signs that they could have no doubt that it was God who was speaking to them. What the patriarchs had received they handed on to their descendants. For the Lord had left it with them on this condition, that they should so propagate it. The children and children's children knew when God dictates within (*Deo intus dictante*) that what they heard was from heaven, not from earth.[72]

This passage is particularly significant for our discussion here because it occurs at the only place in which Calvin writes at some length about the formation of the biblical record.[73] It would be absurd to understand the verb *dictate* here in the modern sense. Calvin's use is identical with the Roman Catholic understanding of the same term. In 1546 (which is contemporaneous to Calvin's writings), we find the following words in the *Decretum de canonicis Scripturis* from the fourth session of the Council of Trent:

> Seeing clearly that this truth and discipline are contained in the written books, and the unwritten traditions which, received by the Apostles from the mouth of Christ himself, or from the apostles themselves, the Holy Ghost dictating (*Spiritu Sancto dictante*), have come down even unto us, transmitted as it were

---

70. *Inst.*, IV, viii, 6 (O. S. V, 138, 12).

71. Dowey, *Knowledge of God* (1994), 91.

72. *Inst.*, IV, viii, 5 (O. s. V, 137, 17-23); Latin supplied.

73. The present writer has not seen the above-quoted passage used in any discussions of the subject of inspiration by others.

> from hand to hand: (the Synod) . . . receives and venerates with an equal affection of piety and reverence, all the books both of the Old and of the New Testament—seeing that one God is the author of both—as also the said traditions, as well those appertaining to faith as to morals, as having been dictated, either by Christ's own word of mouth, or by the Holy Ghost (*a Christo vel a Spiritu Sancto dictatas*), and preserved in the Catholic Church by a continuous succession.[74]

It is interesting that the council members used the verb *dictare* here for the tradition handed down verbally within the church as well as for the written Scripture. We have just noted both uses in Calvin.[75] Likewise, the Roman theologians also call God the author of Scripture, the same term that Calvin employs. Parker makes very helpful remarks as he considers Calvin's doctrine of accommodation:

> God's thoughts and God's language are incomprehensible to man. But revelation is revelation only if it is comprehensible. Therefore, God's thoughts and God's language must become comprehensible, and this takes place when God, so to say, translates them into human thoughts and human language. Calvin frequently expresses this under the simile of an adult (usually here he means a mother) communicating with a child and confining herself to concepts, syntax and vocabulary that he can understand. With a very small child this becomes baby-talk hardly recognizable as the same language that the mother normally speaks. . . . Therefore God accommodates himself to man and expresses his mind in this 'babbling' so that he may communicate his thoughts to him. . . . The revelation of God in Scripture is therefore both direct and indirect. It is direct in that it is God who speaks to man. It is indirect in that God speaks in a way that is alien to himself. Its indirectness however, does not consist in its being mediated through the writer, for to the writer also God speaks in this alien manner, in the way that he individually will understand.[76]

These remarks should make it clear that the doctrine of inspiration was not an issue for Calvin. His interest is not in explaining the mechanics of inspiration but rather the fact that Scripture is *God's* word, which should be above all human authority. This interest becomes clear when

---

74. Schaff, *Creeds of Christendom*, II, 80.

75. *Inst.*, IV, viii, 5 and 6 (O. S. V, 137, 22; 138, 12).

76. Parker, *Calvin's New Testament Commentaries*, 58; also George, *Theology of the Reformers*, 193. References are to *Inst.* I, xiii, 1.

we remember that Calvin's discussion of the formation of the biblical record, in which the word *dictation* appears in connection with both the Old Testament and the New,[77] is situated in the context of "The Power of the Church with Respect to Articles of Faith; and How in the Papacy ... the Church Has been Led to Corrupt All Purity of Doctrine."[78] The purpose of the chapter is to point out that

> ... whatever authority and dignity the Spirit in Scripture accords to either priests or prophets, or apostles, or successors of apostles, it is wholly given not to the men personally, but to the ministry to which they have been appointed; or (to speak more briefly) to the Word, whose ministry is entrusted to them. ... We shall not find that they have been endowed with any authority to teach or to answer, except in the name and Word of the Lord. ... They are to speak nothing but his Word.[79]

Calvin is not trying here to *prove* that Scripture is the Word of God by pointing to a dictation theory of inspiration. Nor is he trying to explain *how* Scripture was conveyed to humans. He is rather dealing with another question altogether, namely the authority of the church vis-à-vis the authority of Scripture. Challenging, Rome he says, «Therefore, if the priest wishes to be heard, let him show himself to be God's messenger; that is, let him faithfully communicate the commands which he has received from his Author.»[80] Then he concludes, "The power of the church, therefore, is not infinite but subject to the Lord's Word and, as it were, enclosed within it."[81]

Thus Calvin's references to dictation are not intended to offer a theory of inspiration. They rather emphasize the fact that the writers of Scripture as well as ministers today "are not to prate whatever they please, but are faithfully to report the commands of Him by whom they have been sent."[82]

> Therefore, none of the prophets opened his mouth unless the Lord had anticipated his words. Hence, it comes that these expressions are so often found among them: 'the Word of the Lord,'

77. *Inst.*, IV, viii, 6 and 8 (O. S. V, 138, 12; 140, 6).
78. *Inst.*, IV, viii, chapter title.
79. *Inst.*, IV, viii, 2 (O. S. V, 134, 13-24).
80. Ibid. (135, 4-6).
81. *Inst.*, IV, viii, 4 (O. S. V, 136, 22ff.).
82. Ibid. (136, 11ff.); cf. Krusche, *Das Wirken*, 161ff.

'the burden of the Lord,' 'Thus saith the Lord,' 'The mouth of the Lord has spoken.'[83]

This passage helps us to understand Calvin's intent in the passages that we have quoted earlier in this chapter. His doctrine of inspiration is not for the purpose of establishing the authority of Scripture, as later Calvinism did,[84] but rather for pointing out that any other authority must be placed under the control of the word. One can say here again with Lehmann, "It is the emphasis upon the *sole* rather than the *supplementary* character of the ultimate scriptural norm that distinguishes the Reformers from their predecessors."[85]

Calvin's purpose becomes still clearer when we remember that in his doctrine of the church, he assigns to ministers the same high office that he assigns to the prophets and apostles. Regarding inspiration he remarks, "Peter says they were *moved*. . . . They followed the Spirit as their guide and obeyed him to such an extent that their mouths became his temple, and he ruled in them."[86] In his related doctrine of the ministry he says:

> Among the many excellent gifts with which God has adorned the human race, it is a singular privilege that he deigns to consecrate to himself the mouths and tongues of men in order that his voice may resound in them. Let us accordingly not in turn dislike to embrace obediently the doctrine of salvation put forth by his command and by his own mouth.[87]

Thus in Calvin's references to inspiration as well as to the ministry, the emphasis is not on the words as such nor on the mechanics but rather on the fact that it is *God's* word that is being spoken, a word that claims subjection without proofs or arguments, a word that does not depend on a church decree or a theory of inspiration to make it certain. Calvin is, however, aware of the fact that

> In every age the prophets and godly teachers have had a difficult struggle with the ungodly, who in their stubbornness can never submit to the yoke of being taught by human word and ministry.

---

83. *Inst.*, IV, viii, 3 (O. S. V, 135, 22–25).
84. See the Appendix.
85. Lehmann, "Reformers' Use of the Bible," 333.
86. *Com.* 2 Pet 1:20 (C. O. LV, 458).
87. *Inst.*, IV, 1, 5 (O. S. V, 9, 11–15).

> This is like blotting out the face of God which shines upon us in teaching.[88]

Accordingly, Calvin would remind us again of the authority of the church, which is an introduction through which we are prepared for faith in the gospel.[89] "Our weakness does not allow us to be dismissed from her school until we have been pupils all our lives."[90]

There are places in which Calvin insists on taking every word of Scripture seriously; however, it is right at these places that he refuses to fall into bibliolatry. In his debate with the Anabaptists, he says, "The letter . . . is dead, and the law of the Lord slays . . . but if through the Spirit it is really branded upon hearts, if it shows forth Christ, it is the word of life"[91] Again in the discussion of predestination he remarks:

> This rashness, therefore, must be restrained by the soberness of faith that in his outward Word, God may sufficiently witness his secret grace to us, provided only the pipe (*canalis*), from which water abundantly flows out for us to drink, does not hinder us from according its due honor to the fountain.[92]

Calvin can make these remarks, for as far as he is concerned, "the Scriptures should be read with the aim of finding Christ in them. Whoever turns aside from this object, even though he wears himself out all his life in learning, will never reach the knowledge of the truth."[93] Thus, in the final analysis, Calvin's doctrine of inspiration is not just a theory but rather a confession of faith. He says:

> Therefore, illumined by his power, we believe neither of our own nor by anyone else's judgment that Scripture is from God; but above human judgment we affirm with utter certainty (just as if we were gazing upon the majesty of God himself) that it has flowed to us from the very mouth of God by the ministry of men.[94]

---

88. Ibid. (9, 29–33).
89. *Inst.*, I, vii, 3 (O. S. III, 68, 9ff.).
90. *Inst.*, IV, I, 4 (O. S. V, 7, 11ff.).
91. *Inst.*, I, ix, 3 (O. S. III, 84, 3–7).
92. *Inst.*, III, xxiv, 3 (O. S. IV, 414, 1–5).
93. *Com.* John 5:39 (C. O. XLVII, 125).
94. *Inst.*, I, vii, 5 (C. O. III, 70, 22–27).

George sums up the matter in these words: "Calvin dealt with the text both reverently and critically."[95]

---

95. George, *Theology of the Reformers*, 195.

Concluding Summary

WE HAVE SEEN THAT the whole of Calvin's *Institutes* is written from the point of view of faith—a faith that is not based on argumentation. Therefore it includes neither proofs of the existence of God nor arguments to demonstrate that Scripture is his word. Speaking as a believer Calvin tells us that "in our ignorance and sloth . . . we need outward helps to beget and increase faith within us, and advance it to its goal."[1] These outward helps are provided in the church and its preaching ministry. "For there is no other way to enter into life unless this mother conceives us in her womb, give us birth, nourish us at her breast."[2]

We have seen that Calvin thinks of Scripture within the context of the church where it is preached and heard. He says: "And in order that the preaching of the gospel might flourish, [God] deposited this treasure in the church. He instituted 'pastors and teachers' (Eph 4:11) through whose lips he might teach his own; he furnished them with authority."[3] Migliore puts it aptly in this way, "The Reformers' view of the authority of scripture was intimately bound to its proclamation of new life and freedom in Christ."[4]

This authority is what Calvin considers to be an "introduction through which we are prepared for faith in the gospel."[5] Thus Scripture for Calvin does not exist in a vacuum; nor is it authoritative in a vacuum "out there." Rather the word has authority in the church and through its preaching ministry to the believers. "The power of the church is therefore

---

1. *Inst.*, IV, i, 1 (O. S. V, 1, 10–13).
2. *Inst.*, IV, i, 4 (O. S. V, 7, 7–9).
3. *Inst.*, IV, i, 1 (O. S. V, 1, 14–17).
4. Migliore, *Faith Seeking Understanding*, 46.
5. *Inst.*, I, vii, 3 (O. S. III, 68, 9ff.).

to be not grudgingly manifested. . . ."[6] "But," Calvin says, "we insist that it be attached to the Word, and do not allow it to be separated from it."[7]

Within the context of the church, Scripture is to be proclaimed by the authority of God. Ministers today should do what the prophets and apostles did in the past. "For, where they are called to office, it is at the same time enjoined upon them not to bring anything of themselves, but to speak from the Lord's mouth."[8]

> The prophets and apostles do not boast either of their keenness or of anything that obtains credit for them as they speak; nor do they dwell upon rational proofs. Rather, they bring forward God's holy name, that by it the whole world may be brought into obedience to him.[9]

This is the manner in which the word is to be presented to people, and here is the objective ground for the authority of Scripture.

This point brought to our attention the question of certainty that was raised by the Roman Church. We have seen that the Roman effort to undermine evangelical doctrine involved the claim that Scripture must be authenticated by the church because it would not be certain unless presented on its authority. Responding to this challenge, Calvin distinguished between the objective and subjective aspects of the authority of Scripture. He argued that Rome raised the question of certainty on the objective level where it does not belong. For, "when that which is set forth is acknowledged to be the Word of God, there is no one so deplorably insolent . . . as to dare impugn the credibility of Him who speaks."[10] Thus on the objective level, Scripture is self-authenticated.[11] "And it is a wicked falsehood that its credibility depends on the judgment of the church."[12]

On the subjective level, Rome claimed that Scripture obtains faith in the hearts of people when they assent to the church. Calvin raised two objections against this teaching. In the first place he averred that if one assents to the church, believers would have no certainty. For, "what will

---

6. *Inst.*, IV, viii, 1 (O. S. V, 134, 6ff.).
7. *Inst.*, IV, viii, 13 (O. S. V, 146, 30 ff.).
8. *Inst.*, IV, viii, 2 (O. S. V, 134, 20–22).
9. *Inst.*, I, vii, 4 (O. S. III, 69, 1–4).
10. *Inst.*, I, vii, 1 (O. S. III, 65, 8–11).
11. *Inst.*, I, vii, 5 (O. S. III, 70, 18).
12. *Inst.*, I, vii, chapter title.

happen to miserable consciences seeking firm assurance of eternal life if all promises of it consist in and depend solely upon the judgment of men?"[13] "The foundation of faith would be frail and unsteady, if it rested on human wisdom."[14]

Moreover, Calvin opposes the notion of assent in itself because it is based on works' righteousness, does not take human sin seriously, and thus leads to fleeting speculations instead of building up firm faith in God's word and truth. "This bare and external proof of the Word of God should have been amply sufficient to engender faith, did not our blindness and perversity prevent it."[15] Sin also stands in the way of those unbelieving people for whom "religion seems to stand by opinion alone."[16] To these Calvin points out that "they who strive to build up firm faith in Scripture through disputation are doing things backwards."[17] That is because "even if anyone clears God's Sacred Word from man's evil speaking, he will not at once imprint upon their hearts that certainty which piety requires."[18] "Because until he [the Spirit] illumines their minds, they ever waver among many doubts!"[19] "Accordingly, without the illumination of the Holy Spirit, the Word can do nothing."[20]

To all alike Calvin would say, "Our mind has such an inclination to vanity that it can never cleave fast to the truth of God and it has such dullness that it is always blind to the light of God's truth."[21] "Accordingly, it [the word of God] cannot penetrate into our minds unless the Spirit, as the inner teacher, through his illumination makes entry for it."[22] Yet "it will not be enough for the mind to be illumined by the Spirit of God unless the heart is also strengthened and supported by his power."[23] We have seen these to be the "two operations of the Spirit in faith" that correspond to "the

---

13. *Inst.*, I, vii, 1 (O. S. III, 66, 8–11).
14. *Com.* Eph 1:13 (C. O. LI, 153).
15. *Inst.*, III, ii, 33 (O. S. IV, 44, 4–6).
16. *Inst.*, I, vii, 4 (O. S. III, 69, 34ff.).
17. Ibid., (O. S. 69, 24ff.).
18. Ibid., (69, 32–34).
19. Ibid. (70, 14ff.).
20. *Inst.*, III, ii, 33 (O. S. IV, 44, 9ff.).
21. Ibid. (44, 6–9).
22. *Inst.*, III, ii, 34 (O. S. IV, 45, 36–38).
23. *Inst.*, III, ii, 33 (O. S. IV, 44, 11ff.).

two parts of which faith consists, as it enlightens, and as it establishes"[24] Illumination must take place before certainty can be achieved and the authority of Scripture fully established in believers' hearts.

Thus we have found that for Calvin the question of authority cannot and should not be differentiated from the question of faith, because in faith we receive Christ clothed with his gospel.[25] There is no separation between what were later termed the formal and material principles of the Reformation.

> Now, therefore, we hold faith to be a knowledge of God's will toward us, perceived from his word. But the foundation of this is a preconceived conviction of God's truth. As for its certainty, as long as your mind is at war with itself, the Word will be of doubtful and weak authority, or rather of none.[26]

"Therefore our mind must be otherwise illumined and our heart strengthened, that the Word of God may obtain full faith among us."[27]

It is in connection with the second operation of the Holy Spirit in faith (the sealing of the heart) that Calvin consistently speaks of the *testimonium Spiritus Sancti internum*. He says:

> 'You have the testimony of the Spirit of God himself, who seals the truth of it in your hearts.' . . . The true conviction which believers have of the word of God, of their own salvation, and of religion in general, does not spring from the judgment of the flesh . . . but from the sealing of the Spirit, who imparts to their consciences such certainty as to remove all doubt.[28]

Accordingly "Scripture Must Be Confirmed by the Witness of the Spirit. Thus May Its Authority Be Established As Certain."[29]

The authority of Scripture in Calvin's theology can therefore be understood in the following manner: Objectively speaking, Scripture is self-authenticated and accordingly it must be presented on God's own authority and his alone. This is the only stable ground on which faith in the word of God can be firm and sure. Looking at the issue from the

---

24. *Com.* Eph 1:13 (C. O. LI. 153).
25. *Inst.*, III, ii, 6 (O. S. IV, 13, 16).
26. Ibid., (15, 10–15).
27. *Inst.*, III, ii, 7 (O. S. IV, 16, 29–31).
28. *Com.* Eph 1:13 (C. O. LI, 153).
29. *Inst.*, I, vii, chapter title.

subjective point of view, Calvin tells us that the authority of Scripture cannot be established as certain in the hearts of people until their minds are illumined and their hearts sealed by the Holy Spirit. The relationship between the illumination and sealing of the spirit can be seen in the following statement: "For as God alone is a fit witness of himself in his Word, so also the Word will not find full credit (*fidem*) in men's hearts before it is sealed by the inward testimony of the Spirit."[30] Out of the certainty of faith the believer makes statements about the inspiration of Scripture. Thus Calvin answered the Roman challenge by propounding the unity of word and Spirit.

In dealing with the Anabaptists, Calvin pointed out that no one can claim to have the Spirit without the word. "The Word is the instrument by which the Lord dispenses the illumination of his Spirit to believers."[31] Moreover, he taught that we can never be sure of the Spirit without the word, "lest under [the Spirit's] sign the Spirit of Satan should creep in, he would have us recognize him in his own image, which he has stamped upon the Scripture."[32] In the final analysis, Calvin says to the Anabaptists:

> By a kind of mutual bond the Lord has joined together the certainty of his Word and of his Spirit so that the perfect religion of the Word may abide in our minds when the Spirit, who causes us to contemplate God's face, shines; and that we in turn may embrace the Spirit with no fear of being deceived when we recognize him in his own image, namely, in the Word.[33]

In the life of faith as Calvin presents it, the believer is united with Christ, from whom he receives a twofold grace of justification and sanctification. This twofold grace brings with it a twofold relationship between God and believers. Thus believers experience a twofold knowledge of God and a corresponding twofold knowledge of themselves. For though restored through Christ (the Second Adam) to what Adam was before the fall, believers are yet sinners; and though illumined, they are still in need of illumination.

---

30. *Inst.*, I, vii, 4 (O. S. III, 70, 3–5); Latin supplied.
31. *Inst.*, I, ix, 3 (O. S. III, 84, 37ff.).
32. *Inst.*, I, ix, 2 (O. S. III, 8, 31–33).
33. *Inst.*, I, ix, 3 (O. S. III, 84, 14–20).

The believer then knows himself or herself as a sinner, a knowledge which corresponds with the knowledge of God as their Redeemer. Within the limits of this experience faith leans and rests only upon the freely given promise in Christ. Thus believers are justified by faith alone, *sola fide*. Here the law is seen in its first use of judgment and condemnation. On the other hand, believers know themselves as restored or being restored to what they were before the fall. They know God as Creator with the "primal and simple knowledge to which the very order of nature would have led us if Adam had remained upright."[34] Within this context believers embrace the word of God in its totality. The law here is seen in its third and principal use, which is its proper purpose. Here it "finds its place among believers in whose hearts the spirit of God already lives and reigns."[35] This is what we have seen to be the believers' experience of sanctification. Thus although justification is not bestowed through works, yet it is not without works.[36] It is as believers respond to their Creator in trust and reverence that biblical authority is established as certain in their heart. It is for this reason that Calvin discusses the authority of Scripture under knowledge of God the Creator. Scripture is authoritative only in the life of faith.

It is in Calvin's discussion of knowledge of God the Redeemer that we find the christocentric side of Calvin's theology with its emphasis on the *sola gratia*. On the other hand, it is within the context of knowledge of God the Creator that we find the theocentric emphasis that explains Calvin's interest in the world. Both aspects are emphasized and are complementary; their relationship can be seen within the tension of the life of faith. Therefore, Calvin's doctrine of authority is not dissonant with his doctrine of faith as it has often been presented. It is rather through faith that the word has full authority.

As for inspiration, we noted that Calvin never gives us a systematic account of a doctrine of inspiration. The opinion of secondary scholars is divided on the understanding of Calvin's position in this regard. Every point of view can find support in one way or another in Calvin's writings. The problem for Calvin in the sixteenth century was not the issue of inspiration. This issue became a problem in the latter part of the nineteenth century and onward beginning with the rise of Biblical criti-

---

34. *Inst.*, I, ii, 1 (O. S. III, 34, 13ff.).
35. *Inst.*, II, vii, 12 (O. S. III, 337, 23–25).
36. *Inst.*, III, xvi, 1 (O. S. IV, 249, 19ff.).

cism. The problem in Calvin's day was that of interpretation since the allegorical method of the Middle Ages continued to predominate. Calvin saw that this method led to idle speculation; he therefore called for the application of the natural, literal, and historical meaning of Scripture.

Furthermore, Calvin never used a doctrine of inspiration to establish the authority of the Scriptures as later Calvinism did. Calvin presented the word of God on God's own authority, with the church acting as an introduction through which humans are prepared for faith in the gospel, i.e. through human ministry. Thus he held the doctrine of the church and ministry in high regard.

It is through the two operations of the Spirit in illuminating the mind and strengthening or sealing the heart that the Scriptures (the word) become authoritative. Word and Spirit are never to be separated.

Appendix

Calvin and Calvinism

We cannot go into the details of the transition from Calvin to Calvinism. Rather, we shall treat the subject briefly within the context of the present study. Probably the best place to begin is the *French Confession*, for it is here that we find a deliberate change from Calvin's doctrine of Scripture.[1] One should remember that the first draft of this confession was written by Calvin and contained thirty-five articles. The first article read:

> Because the foundation of belief, as St. Paul says, is by the Word of God, we believe that the living God is manifest in his law and by his prophets, and finally in the gospel. . . . This doctrine does not derive its authority from men, nor from angels, but from God alone; we believe, too (seeing that it is God who speaks), that He Himself gives the certitude of it to His elect, and seals it in their hearts by His Spirit.[2]

This one article that Calvin wrote was somehow expanded into five, with the last article divided into two, thus making the revised Confession forty articles instead of thirty-five.[3] It seems that two forms of the confession, the shorter in thirty-five articles and the longer in forty, existed side by side until the longer form was adopted by the Synod of La Rochelle in 1571.[4] The fourth article reads as follows:

---

1. Calvin is often discussed and interpreted in the light of some articles in the *French Confession* that he did not write and for which he is not responsible. Cf. K. Barth, *No! Answer to Emil Brunner*, 105; Clavier, *Études sur le Calvinisme*, 23ff., 70.

2. C. O. IX, 739–41 (O. S. II, 310). Cf. Warfield, *Calvin and Calvinism*, 95.

3. Pannier, *Origines de la confession de foi*, 119ff.; cf. Schaff, *Creeds of Christendom*, I, 490 ff., III, 356ff.

4. Pannier, *Origines*, 119ff.; C. O. IX, lix; Schaff, *Creeds of Christendom*, I, 495; Curtis, *History of Creeds and Confessions of Faith*, 224.

> We know these books to be canonical, and the sure rule of our faith, not so much by the common accord and consent of the church, as by the testimony and inward *illumination* of the Holy Spirit, which enables us to distinguish them from other ecclesiastical books upon which, however useful, we cannot found any articles of faith.[5]

It is obvious that this article is very different from what Calvin wrote. Calvin is nevertheless blamed on the basis of this article to be the one who took "the first step . . . where it is expressly stated that the canonicity of the canonical books is an immediate deliverance of the Holy Spirit, independent of the historical judgment of the church."[6] Or again:

> Calvin made the testimony of the Spirit *in* the Word of Christ contingent on a testimony of the Spirit *to* the Word, i.e. to its divine authorship; he observed the essentially personal character of faith and opened the door to the subsequent development of the theory of inspiration, in which the obscurity became total.[7]

It would be more accurate to see the *French Confession* adopted in 1571 as the first move that led to the further steps discussed by Hendry[8] rather than attributing this undertaking to Calvin himself. At any rate, in the original article by Calvin we can see the same thought that we have presented in our study. First he states the objective side of the question, showing that Scripture is authoritative and derives its authority from God alone; then he proceeds to the subjective aspect, showing that believers obtain certainty by the sealing of their hearts by the Holy Spirit.

As we examine the five articles into which the above was expanded, we notice a curious change in the order. The writers of these articles first state the subjective certainty of the believers and they establish the canon on this basis (Article IV). Next they state the objective basis of the authority of Scripture (Article V). Here they say, "We believe that the Word contained in these books has proceeded from God, and receives its authority

---

5. Schaff, *Creeds of Christendom*, III, 361ff.; italics added. The word *illumination* above is an incorrect translation of the French *persuasion* (i.e., "convincing"), which might carry the English reader still further from Calvin's meaning.
6. Hendry, *Holy Spirit in Christian Theology*, 85.
7. Ibid., 85ff.
8. Ibid., 89f.

from him alone, and not from men."[9] The latter statement is true to Calvin. Therefore it is the fourth article that we need to examine more closely.

The striking thing that we find here is the way in which the writers of the article deal with the biblical canon.[10] It should be remembered that the problem of the canon was not a new issue; Calvin had faced the same question before, and it is evident that the Roman Church continued to make a forceful attack in this connection. Yet Calvin dealt with it in a manner different from that of the French Evangelicals. We have already seen that he discussed the canon within the context of the objective authority of Scripture, pointing out that "It is a wicked falsehood that its [Scriptures'] credibility depends on the judgment of the church."[11] Thus Calvin asserted over against the Roman view that Scripture is self-authenticated. Nowhere does he appeal to the inner witness of the Holy Spirit to take the place of the church,[12] for this appeal would confuse the subjective with the objective sides of the question.

As we look again at the fourth article of the longer *French Confession*, we notice that the writers must have been influenced by the debates that were going on between them and the Roman Church.[13] It should be remembered that Calvin argued in debates with his Roman Catholic opponents that the church did not *confer* authority on Scripture with the formation of the canon. On the contrary the church acknowledged the authority of Scripture over itself.[14] The Evangelicals, however, begrudged the church even this subordinate role. Therefore, in an effort to weaken the authority of the church altogether, they tried to replace the authority that Rome claimed for itself with the subjective experience of the believer(s). Thus they made the inner witness of the Holy Spirit the basis of the canon. Accordingly, they tried to establish the objective authority of Scripture on the subjective experience of faith.

Calvin would have opposed such a view. He would not allow the objective authority of Scripture (i.e., its credibility) to depend on some-

---

9. Schaff, *Creeds of Christendom*, III, 362.

10. Article III of the confession contains a list of the canonical books.

11. *Inst.*, I, vii, chapter title.

12. Warfield, *Calvin and Calvinism*, 93ff.; Krusche, *Das Wirken*, 206. This position should be compared with the view of Hendry, *Holy Spirit in Christian Theology*, 84ff.

13. G. Bonet-Maury, "Gallican Confession," Vol. IV, p. 423–24.

14. *Inst.*, I, vii, 2 (O. S. III, 66, 21–67, 7). Cf. Hendry, *Holy Spirit in Christian Theology*, 84ff.

thing outside itself. Moreover, the later approach reverses his meaning. For the *credibility* of the word of God—that is to say, God's truth in itself is not and should not be made dependent upon the *certainty* experienced in faith. For God's truth is not grounded in our certainty; rather our certainty is established on it.[15] This order becomes clear when we remember that the function of the inner witness of the Holy Spirit as Calvin saw it is not to authenticate Scripture, as if the word of God were doubtful in itself, but rather to give *believers* confidence and assurance. It is to heal the wavering of their hearts, enabling them to give full assent to God's word, which is credible and objectively authoritative in itself.

> Indeed, the Word of God is like the sun, shining upon all those to whom it is proclaimed, but with no effect among the blind. Now, all of us are blind by nature in this respect. Accordingly, it cannot penetrate into our minds unless the Spirit, as the inner teacher, through his illumination makes entry for it.[16]
>
> And it will not be enough for the mind to be illumined by the Spirit of God unless the heart is also strengthened and supported by his power . . . . Faith is a singular gift of God, both in that the mind of man is purged so as to be able to taste the truth of God and in that his heart is established therein.[17]

In their effort to combat Rome, the French Evangelicals did not pay much attention to the role of authority that Calvin had assigned to the church. Calvin taught that "the authority of the church is an introduction through which we are prepared for faith in the gospel."[18] He could even say regarding ministers that

---

15. After a lengthy but valuable discussion regarding the canon of Scripture and its accreditation, Dowey concludes as follows: "Calvin offers finally no other standard by which believers can recognize Scripture than the *testimonium internum Spiritus Sancti*, a concept he introduces specifically for the purpose of accrediting Scripture. What is "accredited" (Warfield's term) is not a historico-critical pedigree, but the word of God in the form of Scripture. His whole doctrine of revelation rests confidently upon the correlation of word and Spirit, whereby the previously inspired oracles are identified as such by the subjective illumination of the mind of the believer." Dowey, *Knowledge of God* (1994), 124. Dowey seems here to transfer the "certainty" that the Spirit gives the believers to "confirm" their faith to the "accreditation" of the canon which Dowey had discussed so extensively to come to this concluding remark.

16. *Inst.*, III, ii, 34 *passim*.

17. *Inst.*, III, ii, 33 *passim*.

18. *Inst.*, I, vii, 3 *passim*.

> When the devil cannot alienate us from Christ by hatred of His teaching, he excites either boredom or else contempt of the ministers. Now this admonition of Christ shows that it is unjust that the ungodliness of any whose conduct in their office is wicked or criminal should at all detract from the apostolic dignity. The reason is that we ought to consider God, the author of the ministry, in whom we find nothing worthy of contempt. And then we ought to contemplate Christ Himself who, appointed by the Father to be the sole teacher, speaks by His apostles. Whoever, therefore, does not deign to receive the ministers of the Gospel, rejects Christ in them and God in Christ.[19]

Calvin makes statements like this and yet was not afraid of Roman theologians for he could immediately refute their claims:

> The Papists are foolish and absurd when they turn this into applause for themselves, to establish their tyranny. In the first place they prink themselves out with strange and borrowed feathers which have no connection with Christ's apostles. Secondly, even granting they are apostles, nothing was further from Christ's mind in this passage than to transfer His own right to men—for what else is it to receive those whom Christ sends, but to them, that they may fulfill the office committed to them.[20]

Yet it seems that the French Evangelicals as well as many others felt that to allow the church any authority would leave the door open to Roman claims. Therefore they tried to supplant the authority of the church altogether, replacing it with the inner witness of the Holy Spirit.

In their battle against Rome, the Evangelicals fought on Roman grounds. They failed to appreciate Calvin's doctrine of the church's authority to prepare people for faith in the gospel or its role in preaching God's Word. Nor did they accept Calvin's position that Scripture is self-authenticating. Thus in addressing the issue of the Scriptures' credibility, the Evangelicals sought an outside source of authentication. Accordingly they assigned to the believers' experience of the inner witness of the Holy Spirit the same function that Rome claimed for the church.

The Westminster Confession of Faith in the seventeenth century seems to have assumed the same understanding as the French Evangelicals.[21] The original confession lacked a chapter on the Holy

19. *Com.* John 13:20.
20. Ibid.
21. Hendry, *Holy Spirit in Christian Theology*, 76.

Spirit, although Chapter 1.5 did refer to the Spirit's inner witness. The correlation of word and Spirit, however, which is a prominent motif in Calvin's theology, is lacking in the chapter on the Holy Spirit that was added to the Westminster Confession of Faith in 1903. Hendry comments about this addition as follows:

> If it be true that the Holy spirit points to creativity, the freedom, and the inwardness of the work of God, it could be said that the Westminster Confession of Faith reflects a type of theology which tends to stabilize the relation between God and man within the framework of a rigid system, in which the freedom of God himself is circumscribed (see the doctrine of predestination) and which makes it difficult to distinguish the inwardness of faith from intellectual acceptance of a doctrinal system.[22]

This approach led to the development in later Calvinism of abstractions and an intellectualism that ran counter to Calvin's teaching. Calvinism took up the teaching of the mediaeval Schoolmen and even attempted to present proofs of the existence of God.[23] It is essential to remember that the question here is not about a personal subjective experience, i.e., "what makes *me* certain and confident about *my* faith in Scripture and *my* salvation?" To this question Calvin has said that it is the inner witness of the Holy Spirit which gives this certainty to believers. But we are considering here the objective question concerning Scripture in itself. It is the question of what or who authenticates Scripture. It is the question of the ground of biblical authority. When the Evangelicals claimed that the inner testimony authenticates Scripture, they made the authority of Scripture dependent on the experience of believers. Accordingly, the Evangelicals were vulnerable to the charge of subjectivism and were finally led to formulate a rigid theory of inspiration that would give their doctrine objective grounds that could stand against Rome's objective claims of authority. Proponents of this evangelical view used a vocabulary very similar to that used by Calvin, yet their intentions and meaning differed greatly.

Furthermore, in discussing Calvin and Calvinism, it is worthy of notice, as F. F. Bruce points out that in his commentaries, that Calvin "shows himself not unduly bound by his statements on predestination in the *Institutio*. In fact on this particular subject his commentaries show a flex-

---

22. Hendry, *Westminster Confession for Today*, 117.
23. Torrance, *School of Faith*, lxixff.

ibility which is at times disconcerting to those of his followers who would prefer a line more uniformly consistent with that of the *Institutio*."[24]

A discussion of the difficulties and embarrassments that resulted from this position would take us beyond our purpose.[25] We are concerned here with Calvin's doctrine of biblical authority, avoiding a full discussion of later Calvinism. Therefore, we shall satisfy ourselves with the observations which we have made regarding the differences between Calvin and Calvinism on the question of the inner witness of the Holy Spirit.

24. Bruce, *History of New Testament Study*, 33.

25. For an excellent discussion of this topic see Hendry, *Holy Spirit in Christian Theology*, Chapter IV. Our remarks above, however, have to be borne in mind while reading this chapter.

C*ALVIN'S DOCTRINE OF BIBLICAL Authority* offers a profound new approach to a long-debated topic. Dr. Istafanous draws on Calvin's twofold structure regarding salvation to illuminate the Reformer's twofold knowledge of God with particular focus on Biblical authority. In so doing, Istafanous presents Calvin's view of biblical authority framed within contemporary discussions of inspiration.

Calvin presented justification and sanctification as a twofold grace of God in the 1539 edition of the *Institutes* and in all its subsequent editions. He repeatedly taught this concept in all his commentaries, sermons, and other writings. More than any other Reformer, Calvin used the concept of a twofold grace to express the full relationship between justification and sanctification.

Calvin introduced the concept of a twofold knowledge of God in the definitive edition of the *Institutes* (1559). This framework has been considered by many later scholars as the ordering principle of the *Institutes* and all of Calvin's theology. Istafanous, however, argues that the concept of twofold grace inspired Calvin to introduce the concept of twofold knowledge in 1559. Thus the twofold grace of God provides the key to understanding humans' twofold knowledge of God and themselves specifically and Calvin's theology generally.

The concept of twofold grace explains the way in which believers become blameless before God (justification) and are restored (sanctification). In this way, knowledge of God the Creator (Book I of the *Institutes*) corresponds to knowledge of ourselves as restored to what we would have been had it not been for the fall of Adam. This knowledge is not speculative, hypothetical, or rhetorical. Here the third use of the law is primary and Scripture has full authority.

Believers come to know God as their Redeemer and themselves as sinners simultaneously in the experience of justification, holding only to the promise of grace. This correlation settles the confusion concerning Calvin's concept of the role of Scripture and his understanding of biblical authority.

Bibliography

Allison, L. M. "The Doctrine of Scripture in the Theology of J. Calvin and Francis Turretin." Th. M. thesis, Princeton Theological Seminary, 1958.
Armstrong, Brian G. «Duplex Cognitio Dei, or? The Problem and Relation of Structure, Form, and Purpose in Calvin's Theology.» In *Probing the Reformed Tradition*, 135–153. Louisville: Westminster John Knox, 1989.
Avis, Paul, editor. *Divine Revelation*. Grand Rapids: Eerdmans, 1997.
Baillie, D. M. *God Was in Christ*. New York: Scribner's, 1948.
Bainton, Roland H. *Reformation of the Sixteenth Century*. Boston: Beacon, 1953.
Bakhuizen van den Brink, J. N. "La tradition dans l'église primitive et au XVIe siècle." *RHPR* 36 (1956) 271–81.
———. "The Value of Tradition" In *Reformation and Catholicity*, 271–81. New York: American Church Publications, 1954.
Barth, Karl. *The Doctrine of the Word of God*. Church Dogmatics 1, part I. Translated by T. E. Thompson. Edinburgh: T. and T. Clark, 1936.
———. *The Doctrine of the Word of God*. Church Dogmatics 1, part II. Translated by T. E. Thompson and Harold Knight. Edinburgh: T. and T. Clark, 1956.
———. *The Doctrine of God*. Church Dogmatics 2, part I. Translated by G. T. Thompson. Edinburgh: T. and T. Clark, 1957.
———. "No! Answer to Emil Brunner." In *Natural Theology*, 65–128. Translated by Peter Fraenkel, London: Centenary, 1946.
Barth, Peter. *Das Problem der natürlichen Theologie bei Calvin*. Theologische Existenz heute, 18. Munich: Kaiser Verlag, 1935.
Bauke, Hermann. *Die Probleme der Theologie Calvins*. Leipzig: J. C. Hinrichs'sche Buchhandlung, 1922.
Berkouwer, G. C. *Man: The Image of God*. Translated by D. W. Jellema. Grand Rapids: Eerdmans, 1962.
Biéler, André. *La pensée économique et sociale de Calvin*. Geneva: Librairie de l'Université, 1959.
Bloesch, Donald G., *Essentials of Evangelical Theology*, 1. Peabody, MA: Prince, 2001.
Boisset, Jean. *Sagesse et sainteté dans la pensée de Jean Calvin*. Paris: Presses Universitaires de France, 1959.
Bonet-Maury, Gaston. «Gallican Confession.» *New Schaff-Herzog Encyclopedia of Religious Knowledge*, IV, 423–24.
Breen, Quirinus. *John Calvin: A Study in French Humanism*. Grand Rapids: Eerdmans, 1957.
Briggs, Charles A. *The Bible, the Church, and the Reason*. New York: Charles Scribner's Sons, 1892.
———. "Critical Theories of the Sacred Scriptures in Relation to Their Inspiration." *Presbyterian Review* 2 (1881) 550–79.

Bromiley, Geoffrey W. *Historical Theology, an Introduction*. Grand Rapids: Eerdmans, 1978.
Bruce, F. F . "History of New Testament Study." In *New Testament Interpretation: Essays on Principles and Methods*, 21–59. Grand Rapids: Eerdmans, 1977.
Brunner, Emil. *The Christian Doctrine of God*. Translated by Olive Wyon. Philadelphia: Westminster, 1950.
———. "Nature and Grace." In *Natural Theology*, 15–64, translated by Peter Fraenkel. London: Centenary, 1946.
———. *Revelation and Reason*. Translated by Olive Wyon. Philadelphia: Westminster, 1946.
Brunner, Emil, and Karl Barth. Natural Theology, Translated by Peter Fraenkel. London: Centenary, 1946. Comprising Brunner's essay "Nature and Grace," and Barth's reply, "No!"
Brunner, Peter. *Vom Glauben bei Calvin*. Tübingen: Verlag von J. C. B. Mohr (Paul Siebeck), 1925.
Butin, Philip Walker. *Revelation, Redemption, and Response: Calvin's Trinitarian Understanding of the Divine-Human Relationship*. New York: Oxford University Press, 1995.
Calvin, John. *Calvin: Commentaries*. Translated and edited by Joseph Haroutunian and Louise P. Smith. Library of Christian Classics, 23. Philadelphia: Westminster, 1958.
———. *Calvin's Commentaries*, 46 vols. Edinburgh: Calvin Translation Society, 1843–55.
———. *Calvin's Commentaries*. Edited by David W. Torrance and Thomas F. Torrance. 12 vols. Edinburgh: Oliver and Boyd, 1959.
———. *Calvin's Tracts and Treatises*, with a short life of Calvin by Theodore Beza. Translated by Henry Beveridge. Grand Rapids: Eerdmans, 1958.
———. *Institutes of the Christian Religion*. Translated by John Allen. 7th ed., revised. 2 vols. Philadelphia: Board of Christian Education, 1936.
———. *Institutes of the Christian Religion*. Edited by John T. McNeill. Translated by Ford L. Battles. 2 vols. Library of Christian Classics, 20–21. Philadelphia: Westminster, 1960.
———. *Institutes of the Christian Religion*. Translated by Henry Beveridge. 2 vols. Grand Rapids: Eerdmans, 1957.
———. *Institution de la religion chrétienne* [Geneva 1541]. Edited by Jacques Pannier. Paris: Société les belles lettres, 1936.
———. *Instruction in Faith* (1537). Translated by Paul T. Fuhrmann. Philadelphia: Westminster, 1949.
———. *Ioannis Calvini opera quae supersunt omnia*. Edited by G. Baum, E. Cunitz, E. Reuss, et alii. 59 vols. (Corpus Reformatorum, vols. xxix sqq.). Brunswick: Schwetschke, 1863–1900.
———. *Joannis Calvini opera selecta*. Edited by P. Barth and G. Niesel. 5 vols. Munich: Kaiser Verlag, 1926–36.
———. *On the Christian Faith: Selections from the Institutes, Commentaries and Tracts*. Edited with an introduction by John T. McNeill. New York: Liberal Arts Press, 1957.
———. *Theological Treatises*. Translated by J. K. S. Reid. Library of Christian Classics, 22. Philadelphia: Westminster, 1954.

Clavier, Henri. *Études sur le Calvinisme*. Paris: Librairie Fischbacher, 1936.
Cunliffe-Jones, H. *The Authority of the Biblical Revelation*. London: James Clarke, 1945.
Curtis, William A. *A History of Creeds and Confessions of Faith*. Edinburgh: T. and T. Clark, 1911.
Dakin, A. *Calvinism*. London: Duckworth, 1940.
Daly, Gabriel. "Revelation in the Theology of the Roman Catholic Church." In *Divine Revelation*, 23–44. Grand Rapids: Eerdmans, 1997.
Davies, Rupert E. *The Problem of Authority in the Continental Reformation*. London: Epworth, 1946.
De Greef, Wulfert. *The Writings of John Calvin*. Translated by Lyle D. Bierma. Grand Rapids: Baker, 1989.
DeWitt, John. "The Testimony of the Holy Spirit to the Bible," *Presbyterian and Reformed Review* 6 (1895) 69–85.
Dillenberger, John. *Protestant Thought and Natural Science*. New York: Doubleday, 1960.
Dorner, J. A. *History of Protestant Theology*, vol. 1. Translated by G. Robson and Sophia Taylor. Edinburgh: T. and T. Clark, 1871.
Doumergue, Émile. *Jean Calvin, les hommes et les choses de son temps*, vol. 4. Lausanne: Georges Bridle et cie, éditeurs, 1910.
Dowey, Edward A., Jr. «Continental Reformation: Works of General Interest, Studies in Calvin and Calvinism since 1948.» *CH* 24 (1955) 360–67.
———. "Continental Reformation: Works of General Interest, Studies in Calvin and Calvinism since 1955." *CH* 29 (1960) 187–204.
———. *The Knowledge of God in Calvin's Theology*. New York: Columbia University Press, 1952.
———. *The Knowledge of God in Calvin's Theology*. 3rd ed. Grand Rapids: Eerdmans, 1994.
———. Review of *The Doctrine of the Knowledge of God: A Study in the Theology of John Calvin*, by T. H. L. Parker. *ThTo* 12 (1955) 115–17.
Edgar, William. "Ethics: The Christian Life and Good Works According to Calvin." In *Theological Guide to Calvin's Institutes*, 320–46. Phillipsburg, NJ: P and R, 2008.
Ehrlich, Rudolf J. "Papacy and Scripture." *SJT* 15 (1962) 113–23.
Forstman, H. Jackson. *Word and Spirit, Calvin's Doctrine of Biblical Authority*. Stanford, CA: Stanford University Press, 1962.
Forsyth, P. T. *The Principle of Authority in Relation to Certainty, Sanctity and Society*. London: Independent Press, 1952.
Fuhrmann, Paul T. "Calvin, the Expositor of Scripture." *Interpretation* 6 (1952) 188–209.
———. *God-Centered Religion*. Grand Rapids: Zondervan, 1942.
Fullerton, Kemper. *Prophecy and Authority: A Study in the History of the Doctrine and Interpretation of Scripture*. New York: Macmillan, 1919.
Gaffin, Richard B. "*Justification and Union with Christ*." In *A Theological Guide to Calvin's Institutes*, 248–69. Phillipsburg, NJ: P and R, 2008.
Gamble, Richard C., ed. *The Organizational Structure of Calvin's Theology*. Articles on Calvin and Calvinism, 7. New York: Garland, 1992.
Garcia, Mark A. *Life in Christ*. Colorado Springs, CO: Paternoster, 2008.
George, Timothy. *Theology of the Reformers*, Nashville, TN: Broadman, 1988.

Bibliography

Gerrish, Brian A. "Biblical Authority and the Continental Reformation." *SJT* 10 (1957) 337–60.

———. *Grace and Gratitude*. Minneapolis: Fortress, 1993.

———. *The Old Protestantism and the New: Essays on the Reformation Heritage*. London and New York: T and T Clark, 2004.

Hall, David W., and Peter A. Lillback, eds. *Theological Guide to Calvin's Institutes*. Phillipsburg, NJ: P and R, 2008.

Hamilton, Ian. *Calvin's Doctrine of Scripture: A Contribution to Debate*. Edinburgh: Rutherford, 1984.

Hards, Walter G. "A Critical Translation and Evaluation of the Nucleus of the 1536 Edition of Calvin's Institutes." PhD diss., Princeton Theological Seminary, 1955.

Harkness, Georgia. *John Calvin, the Man and His Ethics*. New York: Abingdon, 1958.

Hendry, G. S. *The Gospel of the Incarnation*. Philadelphia: Westminster, 1958.

———. *The Holy Spirit in Christian Theology*. Philadelphia: Westminster, 1956.

———. *The Westminster Confession for Today*. Richmond, VA: John Knox, 1960.

Heppe, Heinrich. *Reformed Dogmatics*. Translated by G. T. Thompson. London: George Allen and Unwin, 1950.

Hodge, A. A., and B. B. Warfield. "Inspiration." *Presbyterian Review* 2 (1881) 225–60.

Hodge, Casper W. "Witness of the Holy Spirit to the Bible." *Princeton Theological Review* 11 (1913) 41–84.

Horton, Walter M. *Christian Theology, An Ecumenical Approach*. New York: Harper, 1955.

———. "Neo-Orthodox Conceptions of Biblical Authority." *JRT* 5 (1948) 42–56.

Hunter, A. M. *The Teaching of Calvin*. Glasgow: MacLehose, Jackson, 1920.

Jansen, John F. *Calvin's Doctrine of the Work of Christ*. London: James Clarke, 1956.

Johnson, Robert Clyde. *Authority in Protestant Theology*, Philadelphia: Westminster, 1959.

Kantzer, Kenneth S. "Calvin and the Holy Scriptures." In *Inspiration and Interpretation*, 115–55. Grand Rapids: Eerdmans, 1957.

Köstlin, J. "Calvins Institution nach Form und Inhalt, in ihrer geschichtlichen Entwicklung." *TSK* 41 (1868) 6–62, 410–86.

Krusche, Werner. *Das Wirken des Heiligen Geistes nach Calvin*. Göttingen: Vandenhoeck und Ruprecht, 1957.

Lane, Anthony N. S. *Calvin and Bernard of Clairvaux*. Reformed Theology and History, New Series 1. Princeton, NJ: Princeton Theological Seminary, 1996.

Lecerf, Auguste. *Études Calvinistes*. Neuchâtel: Delachaux et Nestlé, 1949.

Lehmann, Paul L. «The Reformers' Use of the Bible.» *ThTo* 3 (1947) 328–44.

Lobstein, P. "La connaissance religieuse d'après Calvin." *RTP* 42 (1909) 53–110.

Luther, Martin. *Commentary on the Galatians*. Translated by Philip S. Watson. London: James Clarke, 1961.

———. *First Principles of the Reformation*. Translated by H. Wace and C. A. Buchheim, Philadelphia: Luther Publication Society, 1885.

MacGregor, G. *Corpus Christi*. Philadelphia: Westminster, 1958.

McNeill, John T. "The Doctrine of the Ministry in Reformed Theology," *CH* 12 (1943) 77–97.

———. *The History and Character of Calvinism*. New York: Oxford University Press, 1954.

———. "The Significance of the Word of God for Calvin" *CH* 28 (1959) 131–46.

———. "Thirty Years of Calvin Study." *CH* 17 (1948) 207–40.
Migliore, Daniel L. *Faith Seeking Understanding*. 2d ed. Grand Rapids: Eerdmans, 2004.
Moore, Dunlop. "Calvin's Doctrine of Holy Scripture." *Presbyterian and Reformed Review* 4 (1893) 49–70.
Muller, Richard A. *Post-Reformation Reformed Dogmatics*, Grand Rapids: Baker, 1993.
Murray, John. *Calvin on Scripture and Divine Sovereignty*. Grand Rapids: Baker, 1960.
Neuser, Wilhelm H., ed. *Calvinus Sacrae Scripturae Professor: Calvin as Confessor of Holy Scripture*. Grand Rapids: Eerdmans, 1994.
Niebuhr, H. Richard. *Christ and Culture*. New York: Harper, 1956.
Niesel, Wilhelm. *The Old and the New in the Church*. London: SCM, 1960.
———. *Les origines de la confession de foi et la discipline des Églises Reformées de France*. Paris: Librairie Félix Alcan, 1936.
———. *The Theology of Calvin*. Translated by Harold Knight. Philadelphia: Westminster, 1956.
Osterhaven, M. Eugene. "Our Knowledge of God According to John Calvin." PhD diss., Princeton Theological Seminary, 1948.
Pannier, Jacques. "L'autorité de l'écriture sainte." *Revue de théologie et des questions religieuses* 15 (1906) 193–211, 367–81.
———. *Le témoignage du Saint-Esprit*. Paris: Librairie Fischbacher, 1893.
Parker, T. H. L. «The Approach to Calvin.» *EvQ* 16 (1944) 165–72.
———. «Calvin's Concept of Revelation.» *SJT* 2 (1949) 337–51.
———. *Calvin's Doctrine of the Knowledge of God*. Edinburgh: Oliver and Boyd, 1952.
———. *Calvin's Doctrine of the Knowledge of God*. Rev. ed. Grand Rapids: Eerdmans, 1959.
———. *Calvin's New Testament Commentaries*. London: SCM, 1971.
———. "John Calvin." In *A History of Christian Doctrine*, 387–99. Philadelphia: Fortress, 1978.
———. *The Oracles of God*. London: Lutterworth Press, 1947.
Partie, Charles. *The Theology of John Calvin*. Louisville: John Knox, 2008.
Piper, Otto A. "The Authority of the Bible." *ThTo* 6 (1949) 159–74.
Preiss, Theo. "The Inner Witness of the Holy Spirit." *Interpretation* 7 (1953) 259–80.
Ramm, Bernard. *The Witness of the Spirit*. Grand Rapids: Eerdmans, 1959.
Raymond, Robert L., *Calvin's Doctrine of Holy Scripture*. In *Theological Guide to Calvin's Institutes*, 44–46. Phillipsburg, NJ: P and R, 2008.
Reid, J. K. S. *The Authority of Scripture, a Study of the Reformation and Post-Reformation Understanding of the Bible*. New York: Harper, 1957.
Reu, M. *Luther and the Scriptures*. Columbus, OH: Wartburg, 1944.
Rome and the Study of Scripture: A Collection of Papal Enactments of the Study of Holy Scripture Together with the Decisions of the Biblical Commission. 5th ed. St. Meinrad, IN: Grail, 1953.
Runia, Klass. *Karl Barth's Doctrine of Holy Scripture*. Grand Rapids: Eerdmans, 1962.
Sabatier, Auguste. *Religions of Authority and the Religion of the Spirit*. Translated by Louis S. Houghton. New York: McClure, Phillips, 1904.
Schaff, Philip. *The Creeds of Christendom*. 3 vols. New York: Harper, 1919.
Schreiner, Susan E. *The Theater of His Glory: Nature and the Natural Order in the Thought of John Calvin*. Durham, N C: Labyrinth, 1991.
———. *Where Shall Wisdom Be Found?: Calvin's Exegesis of Job from Medieval and Modern Perspectives*. Chicago: University of Chicago Press, 1994.

Seeberg, Reinhold. *Lehrbuch der Dogmengeschichte*, vol. 4, part II. 2nd ed. Erlangen: A. Deicherische Verlagsbuchhandlung Werner Scholl, 1920.
———. *Revelation and Inspiration*. London: Harper, 1909.
Stuermann, Walter E. *A Critical Study of Calvin's Concept of Faith*, Tulsa, OK: Tulsa University, 1952.
Tavard, George H. *Holy Writ or Holy Church: The Crisis of the Protestant Reformation*. London: Burns and Oates, 1959.
Taylor, G. A. "John Calvin the Teacher." PhD diss., Duke University, 1953.
Thomas, John N. "The Authority of the Bible." *ThTo* 3 (1946) 159–72.
Todd, John M., ed. *Problèmes de l'autorité*. London: Darton Longman and Todd, 1962.
Torrance, T. F. *Calvin's Doctrine of Man*. Grand Rapids: Eerdmans, 1957.
———. *The School of Faith*, London: James Clarke, 1959.
Van Buren, Paul. *Christ in Our Place*. Edinburgh: Oliver and Boyd, 1957.
Venema, Cornelis Paul. *Accepted and Renewed in Christ: The Twofold Grace of God and the Interpretation of Calvin's Theology*. Göttingen: Vandenhoeck und Ruprecht, 2007.
———. "The Twofold Nature of the Gospel in Calvin's Theology: The 'Duplex gratia Dei' and the Interpretation of Calvin's Theology." PhD diss., Princeton Theological Seminary, 1985.
Wallace, Ronald S. *Calvin, Geneva and the Reformation*. Grand Rapids: Baker, 1990.
———. *Calvin's Doctrine of the Christian Life*. Edinburgh: Oliver and Boyd, 1959.
———. *Calvin's Doctrine of the Word and Sacrament*. Grand Rapids: Eerdmans, 1957.
Walwoord, J. F. *Inspiration and Interpretation*. Grand Rapids: Eerdmans, 1957.
Warfield, B. B. *Calvin and Calvinism*. New York: Oxford University Press, 1931.
———. "Inspiration." *Presbyterian Review*, 2 (1881) 225–60.
Wendel, François. *Calvin, sources et évolution de sa pensée religieuse*. Paris: Presses Universitaires de France, 1950.
Willis, Edward David. *Calvin's Catholic Christology: The Function of the So-called Extra Calvinisticum in Calvin's Theology*. Studies in Medieval and Reformed Thought, 2. Leiden: Brill, 1966.
World Council of Churches, Commission on Faith and Order. *Old and New in the Church*. London: WCC, 1961.

Subject/Name Index

Abraham, 161
Anabaptists xx; xlii; xlv; 4; 6; 150; 152; 154; 165; 170; 177
Apostles' Creed xxiv; xxxiv; 6 n. 29.
Armstrong, Brian G., xxxii; xxxii n.96; xxxiii; xxxiv; xxxiv n.103, 105; 65; 65 n.112; 83; 88; 88 n.223.
Avis, Paul, xli n.131

Baillie, D. M., 46; 46 n.43.
Bainton, Ronald H., xx n.14
Barth, Karl, xxiii n.34; 3 n.5; 108 n.76; 134 n.62; 157 n.14; 181 n.1
    Controversy with Brunner 109 n.76
Barth, Peter, 109 n.76; 121.
Battles, Ford L., xvii n.2; xxxvi; xxxiix n.121; 19 n.69; 63 n.104; 125 n.27; 154; 160; 163.
Bauke, Hermann, xxiii n.35; 157 n.14
Berkouwer, G. C. 47 n. 47
Biblical Criticism xl; 5;17;18;136;145
Bibliocentric xxiii
Biéler, André, 118 n. 124.
Bierma, Lyle D., xxxvii n.115.
Bloesch, Donald G.W, 139; 139 n.89; 151 n.143; 163 n.58.
Boisset, Jean, 18 n.66.
Bonet-Maury, G., 183 n. 13
Briggs, Charles A., xxii; xxii n.33,34; xli
Bromiley, Geoffrey W., xxxix; xxxix n. 126; 86 n.216
Brunner, Emil, 108 n. 76; 181 n.1.
    Controversy with Barth, 108 n. 76; 181 n.1.
Büsser, Fritz, xxxvi
Butin, Philip Walker,xxxiv; xxxiv n.106; xxv; 9; 9 n.38; 11 n.41; 85; 85 n.210; 118 n.125.

Catholics (Catholic Church) xix; xx n.13; xxi, xxiix n.72; xxix; xl; xli n.131; xlii; xliii; xlv, 6, 58; 69; 77; 78; 79; 83; 86; 96; 121; 126; 130; 138; 139; 150; 152; 167; 183.
Certainty xix; xliv; 24; 43; 44; 56; 79; 120; 122–128; 130; 131; 132; 134–139; 141–143; 145; 146; 148; 150–153; 171; 174–177; 182; 184; 184 n.15; 186.
Christocentric, xxiii; xxvi; 47 n.47; 118; 158; 178.
Christological Formula of Chalcedon, 46; 88
Christology, xxiix n.72; xxix; xxx; 16; 117; 118.
Conscience, 24; 43; 78; 79; 84; 97; 104; 131; 135; 143; 153; 155; 175; 176.
Correlative Character of Knowledge of God, xxxiix n.122; 7; 14; 51.
Clavier, Henri, 160; 160 n.37; 181 n.1
Cunliffe-Jones, H. xxxvii n.117; 69 n.128.
Curtis, William A., 181 n.4.

Dakin, A., 6 n.28
Davies, Rupert E., xxiii n.35; 157 n. 14.
Daly, Gabriel, xli; xli n.131.
De Greef, Wulfert, xxxvii n.115.
Dei Verbum xl; xli n.131; 159.
Dialectical Relationship xxv; xxvi; xxvii; xxix; xxx; xxxiv; 33; 53 n.63; 65; 89.
Dillenberger, John, 118 n.124.
Dorner, J. A., 134 n.62.

Subject/Name Index

Doumergue, E., 138 n.81; 147 n.118; 159 n.25, 27; 122; 132
Dowey, Edward A., xvii n1; xxiv; xxiv n.42,47; xxv; xxvi; xxvi n.61; xxvii; xxvii n.67; xxviii; xxiix; xxiix n. 70,71; xxix; xxxi; xxxii; xxxiv; xxxv; xxxvi; xxxiix; xxxiix n. 121,122; xlii; 5; 5 n.24; 6; 6 n.27,28,29; 13; 7; 11 n.41; 13; 13 n.52; 16 n.64; 18 n.67; 25; 25 n.100; 28; 28 n.115; 29; 29 n.117; 33; 33 n.131; 44 n.33; 51; 51 n.59; 53 n.63; 64; 64 n.106; 66 n.115; 80 n.185; 82 n.193; 85; 85 n.208; 86; 88; 88 n.220; 89; 89 n.226; 103; 103 n.51; 111; 111 n.88; 114 n.104; 118 n.124; 121 n.11; 129 n.45; 134 n.63; 137; 137 n.74; 138 n.81; 148 n.125; 157; 157 n.12; 161 n.43,48; 165; 165 n.65; 166; 166 n.71; 184 n.15.
Duplex Gratia Dei (Christi), xxx; xxxiv; xxxvi; xxxiix; xxxix; xl; 37; 65; 66; 69; 70; 76; 82; 84; 85; 87; 88; 89.
Duplex Cognitio Domini, xxiv; xxiix; xxxii; xxxii n.96; xxxiv; xxxv; xxxvi; xxxix; 3; 6; 9; 13; 15; 17; 18; 65; 65 n.112; 66; 69; 70; 76; 82; 85; 87; 88; 89; 189.

Editio Princeps of the Institutes 15; 87
Ehrlich, Rudolf J., xliii n.142

Fisher, G. P., xxxvii n.117; 69 n.128; 77 n.174.
Forstman, H. Jackson, xxvii; xxvii n.65; xli; xli n.132; 57; 57 n.84; 64 n.110; 144 n.110; 154 n.1; 158; 158 n. 16,17.
Francis I., King (Address to), xvii; xiix; xix; 120.
Fuhrmann, Paul T., 3 n.2; 100 n. 35; 159; 159 n.33.

Gamble, Richard C, xxxvi; xxxvi n.114; 88 n.222; 156; 156 n.66.
Garcia, Mark A., xxxiv; xxxiv n. 104; 66 n. 115; 88 n.217; 115 n.111.
George, Timothy, xxxvii n. 116; 86; 86 n. 215; 136; 137 n.73; 161 n.45; 168 n.76; 171; 171 n. 95.
Gerrish, Brian Albert, xxiv; xxvi; xxvi n.62,63,64; xxvii; 12 n.49; 158 n.16; 161 n.43.

Hall, David W. & Lillback, Peter A., 86 n.213; 158 n.23.
Hamilton, Ian, 164; 164 n.62.
Hards, Walter, G., 8 n.34
Harkness, Georgia, 118 n. 124.
Hendry, G. S. 117; 117 n.119; 136; 136 n.70;182; 182 n.6; 183 n.12,14; 185 n.21; 186; 186 n.22; 187 n.25.
Heppe, Heinrich, 159; 159 n.36.
Hodge, A. A., xxii.
Hodge, Casper W., xxii; xxii n.30,34; 129 n.45; 136 n. 70.
Holy Spirit, Illumination, xliv; 30; 93–95; 101; 106; 107; 119; 122; 133; 137; 138; 140; 141; 143; 152; 175–177; 179; 182; 182 n.5; 184; 184 n.15.
Holy Spirit, Sealing, xliv; 4; 95; 119; 122; 123; 124; 126; 133; 135; 138; 142; 143; 176; 177; 179; 182.
Horton, Walter M., xliii n.142.
Hunter, A. M., xxiii n.35; 53 n.63; 157 n.14.

Inspiration, xxii; xxii n.30; xxiii; xxiii n.35; xl; xli; xlii; xliii; xliv; xliv n.144; 150; 154–160; 162; 164; 165; 166; 166 n.73; 168; 169; 177–179; 182; 188.
 Case for Verbal Inerrancy, 155 ff
 Case against Verbal Inerrancy, 159 ff

Subject/Name Index 197

Jansen, John F., 67; 67 n.122; 100 n.35.
Johnson, Robert Clyde, xvii n.1; xxi n.18; xliv n.144; 158 n.22.
Justification, xxx; xxxi; xxxiii; xxxiv; xxxix; xl; 18; 64; 65; 66; 66 n.115; 68; 69; 74–78; 78 n.178; 79; 80–85 n.212; 86–88; 102; 106; 114; 120; 177–188.

Kantzer, Kenneth S., xxii n. 34; 157 n.14.
Köstlin, J., xxiv; xxiv n.46; xxxv; xxxvi; 6 n. 28.
Krusche, Werner, xxix; xlii; xlii n.137; 47 n.46; 66 n.115; 68 n.123; 80 n.186; 95 n.14; 121 n.11; 126 n.33; 129 n.43; 132 n.55; 134 n. 62; 137 n.75; 138 n.82; 145 n.113; 169 n.82; 183 n.12.

Law, xx; xxiii; xxxi; 34; 35; 45; 67; 78; 103; 104; 105; 106; 113; 114; 114 n.104; 105; 115; 115 n.111; 118; 151; 152; 155; 156; 170; 178; 181; 188.
Lehmann, Paul L., xx; xx n.17; 169; 169 n.85.
Leith, John, xxxvi.
Lobstein, P., xxi; xxi n.25; xxii; xxiii n.35; 4; 4 n.7; 5; 6; 6 n.31.
Luther, Martin, xx; xx n.13; xxi; 32; 85; 115; 115 n.111.
Lutheran, 100.

MacGregor, G., 99 n.31; 144 n.110.
McClelland, Joseph, xxxvi.
McKee, Elsie A. & Armstrong, Brian G., xxxii n.96; xxxiv n.103,105; 88 n.223.
McNeill, John T., 16 n. 64; 160; 160 n. 40.
Migliore, Daniel L., 173; 173 n.4.
Moore, Dunlop, xxii n.34; 157 n. 14.
Murray, John, xxii n.34; 126 n.33; 157 n.14.

Natural Theology, xxvii; 108; 109 n.76.
Neuser, Wilhelm H., xxix n.79; 162; 162 n.52; 163; 163 n.56.
Niebuhr, H. Richard 118 n.123.
Niesel, Wilhelm xxiii; xxiii n.37; xxx; 47 n.47; 68 n.125; 84 n. 205; 86 n.214.

Offices of Christ, 67 n. 122; 77.
  As King, 67; 67 n.122; 68; 73; 80; 85.
  As Priest, 67; 67 n.122; 68; 75; 80; 85.
Osiander, 77; 78; 78 n.178; 79.
Osterhaven, M. Eugene, 5; 5 n. 22; 12 n.49.

Pannier, Jacques, xxi; xxi n.22,23; 159; 159 n.30,35; 181 n.3,4.
Parker, T. H. L., xxiv; xxiv n.40; xxvii; xxvii n.68; xxiix; xxxi; xxxvi; xxxvii; 3 n.5; 5; 5 n.23,25; 29 n.117; 36; 36 n.145; 51 n.59; 68; 69 n. 128; 77 n.174; 100; 100 n.37; 116; 116 n.113; 121 n.9; 158 n.23; 135; 164; 164 n.63; 167; 168 n.76.
Preiss, Theo 136 n.70; 146; 146 n.117; 154 n.2.
Providentissimus Deus xl.

Reid, J. K. S. xxiv; xxiv n.41; xli n.132; 139 n.84; 156 n.7; 160; 160 n.38.
Reformation, xx; xx n.13; xxiii; xxiii n.35,36; xxv; xxxiii; xxxiv; xli; xliii; xliii n.139; 4; 64; 79; 83; 84; 123; 130; 137; 145; 157 n.14; 158 n.16; 161 n.43; 176.
Renaissance, xxxiii; xxxiv.
Restore, Restoration, xxvii; xxxiix; xxxix; 31; 32; 33; 35; 36; 44–53; 53 n.63; 55; 63; 65; 70–74; 80; 86; 88; 101; 104; 107; 108; 109 n.76; 113; 115–118; 125; 177; 178; 188.
Reu, M., xx n.13.
Rhetorical, xl; 88.
Runia, Klass, xxiii n.34; 134 n.62; 157 n.14.

Sabatier, Auguste xxi; xxi n.19; xxii; 159; 159 n.30.
Sadoleto, 80; 101 n. 40; 130; 142 n.102;152.
Sanctification, xxx; xxi; xxxiii; xxxiv; xxxix; xl; 65;67–74; 77–85; 85 n.212; 86–88; 113; 115; 125; 177; 178.
Schaff, Philip, 167 n.74; 181 n.3,4; 182 n.5; 183 n.9.
Schoolmen, xix; xlv; 11 n.41; 39–41; 50; 54; 58–61; 69; 103; 114; 119–123; 131; 139; 140; 186.
Seeberg, Reinhold, xxiii n.35.
Simul istus et peccator, 32; 45; 85.
Sola Gratia, 65; 75; 80; 85 n.212; 178.
Sola Fide, 137; 178.
Sola Scriptura, xx; xl; xlii; xliii; 137.
Soteriology, xxxiv; 117.
Spectacles, 2; 107–109; 109 n.76.
Schreiner, Suzan E. 31 n.124; 109 n.76; 117 n.116; 165 n.67.
Stuermann, Walter E., 44; 44 n.33; 112; 112 n.98.

Taylor, G. A., 134 n.62; 140 n. 91; 162; 162 n. 49.
Testimonium Internum Spiritus Sancti, xliv; xliv n.144; 12; 13; 124; 138; 140; 145; 146; 155; 184 n.15.
Testimony of the Holy Spirit, 5; 82 .193; 125; 129; 132; 135; 136; 136 n.70; 138; 141–143; 146–150; 154; 176; 177; 182.
Todd, John M., xliii n.142.
Torrance, T. F., 3 n. 3; 94 n. 11; 97 n. 25; 102; 102 n. 46; 137 n.80; 186 n. 23.
Trinity, xxvii; xxiix; xxix; xxxiv; xli; 29; 82.
Twofold Grace, xxx; xxx n.83; xxxi; xxxv; xxxiix; xxxix; xliii; 53 n.63; 66; 76; 69; 76; 77; 79; 82; 84; 87; 115; 116; 188.
Twofold Knowledge of God, xxxvi; xlii; xliii; 7; 12; 13; 15; 18–20; 25; 32; 34; 36; 46; 53 n.63; 76; 80; 86; 188.
Twofold Knowledge of Ourselves, xxxvi; xxxiix; xlii; 5; 7; 14; 17; 18; 18 n.67; 46; 51; 51 n.59; 115.

Van Buren, Paul, 66 n.115; 67 n.118; 68 n.125; 84 n.205.
Van den Brink, xliii n.140.
Venema, Cornelis Paul, xxx; xxx n. 83; xxxi; xxxii; xxxiix; xxxix; xxxix n.123; xl; xl n.128; 88; 88 n.218; 89; 89 n.225.

Wallace, Ronald S., xlii; xlii n.136,138; 23 n.83; 35 n.144; 67 n.125; 100 n.34; 122 n.14,15; 125 n.30; 161 n. 44,47.
Walvoord, J. F., xxii. n.34
Warfield, B. B., xxvii n.1; xxii, xxii n. 30,32,34; xxiii; xli; 4; 4 n.13; 5; 12; 12 n.49; 13; 13 n.51; 129 n.45; 134 n.63; 136 n.70; 147; 147 n.119; 148; 157; 157 n.15; 161; 161 n.48; 181 n.2; 183 n.12; 184 n.15.
Wendel, François, xxiv; 6 n.28; 51 n.59; 84 n.205.
Willis, Edward David, xxiix; xxiix n.72; xxix; 11 n.41.

Zwinglian 100.

www.ingramcontent.com/pod-product-compliance
Lightning Source LLC
Chambersburg PA
CBHW062000220426

43662CB00011B/1758